Contents

Oxford School Shakespeare

King Lear

Edited by

Roma Gill, OBE

M.A. *Cantab.*, B. Litt. *Oxon*

Oxford University Press

Oxford University Press, Great Clarendon Street, Oxford OX2 6DP

Oxford New York
Athens Auckland Bangkok Bogota Bombay
Buenos Aires Calcutta Cape Town Dar es Salaam Delhi
Florence Hong Kong Istanbul Karachi
Kuala Lumpur Madras Madrid Melbourne
Mexico City Nairobi Paris Singapore
Taipei Tokyo Toronto Warsaw

and associated companies in
Berlin Ibadan

Oxford is a trade mark of Oxford University Press

© Oxford University Press 1994
Reprinted 1994, 1996, 1997, 1998
Trade edition first published 1996
Reprinted 1997, 1998

ISBN 0 19 831977 0 (School edition)   3 5 7 9 10 8 6 4 2
ISBN 0 19 831994 0 (Trade edition)   3 5 7 9 10 8 6 4 2

Illustrations by Victor G Ambrus

Cover photograph from Photostage (Donald Cooper)
shows Brian Cox in the 1990 National Theatre production of
King Lear.

For Jonathan

Oxford School Shakespeare
edited by Roma Gill

A Midsummer Night's Dream	The Taming of the Shrew
Romeo and Juliet	Othello
As You Like It	Hamlet
Macbeth	King Lear
Julius Caesar	Henry V
The Merchant of Venice	The Winter's Tale
Henry IV Part I	Antony and Cleopatra
Twelfth Night	The Tempest

Printed in Great Britain at the University Press, Cambridge

Introduction

In 1603 an old gentleman, Brian Annesley, was declared unfit to manage his own affairs. His two elder daughters tried to have him certified as insane, so that they could get control of his estate—but his youngest daughter (whose name was Cordell) protected her father and cared for him until he died. Shakespeare must have known the story—there was just as much gossip in the seventeenth century as there is today—and he could even have known Cordell who, after her father's death, married Sir William Harvey whose stepson, the Earl of Southampton, may well have been the young man described as the 'only begetter' of Shakespeare's Sonnets.

It is tempting to suggest—though it can never be more than supposition—that this human story was what triggered off Shakespeare's imagination to write his greatest masterpiece, a play which ranks as drama with Sophocles's great Theban trilogy—*Oedipus, Oedipus at Colonus,* and *Antigone.* As a product of the human imagination it takes its place in modern western civilization with Michelangelo's frescoes on the ceilings of the Sistine Chapel and with Bach's composition in the B Minor Mass.

King Lear's major theme—ingratitude—was very close to Shakespeare's heart. In *As You Like It* Amiens sings of the winter wind and the freezing cold which, no matter how severe, cannot hurt so much:

> Blow, blow, thou winter wind,
> Thou art not so unkind
>   As man's ingratitude . . .
> Freeze, freeze, thou bitter sky,
> That does not bite so nigh
>   As benefits forgot.   (2, 7, 175–7, 185–7)

In *Twelfth Night* Viola seems to speak with the author's voice when she tells Antonio

> I hate ingratitude more in a man
> Than lying, vainness, babbling drunkenness,
> Or any taint of vice whose strong corruption
> Inhabits our frail blood.   (3, 4, 352–5)

And *Timon of Athens*, the most bitter of Shakespeare's tragedies, shows a rich man who is deserted in his hour of need by all the friends who had once enjoyed his generosity.

The story of King Lear and his three daughters was familiar to Shakespeare. There were many different versions which could have inspired him, and his play gives evidence of at least three which certainly influenced him: the historical account as it was given by Raphael Holinshed; the old play *King Leir* which was written by an unknown dramatist and performed (but not published) before *King Lear*; and a few stanzas included in Edmund Spenser's epic poem *The Faerie Queene*.

These gave Shakespeare the outline for his play, as well as words and phrases to flesh out the skeleton. But he ranged beyond the histories, and hewed the materials for *King Lear* from many a rich (if unsuspected) quarry. In Sir Philip Sidney's *Arcadia*, Shakespeare found the fictional history of two sons and their behaviour towards their father, 'the Paphlagonian king'. This became, in *King Lear*, the secondary plot concerning Gloucester and his sons. It is more than a sub-plot, being very closely intertwined with the play's main action which it both imitates (in the rejection of the loving child) and resolves. For the assumed madness of Edgar, the rejected son, Shakespeare had recourse to a different kind of publication, *A Declaration of Egregious Popishe Impostures*, whose author, Samuel Harsnett, was attacking beliefs in diabolic 'possession'.[1]

The Fool got into the play by himself! Shakespeare was always a practical man of the theatre, and he understood the structure and resources of the company, the King's Men, with which he was working. At the time Shakespeare wrote *King Lear* the company enjoyed the services of a very good comic actor, Robert Armin, who had to be given a role—and who might even have supplied some of his own 'gags'! It is not impossible to think that the Fool's part could have been 'doubled' with that of Cordelia: the Fool does not appear until Scene 4 of *Act 1*, when Cordelia has left England for France, and he disappears again after *Act 3*, Scene 6, shortly before her arrival at Dover.

But Shakespeare made one alteration of his own, for which there seems to be no precedent. In every other account, the old king is finally united with his youngest daughter and they are allowed to enjoy a few years of happiness together. Shakespeare's contemporary audiences, acquainted like him with the familiar

---

[1]   For more details of these sources see Appendix, p.135.

stories, would have expected such a development—and there are times when the dramatist seems to encourage such expectations, raising hopes only to dash them down! In the seventeenth century Shakespeare's own authority was overruled in this matter when Nahum Tate took a decisive hand in the play. He twisted the ending to make romantic comedy, where Cordelia became the wife of Edgar and they jointly ruled over the kingdom, approved by a delighted and benevolent Lear. Tate's version held the English stage from 1681 until 1834; many of the great scholars and critics of the eighteenth and nineteenth centuries knew Shakespeare's masterpiece only from their studies. The twentieth century has brought *King Lear* back into the theatre, which is its true home.

King Lear: synopsis

King Lear is the most complicated of all Shakespeare's plays. There are two plots—the main one concerning the king and his three daughters; and the sub-plot of Gloucester and his two sons. The plots are intricately interwoven with each other, as the characters from Gloucester's sub-plot become involved with those in the king's main action. At the end of the play, the two plots are finally resolved together.

King Lear has planned to divide his kingdom between his three daughters, but when the youngest, Cordelia, incurs his displeasure he casts her off and gives her share of the land to her sisters—on whom he soon becomes totally dependent. They are greedy and selfish, and eventually dispossess their father entirely. They turn him out of doors into a wild and stormy night with only his Fool and a devoted servant, Kent, as companions. But Gloucester follows them, and leads the king to find shelter in a deserted 'hovel'.

Gloucester has griefs of his own: early in the play we saw how his younger son, Edmund, deceived him into thinking that Edgar, his elder son, was plotting against his father's life. A search warrant was issued against Edgar who, to avoid arrest, disguised himself as 'Poor Tom', a crazy beggar. He, too, has taken refuge from the storm, and in the 'hovel' the king and the Fool encounter the madman.

Gloucester's other son, meanwhile, has been worming his way into the favour of King Lear's elder daughters, Goneril and Regan, and their husbands, the Dukes of Albany and Cornwall. These are now rulers of the kingdom—and Edmund is ambitious! He betrays his father by revealing the help that Gloucester has given to the outcast Lear, and he is rewarded for this with the title 'Earl of Gloucester', which has been stripped from his father.

The Dukes of Albany and Cornwall begin to quarrel, each wanting the other's share of Lear's kingdom. They unite only to face a threatened invasion from France—whose troops are led by Lear's youngest daughter. Cordelia is now married to the King of France, and she is coming to rescue her father and restore him to his throne.

But by this time Lear's sufferings have driven him mad. He is led to a place of safety by the old Earl of Gloucester, and for some time withdraws from the action. Gloucester, however, is arrested and charged, on the evidence of his son, with aiding and abetting a known traitor—King Lear. The Duke of Cornwall tears out Gloucester's eyes, and the blind old man, expelled from his castle, is put into the care of 'Poor Tom'—who is actually, of course, the loving son (i.e. Edgar) whom Gloucester had once rejected and outlawed. Edgar leads his father towards Dover, where he plans to take his own life. Cornwall dies, wounded by one of his own servants who was outraged by his cruelty.

Lear's elder daughters have both fallen in love with Edmund, and are jealous of each other. Regan is now a widow, and Goneril has begun to despise her husband, Albany, who is horrified by the way that the two sisters have treated their father. Cordelia arrives in England and finds her father. She asks for the Doctor's help to cure his madness, and prepares to do battle with the armies of her sisters.

Edgar leads his father in the direction of Dover, but frustrates his suicide attempt; he then saves his father's life for a second time when Goneril's messenger, Oswald, carrying a letter from Goneril to Edmund, recognizes Gloucester and tries to kill him. Edgar kills Oswald, and reads the letter he is carrying. From this, Edgar learns that Goneril wants Edmund to kill her husband so that she and Edmund can be married. Edgar gives the letter to Albany.

Lear recovers from his madness sufficiently to recognize Cordelia, but their joy at their reunion is shortlived. The battle is fought between the invading French forces (who are fighting for the rights of Cordelia and her father) and the English armies, defending the kingdom of Goneril and Regan. The French army is defeated; Cordelia and Lear are taken to prison. Edmund arranges for Cordelia to be murdered.

Albany denounces Edmund, and Edgar (in another disguise) challenges his brother to a duel. Edmund is fatally wounded, but before he dies he learns of his father's death and of the deaths of Goneril and Regan (Goneril poisoned her sister, and then stabbed herself). Edmund makes a last-minute attempt to save Cordelia's life, but it is too late: she was hanged on the instructions he had given earlier. Lear carries in the body of his youngest daughter. His grief is extreme, and shortly he is dead too. Albany yields the kingdom to Edgar, who has the last words of the play.

Leading Characters in the Play

King Lear

An autocratic ruler who has governed Britain, without let or hindrance, for a very long time. He is now over eighty years old and, anticipating the trouble that might arise after his death, when the land will be divided between his three daughters (he has no son to inherit his kingdom), he has decided to make the division himself before he dies. In this way he can control the way the country is split up—and make sure that his favourite daughter gets the richest area. Then he will abdicate and surrender all his power—but he will continue to enjoy his royal status with none of the responsibilities of a king. When things do not work out according to his plans, he is outraged, bewildered, deeply hurt, and eventually driven out of his mind.

His daughters

Goneril, the eldest, is glib of tongue and satisfies her father's demands for flattery until she has secured her desires. Then she shows herself to be cold, heartless, and selfish. She scorns her husband, and her passion for Edmund leads her to plot Albany's death, to poison her sister Regan, and—when her lust is finally frustrated—to kill herself.

Regan is very much like her older sister. She can command the same oily flattery when it suits her purpose, and she is no less heartless and selfish when her real nature is revealed. In lust and jealousy she is her sister's equal, and it may be argued which of the two is capable of the greater cruelty.

Cordelia, Lear's youngest and favourite daughter, has nothing in common with Goneril and Regan. She staunchly refuses to flatter her father, preferring rather to bear his displeasure than to emulate her sisters' empty boasts. Throughout the central part of the play she is away in France, returning at the end of *Act 4* to rescue the king from his persecutors.

Their husbands

Albany is married to Goneril. At first he seems a mild-mannered husband, who dares do no more than remonstrate with his wife about her callous indifference to her father's sufferings. But when he realizes the full monstrosity of the two sisters in their dealings with both Lear and Gloucester—and when he understands the threat to his own life—he is moved to action.

Cornwall, Regan's husband, is a brute. It is he who is responsible for putting Kent in the stocks in *Act 2,* Scene 2, and for locking the castle gates (in *Act 2,* Scene 4) so that Lear is left to the mercy of the storm. His great scene is the one (*Act 3,* Scene 7) where, with evident relish, he tears out the eyes of the helpless Gloucester.

The King of **France** chooses to marry Cordelia after she has been disinherited by her father and rejected by her other suitor. France's part in the play is finished at the end of the first scene, when he takes his bride back to his own country. We hear of his anger, and we know about his threat to invade Britain, but it is Cordelia who leads his army and employs it to rescue her father.

Gloucester
On his first appearance he seems a sophisticated, urbane character, laughing about his illegitimate son, Edmund. He is, however, superstitious and easily deceived by Edmund into rejecting Edgar, his legitimate son. Gloucester is too weak to stand against Cornwall (who is his overlord), but at last he finds courage to go to the aid of the king. But he is forced to pay a heavy penalty for all his mistakes.

His sons
Edgar, the elder of the two, develops in character and stature as the play progresses. He is slandered by his brother and outlawed by his father. To escape detection, he disguises himself as a 'Bedlam beggar'—one of the lunatics who had licence to beg throughout the country. He gives a splendid performance as 'Poor Tom', imitating the cries and fantastic behaviour of a madman (learned out of Harsnett's *Declaration of Egregious Popishe Impostures*—see Appendix, p. 141). In this persona he encounters his blind father and the mad old king, and at the end of the play he is able to offer some relief to both. He grows wiser and more self-confident through his exposure to suffering, and he emerges from his experiences with a new strength.

Edmund is wilful and ruthless. Perhaps his life has been warped by his illegitimacy, making him determined to be revenged on the society which casts a stigma on his birth. He is clever, intelligent, and attractive—able to draw the loves of two sisters with his sexual magnetism, and to charm an audience with his sardonic wit.

Kent

The Earl of **Kent** is King Lear's most steadfast supporter. Banished by Lear for his boldness in daring to reprove the king's behaviour, he nevertheless returns to serve his master in disguise, calling himself 'Caius'. He retains his former outspokenness, however, although it gets him into still more trouble. Kent does valuable service to the king (and to the play!) by keeping in touch with Cordelia, to whom he is devoted. But right to the end Kent is something of a mystery man, seeming to be in the service of a greater master than Lear.

The Fool

The part of Lear's **Fool** was created for the actor Robert Armin, who had acted in other plays of Shakespeare's (most notably as Feste in *Twelfth Night*, where some of a fool's duties are described by Viola—*Act 3*, 1, 59–67). He brought his own brand of comedy to the part, and some critics think that it was he who supplied the Fool's strange prophecy at the end of *Act 3*, Scene 2. A court fool was granted all sorts of licence in the performance of his duty, but his position was a sensitive one: royal favour was always unpredict-able, and it was dangerous for the fool to overstep the limits of his licence. At first Lear's Fool seems bitter about his master's rejection of Cordelia, and his jests are aimed at making Lear understand the full extent of his own folly. Later, when he is cold and frightened on the heath, his manic attempts to joke about the situation only increase the pathos. The Fool disappears when he is no longer needed (at the end of *Act 3*, Scene 6); we never learn what has become of him.

King Lear: commentary

Act I

Scene 1   Two noblemen, the Earl of Kent and the Earl of Gloucester, are
holding what appears to be a fairly casual conversation, discussing
the way that their king is planning to divide up his kingdom. They
do not seem to be in the least distressed that the country is to be
split between different rulers, and very soon the subject is
forgotten. Gloucester is accompanied by a young man whom he
introduces as his illegitimate son, Edmund. Gloucester jokes about
Edmund's illegitimacy, and Kent replies to him with polite
surprise. Edmund is silent. Perhaps he is not within earshot;
perhaps he has heard these jokes before and is not embarrassed by
them; or perhaps he hears—and hides his thoughts, even when his
father talks of sending him away from the court.

The first thirty lines of the play are spoken in an easy, relaxed
prose. They serve as a kind of prologue, in which a great deal of
information is imparted and the two plots of the play are introduced together.

The private conversation is hushed when the trumpets
announce the entry of the royal procession for Lear's ceremony of
abdication. Verse is now the proper medium of communication,
and Lear speaks with measured dignity about the division of his
kingdom. It is to be shared between his three daughters, and Lear
means to give the best portion to the most deserving—the one
who can make the greatest show of love. He has no male heir (who
would automatically succeed his father), and the land will inevitably be divided after Lear's death. Lear intends 'that future strife
May be averted now'. He has already apportioned the land
between his daughters, so the 'love test' is in fact meaningless: but
the king enjoys flattery!

Goneril readily plays her part, giving a fulsome description of
her love that quickly wins her father's approval. Regan joins in the
competition, seeking to excel her sister. Again, Lear is satisfied,
and he turns with great expectation to his youngest daughter,
making no secret of the fact that Cordelia is his favourite, and that

for her he has reserved 'A third more opulent' than those awarded to Goneril and Regan. But Cordelia's 'asides' (thoughts spoken for no one—except the audience—to hear) have prepared us for the kind of reply she will give to her father. She disliked the way Goneril was boasting of her feelings, deciding that she herself would 'Love, and be silent'. This determination is strengthened when she hears Regan's even more excessive claims, and recognizes their hypocrisy.

Cordelia answers her father plainly, with sincerity, intelligence—and real love, which acknowledges the limitations, as well as the extent, of filial love. But Lear does not understand this. He is disappointed, and he feels rejected—so he in turn rejects his daughter. His language is as violent as hers is plain: where Cordelia spoke of the simple, natural relationship of parent and child, Lear invokes pagan gods and supernatural phenomena.

When the division of the kingdom is finally made, there is none of the ceremony that we have been led to expect. Lear states his conditions, insisting that he should keep one hundred knights as his personal retinue; and then he hands over the crown to his two sons-in-law: 'This coronet part between you'.

The Earl of Kent speaks a note of respectful common sense, but when Lear refuses to listen, Kent's language becomes increasingly forceful. His bluntness only inflames Lear's wrath, and the two men engage in a short verbal skirmish from which they have to be separated by Albany and Cornwall. This is reflected in the verse of the play as the characters break into each other's pentameter lines:

> **Kent**
> My life I never held but as a pawn
> To wage against thine enemies; nor fear to lose it,
> Thy safety being motive.
> > **Lear**
> >   Out of my sight!
> > **Kent**
> See better, Lear; and let me still remain
> The true blank of thine eye.
> > **Lear**
> Now, by Apollo—
> > **Kent**
> >   Now, by Apollo, king,
> Thou swear'st thy gods in vain.

Lear
                                        O vassal! miscreant!
   Albany, Cornwall
  Dear sir, forbear.

    Lear regains control of the situation and (although he has just resigned all power along with his kingdom) pronounces a sentence of banishment on his most loyal courtier.

    Kent accepts his sentence with calm resignation—indeed, he almost seems to welcome the thought of being exiled from an oppressive regime. The rhymed couplets of his speech halt the movement of the scene for a few moments, allowing the audience to assimilate what they have just witnessed and (with the actors!) to take a short break from the rising passions. Kent sums up the action of the scene to this point and suggests the direction in which it will move. We have learned that Kent's judgement is to be trusted—and we can be fairly sure that there will be no 'good effects' arising from the 'words of love' that were spoken by Goneril and Regan.

    The business of the scene is resumed when Lear, now icily in control of himself, offers Cordelia to one of her suitors, the Duke of Burgundy. Cordelia is now, in her father's eyes, a mere trading commodity whose 'price is fallen'. Burgundy seems to share something of this attitude, but Cordelia's other suitor, the King of France, asks the reasons for Lear's sudden change of heart. Cordelia breaks her silence, and defends herself with a forceful modesty which is also an indictment of her sisters. The King of France knows how to value Cordelia, and he claims her as his wife. Before she parts from Goneril and Regan, Cordelia lets them know that she understands their falsehood. Rhymed couplets again signal the close of an episode in this long first scene of the play.

    The scene ends as it began—in prose. Goneril and Regan discuss what has happened and make their own plans for the future. For a moment we see Lear through *their* eyes: he is an old man 'full of changes', prone to 'unruly waywardness', and liable to 'unconstant starts'. Regan is thoughtful, but Goneril is ready for action!

Scene 2 Edmund, who left the stage in Scene 1 (at line 34) and did not witness Lear's disinheritance of Cordelia, now presents himself, alone, to the audience. He is no longer the reserved—even shy— young man who was so polite when he was introduced to Kent;

instead he is bold, confident, and rebellious. He resents the position of a younger brother; and he also resents the attitude with which society regards his illegitimate birth: 'Why brand they us With base? with baseness? bastardy? base, base?'.

Edmund knows that he is in appearance quite as handsome as his legitimate older brother (Kent praised Edmund's good looks in *I, I, 17*), and he is determined to prove his superior in ability. Edmund rejoices in the thought (which was quite common at the time Shakespeare wrote *King Lear*) that an illegitimate child, conceived in an act of sexual passion, might have more vigour than a child whose conception was the result of the parents' marital duty! Certainly Edmund shows a lot of energy in his first speech, which makes him very attractive to audiences (or readers); we are taken into his confidence through the direct address of the soliloquy, and the wit of his argument compels our sympathy.

Gloucester enters, lamenting the general state of affairs in the world. He insists on reading a letter which Edmund is pretending to hide from him, and learns that Edgar, his elder son, is plotting against his life. Although we have not met Edgar, we have learned (from his own soliloquy) that Edmund is not to be trusted: this letter is the 'invention' of which he boasted in line 20. But Gloucester, it seems, is easily fooled: he recognizes Edgar's (supposed) treachery as part of the general social disorder which was predicted by recent supernatural phenomena (the 'late eclipses in the sun and moon').

After Gloucester's departure, Edmund has a moment to scoff at his father's superstition and gullibility, and to congratulate himself on the success—so far—of his scheme. At a most opportune moment, Edgar appears. It is time for Edmund to assume another role: now he is the caring brother, anxious to protect Edgar from his father's wrath.

The scene ends as it began: Edmund speaks his mind where he can be heard only by the audience, who must applaud—but not approve—the skill with which he has duped both Gloucester and Edgar.

Scene 3　　Time has passed, and Goneril (with whom Lear is spending the first month, as he had arranged in Scene 1, lines 131–4) is already looking for an excuse to break the agreement: her father is proving a difficult guest, and his bodyguard of a hundred knights disrupts her own household. But these are mere pretexts. Goneril is wanting to start a quarrel!

Scene 4   We have already seen the true worth of the boasted love of Goneril and Regan. In contrast is the real love and loyalty of Kent who has disguised himself as 'Caius' and come to find service with his former master. It is useful for us—audience or readers—to be reminded at this point in the play that Lear is more than an 'Idle old man' (*1, 3, 17*). Kent tells him—and we should be able to *see*—that Lear is still able to command respect:

> **Kent**
> . . . you have that in your countenance which I would fain call master.
> **Lear**
> What's that?
> **Kent**
> Authority.

This, however, is not generally apparent, as the episode with Oswald amply demonstrates. Lear's Knight remarks the lack of 'ceremonious affection' in the treatment of his master, and Lear himself has 'perceived a most faint neglect of late'. But the diminution in Lear's status is declared by Oswald: Lear demands acknowledgement—'Who am I, sir?'—and Oswald replies without hesitation, 'My lady's father'. Lear is beginning to understand the folly of his actions, and his Fool is introduced here to drive home the lesson:

> **Fool**
> . . . Would I had two coxcombs and two daughters!
> **Lear**
> Why, my boy?
> **Fool**
> If I gave them all my living, I'd keep my coxcombs myself.

Although he is threatened with the whip, the Fool persists in his jests—which become increasingly bitter to Lear. The Fool's mad capering is momentarily silenced by Goneril. Lear listens to Goneril's criticisms with bewilderment, unable to believe what he is hearing. Once again he tries to compel recognition: 'Who is it that can tell me who I am?' This time it is the Fool who replies: 'Lear's shadow'. Goneril repeats her accusations, requesting Lear to curb the behaviour and reduce the number of his followers.

But Lear's followers, the one hundred knights whom he reserved in his service (*1, 1, 132*), are a sign of his status and identity as a king; Lear will not relinquish this.

Defending his knights, Lear prepares to leave Goneril's house. Albany, Goneril's husband, denies having any part in

Goneril's unkindness, and Lear seems to accept this. But he prays to the goddess Nature, imploring a curse of sterility on Goneril. His language is strange and terrifying: the Latinate words— 'derogate body', for instance, and 'cadent tears'—give awesome solemnity. He sweeps out of the room in a dignified rage—only to burst in again almost immediately in a furious temper, weeping passionate tears because Goneril's threat has been fulfilled: his train of followers has already been cut in half. With uncontrolled anger he once more curses Goneril before rushing away to find Regan, confident that she will prove 'kind and comfortable'.

We can be sure, however, that this will not be the case. Goneril sends Oswald with a letter to her sister, which will prepare Regan for the coming of their father; it is unlikely that she will 'sustain him and his hundred knights' when Goneril has 'show'd the unfitness'.

Albany and Goneril are left alone together, and Albany makes an attempt to reproach his wife for her treatment of Lear. Goneril is unrepentant, and defends her conduct, scorning Albany for what she calls his 'milky gentleness'—which, she implies, is mere weakness. Albany's warning, expressed in an easy couplet, sounds trite and unconvincing: Goneril is not worried, and Albany himself can only be resigned to wait and see what happens—'Well, well; th'event'.

Scene 5   Lear, too, sends a letter to Regan, no doubt telling her of Goneril's unkindness and preparing her for his unexpected arrival. In Lear's first words to Kent—'Go you before to Gloucester'—the careful reader finds a problem which is unnoticed in the theatre. Regan is *not* at Gloucester (if—as some editors assume—it is the town that is referred to), nor is she *yet* visiting the Earl of Gloucester. Kent must travel (as he explains in *Act 2*, Scene 4, lines 26–36) first to Regan's residence, and afterwards to Gloucester's castle in pursuit of Regan and her husband.

Shakespeare, it seems, has made a careless mistake—and one which is hardly worth noticing, *except* that it can usefully draw our attention to the magnificently complex achievement whereby Shakespeare melds (the American word— = *melts* and *welds*—is most apt) his two plots. At the moment, the plots—of Lear and his daughters, and of Gloucester and his sons—are fairly distinct. But the merger begins in *Act 2*, when the characters assemble in Gloucester's castle; Shakespeare is anticipating this when he makes Lear send Kent to Gloucester.

This scene does little to further the action: Lear waits for his horses to be saddled in preparation for the journey to Regan's home and, to pass the time, his Fool makes jokes. These do not entertain Lear (it is doubtful whether he is even listening), nor do they particularly amuse the audience. They do, however, effect an easing of the tension which has been occasioned by the relentlessly swift action of the play so far. The 'all-licens'd fool' speaks to Lear, as only he can, in the language of homely common sense. The world seems to be turned upside-down when Folly laughs at Majesty.

Act 2

Scene 1   The two plots begin to fuse. Gloucester has just been informed that Regan and Cornwall (whom he describes as his 'arch and patron'—i.e. his overlord) will shortly be arriving at his castle. Now Edmund is given the news, and he hears also of the dissension between Albany and Cornwall (Lear's division of his kingdom has not succeeded in averting this, as he had hoped—*1, 1, 44*). Edmund welcomes the news, seeing at once how he can use this changed situation to his own advantage. Calling Edgar, and acting in his role of loving brother, he advises instant flight; then, switching to his character of loyal son, he pretends to fight Edgar. Edmund is thus able to manipulate both his brother and his father.

When Gloucester comes on the scene, Edmund's performance is masterly. He must now give fuel to his father's suspicions of Edgar, and at the same time allow Edgar to get well away from the castle. Playing on Gloucester's superstitious nature, he tells how he found Edgar 'Mumbling of wicked charms, conjuring the moon To stand auspicious mistress'. He draws attention to his own wound—and perhaps the gesture that must accompany his 'Fled this way' is to point in the opposite direction to Edgar's actual exit. With assumed self-righteousness he describes his argument with Edgar, and gives a melodramatic account of their fight. Of course Gloucester is convinced—and his reaction ('Not in this land shall he remain uncaught; And found—dispatch') encourages Edmund to press his accusations still further.

By the time Cornwall and Regan arrive, Gloucester is almost wild with rage. He confides in them, finding sympathetic hearers.

Regan associates Edgar with her father's followers, whom she terms 'the riotous knights', and Edmund is quick to support her in this opinion. The mock fight with Edgar, and Edmund's self-inflicted wound, have drawn him to the attention of Cornwall, who now takes Edmund under his patronage—'you shall be ours'.

At this juncture the two plots become one, interdependent on each other for their different crises and solutions.

Cornwall starts to explain why they have now come to visit Gloucester, but Regan interrupts him. Like Goneril (see *Act 1*, Scene 4), she dominates her husband. Now she tells Gloucester about the letters she has received from Lear and Goneril. She will answer them when she is *away* from home: in this way, her father will not be able to come to her house before she and Goneril have decided on a plan of action. They have apparently chosen Gloucester's castle for their meeting-place because Cornwall is Gloucester's overlord, his 'arch and patron'.

Scene 2   Kent and Oswald, the messengers from Lear and Goneril, have followed Regan and Cornwall to Gloucester's castle. Here they confront each other. Oswald is slow to recognize Kent (who is, of course, in his disguise as 'Caius'), but Kent bears a grudge against Oswald for the insolence of his conduct to the king in *Act 1*, Scene 4 (and also—as we learn in Scene 4, lines 26–36—for his reception when he arrived at Regan's castle). He is ready to quarrel, and looses a stream of comic abuse at Oswald, who is first surprised and then frightened when Kent begins to beat him. His cries for help bring Cornwall, Regan, and Gloucester out to see what is happening.

Kent continues to insult Oswald, to the bewilderment of his audience. He extends his insults to include Cornwall and Regan—and this conduct cannot go unpunished! Cornwall calls for the stocks (see picture, p. 44). Such discipline was considered appropriate for the misbehaviour of servants in any great house, but Kent is the king's messenger and Cornwall should not dishonour him in this way. Kent's objections, however, only make Cornwall—and Regan—more determined, and even Gloucester's words carry no weight with them. Gloucester is embarrassed, but he is also afraid of Cornwall, 'Whose disposition, all the world well knows, Will not be rubb'd nor stopp'd'. He must obey his 'arch and patron'.

Kent accepts his shameful punishment with dignity, and consoles himself (and the audience) by reading a letter from Cordelia which somehow promises to 'give Losses their remedies'.

For readers of the play, this letter can present difficulties: when did Kent get the letter, and how did Cordelia learn of his 'obscured course'—since he has been serving Lear in this disguise for no more than two days? Shakespeare is ignoring any time-scheme—and theatre audiences will be too caught up in the action to notice. It is important only that we should be prepared for Cordelia's coming.

Scene 3   Kent sleeps in the stocks, and the attention of the audience is drawn to another part of the stage where Edgar describes how, in order to avoid capture, he will disguise himself as a 'Bedlam beggar'. Shakespeare had been reading a book by Samuel Harsnett (see Appendix, p. 141) which described the appearance of such licensed beggars—and of the rogues and vagabonds who *pretended* to be 'Bedlam beggars'. After his soliloquy Edgar leaves the stage; he has established his new identity, and can safely disappear from the action of the play for some time.

Once again we focus our attention on the stocks. This short Scene 3 has allowed for time to pass—perhaps the entire day.

Scene 4   Lear, accompanied by his Fool and with a Gentleman in attendance, arrives before Gloucester's castle in pursuit of Regan and Cornwall. Outside the castle, he discovers his messenger, Kent, confined in the stocks. When he hears Kent's account of the way he has been treated, Lear is suffused with rage and goes inside to find his daughter.

The Fool, in his own fashion, answers Kent's questions until Lear returns with Gloucester. Regan and Cornwall have refused to answer Lear's summons, and he is further incensed with their excuses. But he controls himself, and even tries to make some allowances—until he once more catches sight of Kent in the stocks, when his anger is re-kindled. Gloucester is anxious to make peace; Lear feels that he is choking with passion; and the Fool's jests grow even wilder.

At last Cornwall and Regan come to meet Lear. He greets them coolly, but then—turning to Regan—breaks into an impassioned denunciation of Goneril which ends with a cry for help and comfort: 'O Regan!'. But instead of the sympathy he expected, he finds that Regan takes her sister's side, defending Goneril's actions and recommending that Lear should return and ask for Goneril's forgiveness. Lear cannot believe what he is hearing. He repeats his complaints, and reiterates his curses on Goneril. Regan is not impressed, and Cornwall scoffs at the king.

Lear still has some hopes, however, that Regan will not be like her sister, but when Goneril arrives he sees Regan take her by the hand—a mark of solidarity. Goneril and Regan (backed by Cornwall) stand together in opposition to Lear. He tries to bargain with them about the number of his attendant knights, but they are adamant in their insistence that the knights must be reduced in number. Their arguments are eminently reasonable: 'How, in one house, Should many people, under two commands, Hold amity': Lear could 'receive attendance From those that she [Goneril] calls servants'; and if the servants were unsatisfactory, his daughters 'could control them'. But the hundred knights represent his independence—even, his majesty—to Lear; and he clings to this number. Relentlessly his daughters strip away these remnants of Lear's power until at last Regan asks why he should need *any* of his knights.

At this, Lear's temper explodes, and he is almost speechless with fury:

> I will have such revenges on you both
> That all the world shall—I will do such things,
> What they are, yet I know not, but they shall be
> The terrors of the earth.

Refusing to weep, but fearing for his own sanity, Lear rushes out into the night. He takes the Fool with him, and Gloucester follows them. We hear the distant rumble of thunder.

The scene, in which so many and such violent passions have been displayed, ends quietly. Goneril and Regan begin to make excuses for themselves. When Gloucester returns to report the king's departure and the gathering storm, the two sisters are ruthless: Lear must learn his lesson. Gloucester would show pity, but Cornwall takes command and Gloucester must obey the order to 'Shut up your doors'.

Act 3

Scene 1   Outside the castle is deserted heathland where (as Gloucester told us in the last scene) 'for many miles about There's scarce a bush'. A storm is raging, and a Gentleman (perhaps the last remnant of Lear's original entourage) describes how Lear seems to have allied himself with the cosmic powers. Kent (who is still disguised as 'Caius') imparts strange information to the Gentleman, telling him of quarrels between Albany and Cornwall, and of an impending French invasion (which he learned, perhaps, from Cordelia's letter in *Act 2*, Scene 2). The Gentleman must go to Dover, where he will be sure to meet Cordelia and learn the truth about the man he is now speaking to.

The scene offers more hope of comfort: when Cordelia returns, all will be well.

Kent and the Gentleman separate to resume their search for Lear; as they leave the stage, the king himself enters.

Scene 2 We see now what the Gentleman had described in the previous scene: Lear tries to 'out-storm' the elements, whilst the Fool 'labours to out-jest His heart-strook injuries'. Shakespeare is supremely tactful here. To have shown any more of the king's passion might have exposed him to ridicule—and would certainly have taxed any actor's vocal powers. And any more of the Fool's hysterical jokes might very well have produced the *wrong* kind of laughter.

Just as Lear is resolving to be patient, Kent comes upon the scene. His presence seems to set off Lear's passion again, and now he hears in the storm the wrath of the gods threatening judgement and punishment for the crimes of human beings. Kent attempts to persuade him to take shelter, but Lear at first resists; then, catching sight of the shivering Fool, he takes pity on him and consents to go inside. This may be a turning point for Lear: he begins to think of others before himself.

The Fool responds with the snatch of a song—whose tune would be immediately recognizable to Shakespeare's first audiences. It is the song that was sung in Shakespeare's play *Twelfth Night* by Robert Armin, who now plays the part of the Fool in *King Lear*. The verse lines are adapted to the present situation, but the refrain—'the rain it raineth every day'—is the same.

With this song, and the Fool's prophecy that follows it, the actor seems to step out of his character to remind the audience that some things *never* change: Lear's dilemma would be the same today (in the seventeenth—or even the twentieth—century), because the ideal world is yet to come. The words of the prophecy (which parody some lines quoted in a sixteenth-century book of poetical theory[2]) may not have been written by Shakespeare—Armin himself was quite capable of writing this sort of verse.

---

[2] *The Art of English Poesie* by Richard Puttenham.

The Fool's speech to the audience is dramatically useful because it helps with the first transition between the outdoor scene on the heath and the scene indoors in Gloucester's castle.

Scene 3 Gloucester, very agitated, takes Edmund into his confidence. Goneril and Regan have hardened in their attitude to Lear, and have threatened Gloucester with their 'perpetual displeasure' if he shows any sympathy towards their father. They have already taken possession of Gloucester's house. Gloucester knows that Albany and Cornwall are at odds with each other, and he has just learned —by letter—of some new danger from 'a power already footed'. We can guess that this letter, like the one that Kent was reading at the end of Scene 1, gives news of an invasion by the army of the King of France. It seems likely that France, who left England 'in choler' (*1*, 2, 23), has returned to take by force that portion of Lear's kingdom which Cordelia should rightfully have inherited.

Gloucester advises Edmund that they must now support King Lear against his daughters, and he is determined—even at the risk of his own life—to give comfort to his 'old master'. Edmund is sympathetic—but after Gloucester has left the stage, he discloses his own intentions to the audience: he will betray his father's confidence; reveal the incriminating letter; and hope to profit by Gloucester's certain downfall. The slick, self-congratulatory verse of Edmund's lines is in striking contrast with Gloucester's rambling prose. The hopes raised by Gloucester's letter now seem to be threatened by the intended treachery of Gloucester's son.

Scene 4 We return to the wild heath where Kent is shepherding Lear to take refuge from the storm. The king is reluctant to go inside, arguing that the suffering of his body eases the anguish of his mind. But he sends Kent and the Fool in to find comfort—yet another sign that he is taking thought for others. And when he is alone he prays, recognizing his responsibility for the 'Poor naked wretches' who share with him the miseries of the storm.

Suddenly the Fool rushes out to him, scared out of his wits by something that is lurking in the hovel. It is Edgar, totally submerged in his character of Poor Tom (for which we were prepared in *Act 2*, Scene 2). His appearance is the last straw for Lear, who finally succumbs to the madness he had feared ever since his daughters first showed their real natures. In his madness, he assumes that Poor Tom is in the same condition as he himself: 'nothing could have subdu'd nature To such a lowness but his unkind daughters'. Edgar gives a superb performance as Poor Tom, naked except for a blanket around his loins. The storm rumbles still. Lear watches and listens; in Tom he finds the truth about human nature, the essence of humanity unadulterated by the trappings of civilization. Tearing off his clothes, Lear tries to become like Tom, but he is restrained by the Fool.

There is an interruption in the mad frenzy when Gloucester arrives, coming in search of Lear. Then Edgar, with renewed vigour, resumes his performance as Poor Tom, and Lear's genuine madness responds to his assumed lunacy. His pity for Lear reminds Gloucester of his own situation and he tells Kent of the son who (as he believes) has tried to kill him:

> I lov'd him, friend,
> No father his son dearer; true to tell thee,
> The grief hath craz'd my wits.

If Edgar hears this—and I think he must—he can only respond with the beggar's cry, 'Tom's a-cold'.

Once again, Kent shepherds the sad, mad little party into the hovel.

Scene 5   Inside Gloucester's castle, Edmund has betrayed his father to Cornwall, and now he is playing a new role: he is a loyal subject who has sacrificed his own father for the good of his country! He gets his reward—his father's title, 'Earl of Gloucester'. An 'aside' spoken to the audience leaves his hypocrisy in no doubt. But Gloucester himself is in serious danger.

Scene 6   Lear, in his new and very real madness, joins with Edgar (in his pretended insanity as Poor Tom) and the Fool to hold a trial of Goneril (represented by 'a joint-stool') and Regan. The king's madness distresses Kent, and moves Edgar to tears—he can hardly sustain his performance. At last Kent succeeds in persuading the king to rest and Lear, believing himself to be in his own bed, falls asleep.

The Fool, responding to Lear's decision to 'go to supper i'th'morning', makes his final comment: 'I'll go to bed at noon'. If supper is to be eaten in the morning, then it is logical to go to bed in the middle of the day: the world is completely upside-down. He helps to carry Lear out to the cart in which he will be conveyed to Dover, and then the Fool disappears from the play's action. Being quite insane, the king has no further need of a fool.

Gloucester has arranged for Lear to be taken to Dover (where

he will be able to meet Cordelia and the French troops) because
the king's life is now in danger. And Gloucester must know that he
is putting his own life at risk. When the king's party has left,
Edgar, now in his own person, comments on the king's suffering
and finds a parallel with his own: 'He childed as I father'd'. He
recognizes the present danger, but the audience can take comfort
from the knowledge that he intends to reveal himself when the
time is ripe.

His soliloquy is of great value in showing the development,
through suffering, of Edgar's character; and the speech is immediately useful because it allows the audience to imagine that a little
time is elapsing. And it makes a break between the different
tensions of Scene 6 and Scene 7.

Scene 7   Cornwall is preparing to deal with 'the traitor Gloucester' following Edmund's betrayal of his father in Scene 6; the French army
has landed in England—and it is only right that the rulers,
Cornwall and Albany, should defend their territory and punish
anyone suspected of aiding the invaders. But Regan and Goneril
are blood-thirsty, and Cornwall, although he knows that Gloucester should be given a public trial, is equally vindictive. He sends
Edmund out of the room—in company with Goneril—and orders
the servants to bring Gloucester before him, bound as though he
were a common thief and not a nobleman.

Cornwall and Regan exult in the humiliation of their
prisoner, interrogating him with relentless violence until he is
forced to disclose the king's whereabouts. When the questions
persist, Gloucester—terrified though he is—speaks out against the
pitiless treatment that Lear has received at his daughters' hands;
he tells Regan that he hopes to see retaliation from some divine
justice, and he is answered 'See't shalt thou never'. Gloucester is
bound to a chair, and Cornwall claws out one of his eyes.
Gloucester screams in agony, but Regan, jubilant in his anguish,
demands his other eye, too.

Cornwall's servants are revolted by this obscene torture, and
one of them draws his sword against his master. Whilst they are
fighting, Regan snatches a sword from another servant and stabs
from behind, killing her husband's assailant—but not before
Cornwall himself is wounded. Undeterred, however, Cornwall
renews his assault on Gloucester and tears out his other eye.
When Gloucester calls on his son, Edmund, for help, Regan takes
great delight in telling him that it was Edmund who first betrayed
his father:

> Thou call'st on him that hates thee; it was he
> That made the overture of thy treasons to us.

Gloucester is bundled out of the room and Cornwall, bleeding heavily, retires with Regan. Only the servants are left to bring this outrageous scene to a close with the compassion of their common humanity.

It is many years since Shakespeare presented a scene of such physical brutality—and even then (in *Titus Andronicus, c.* 1591) almost all the actual violence took place off-stage. But in *King Lear* Shakespeare wants to show, as far as it is possible in the theatre, the depths to which human beings can sink and the extent of 'man's inhumanity to man'.

Act 4

Scene 1   Edgar, still in his disguise as Poor Tom but speaking in his own person, is cheering himself up with the thought that things cannot get any worse, and so they must improve. But this philosophical meditation proves to be ironic (proleptic—anticipatory—irony is characteristic of this play). Edgar's thoughts are interrupted when he sees his father and overhears Gloucester's conversation with the old man who is leading him. Although he is sightless, Gloucester can at last see the truth: he now knows which of his two sons was to be trusted.

Greatly distressed by the appearance of his father, Edgar reverts—with some difficulty—to the speech of the mad beggar and agrees to lead Gloucester to Dover. Gloucester's predicament has brought him, like Lear (in *Act 3*, Scene 2), to a heightened awareness of the needs of the suffering poor, and he, too, prays for a fairer distribution of wealth in a world where 'each man [will] have enough'. But for himself, he is desperate, and he means to put an end to his misery when 'Poor Tom' has led him to the top of Dover cliff.

Scene 2   Arriving at Albany's castle, Goneril and Edmund (who seem to be very intimate) are met by Oswald, who describes a strange alteration in the character of Albany: 'What most he should dislike seems pleasant to him; What like, offensive'. Goneril is immediately scornful of her husband's 'cowish terror'—but she can see how she and Edmund may be able to take advantage of this. She sends Edmund back to raise up Cornwall and his troops, giving him a token of her affection which he can wear as a public declaration of their private relationship—just as a medieval knight would wear his mistress's scarf in a tournament.

We have been prepared (by Oswald) to see a change in Albany—but even so, we can be surprised by the vehemence of his denunciation of Goneril. Albany has been absent from the stage since *Act 1*, Scene 4, where he offered no more than a mild remonstration to his wife. But now he confronts her with sheer disgust, accusing her of such monstrous and unnatural crimes against her father that, if they are not punished by divine retribution, will lead the whole world to disaster:

> It will come,
> Humanity must perforce prey on itself,
> Like monsters of the deep.

This image of cannibalism, indicating the total collapse of all moral and natural law and order, was not uncommon in Elizabethan literature; Shakespeare has used it twice before—in *Troilus and Cressida* (1, 3, 123–4), and in a scene which he added to *Sir Thomas More*, a play written by several different dramatists of whom Shakespeare was easily the most distinguished. In Shakespeare's scene, More prophesies a future chaos where 'men like ravenous fishes Would feed on one another' (lines 86–7).

Goneril is unmoved, however, and repeats her charges of cowardice to Albany. Husband and wife argue bitterly—it is a verbal fight, which is interrupted only when a Messenger arrives and blurts out his news: 'the Duke of Cornwall's dead'. The news of Cornwall's death means less to Albany than the occasion for it. The blinding of Gloucester horrifies him for the deed itself, but he can see in it the working of some divine power.

The information disturbs Goneril: she is glad to know that the old man has been made to suffer, but jealous and suspicious of Regan's dealings with *her* Gloucester—that is, with Edmund. Goneril leaves the stage to write some letters; when she is gone, Albany learns from the Messenger how Edmund had betrayed his father and left the house so that Cornwall and Regan 'Might have the freer course' in punishing Gloucester for his support of the king. Albany at last declares which side *he* is on:

> Gloucester, I live
> To thank thee for the love thou show'dst the king,
> And to revenge thine eyes.

Scene 3   The Gentleman who was sent to meet Cordelia (in *Act 3*, Scene 1) has returned to Kent, who questions him about the French army that has landed at Dover. The King of France, it seems, has suddenly returned home, and the Gentleman explains that some official business needed his immediate personal attention. His explanation is rather vague—but Shakespeare has *always* been (deliberately) vague about the real reasons for this French presence in England—probably because the English audiences of his time would have felt uneasy about such an invasion of their country. But now it is clear that Cordelia is going to use her husband's army solely for the purpose of rescuing and relieving her father.

     In lines of rare lyrical beauty, the Gentleman speaks of Cordelia's reactions when he gave her the letter from Kent. Images of richness—the pearls and diamonds—are used to describe the blessed relief that comes from the 'holy water' of Cordelia's unselfish tears. At the beginning of the play, Shakespeare took great care to show that the action was set in a pagan, pre-Christian, world (see *1*, 1, 159). But in presenting Cordelia as a redemptive power, his language is charged with biblical overtones—most especially in the next scene (lines 23–4), where Cordelia takes up her father's cause with words that echo those of Jesus in the Gospel of St Luke.

     Kent must now tell how 'the poor distressed Lear' has some lucid moments when he knows where he is and remembers what he has done. But when he is like this, 'in his better tune', he is so overcome with shame that he refuses to meet Cordelia. Kent takes the Gentleman to see the king.

     This scene is not present in the Folio text whose readers are consequently unprepared for the reappearance of Cordelia (who has had no active part in the play since the end of *Act 1*, Scene 1).

Scene 4   Cordelia now enters, *'with drum and colours'*, discussing her father's madness with a Doctor. Lear has been seen wearing a crown made up of what Cordelia calls 'all the idle weeds that grow In our sustaining corn'. His disordered mind is thus linked, emblematically, with the rich cornfield overgrown with weeds— which itself seems to represent the torn and divided land of Lear's kingdom under the sway of its new rulers.

     To treat Lear's distraction, the Doctor prescribes the most natural of all remedies—what Shakespeare described in another play as 'The season of all natures, sleep' (*Macbeth*, *3*, 4, 141).

     Entrusting her father's person to the Doctor's care, Cordelia prepares to fight for his rights against the advancing English armies: 'O dear father! It is thy business that I go about' (see Luke 2:49, 'I must go about my father's business'). Before she leaves the stage, however, Cordelia declares (for the more assurance of Shakespeare's contemporary audience) the reason for the presence of a French army on English soil:

> No blown ambition doth our arms incite,
> But love, dear love, and our ag'd father's right.

Scene 5   Oswald has reached Regan's castle, bringing the letter that Goneril sent to her sister (in *Act 4*, Scene 2), and also carrying Goneril's letter to Edmund. This arouses Regan's suspicions, throwing her into some confusion. She tries to get Oswald to let her read the second letter, explaining that Edmund is away on important business: the spectacle of the blinded Gloucester is turning people against Cornwall and Regan, so Edmund has gone to find his father and 'In pity of his misery, to dispatch His nighted life'.

The information seems partly to be spoken as an 'aside' (when Regan regrets that they did not kill Gloucester at once), and partly offered as a kind of humanitarian excuse. But Oswald is a loyal servant to his mistress, Goneril, and he shows no reaction. His impassiveness forces Regan to a declaration of her jealousy and her desires, and she too (like Goneril in Scene 2) has a token of her love to give to Edmund. Their love—or lust—for Edmund is driving a wedge between the two sisters.

Scene 6   Edgar and his blind father are walking towards Dover. The 'Poor Tom' disguise is now completely discarded: Edgar wears the clothes provided by the servant (in Scene 1) and speaks with his normal tones and language. The ground they tread on is quite level. But Edgar must persuade Gloucester that they are reaching the summit of a high cliff. He points out graphic details—crows 'scarce so gross as beetles', the samphire-gatherer who 'seems no bigger than his head', and the fishermen who 'Appear like mice'— and he even creates, by commenting on its absence, the sound of the sea. His description certainly convinces Gloucester—and would almost deceive audience and readers into accepting this for truth, as Shakespeare's verbal compensation for the lack of scenic resources in the theatre of his day!

Gloucester parts from his guide (who confides in the audience the reason for his play-acting like this: 'Why I do trifle thus with his despair Is done to cure it'). Gloucester prays to the 'mighty gods', asking their forgiveness for his weakness (because he cannot endure his present existence) and for their blessing on Edgar. He then throws himself—as he imagines—over the edge of the cliff. Actually, of course, he falls flat on the ground! The situation is grotesque—even comical; but there is no *laughter* in the spectacle of a blind man desperately trying to kill himself.

Edgar now 'finds' his father, and again he creates in Gloucester's mind the image of a tall cliff, more than the height of the masts of ten ships, standing one upon the other. But this time we are looking *upwards,* and Gloucester must be persuaded that he has indeed fallen down and lies on the beach: it is a miracle that he is unharmed! Edgar describes a monstrous creature seen at the top of the cliff and Gloucester (still as gullible as he ever was) is certain that this was 'the fiend'—the devil himself. In Elizabethan thought, the devil was always ready to lead human beings to the ultimate desperation in which they would commit suicide and thereby incur eternal damnation. Gloucester is willing to accept a lesson from his preservation, and endure his affliction with all patience.

As one crisis is resolved, a new one comes to the fore. Lear comes on to the scene, *'fantastically dressed with wild flowers'.* We have been prepared for this latest stage in his madness, so the sight is not totally surprising—although we should still respond with something of the anguish that Edgar articulates: 'O thou side-piercing sight!' The king is locked in his own world, into which there is no entry for Gloucester and Edgar, who can only stand and grieve.

In his madness, Lear's mind jumps from one subject to another, sometimes through word-associations ('peace' suggests 'piece' and 'bills' prompts 'birds'). The first of these 'mad' speeches accustoms us to Shakespeare's technique in creating a language for madness: the content of the speech is negligible. But when he looks on Gloucester, Lear sees 'Goneril, with a white beard!' and this starts off a new chain of thought-processes which (at least for the play's audience) are more accessible because more relevant to the king's situation.

Hearing the word 'king' spoken by Gloucester, Lear's mind fastens on this and it moves him from the idea of the king's pardon for a crime and the crime of adultery to a passionate denunciation of female sexuality where his horrified imaginings reveal a 'sulphurous pit—burning, scalding, Stench, consumption'.

At this point some slight respite is needed—for Gloucester and Edgar to voice their reactions, for the audience to draw its

breath after this onslaught, and for Lear himself (and the actor
playing this part). The relief is given in the prose exchange
between Lear and Gloucester, which almost becomes *comic* relief
(although it is not funny) when Lear identifies Gloucester as
'blind Cupid' and when he plays 'handy-dandy' with the
magistrate and the thief—let them change places, and then can
you tell which is which?

There is nothing comic in the tirade that follows, where Lear
inveighs against the power of wealth and the corruption of justice.
At the climax of the speech he pauses, relapsing momentarily into
the madness of exhaustion and ordering the (imagined) footmen
to pull off his boots. His recognition of Gloucester sounds like
sanity, and he preaches patience with a wisdom acquired through
suffering whilst Gloucester weeps in pity of his master.

His attention is suddenly diverted away from his preaching
and he praises 'a good block'. Perhaps 'stage' (in the same line)
has suggested something to him (scaffold, executioner's block,
mounting-block, hat-block?) which leads him to the notion of felt-
shod cavalry who could take his daughters' husbands by surprise
and exact revenge upon them. But it is Lear himself who is taken
by surprise when the Gentleman—making a rather clumsy
move—orders Cordelia's attendants to 'lay hands upon him'. Lear
evades capture and, although the Gentleman now speaks in
conciliatory tones—humouring a madman and honouring a
king—he succeeds in running away, chased by the attendants.

The Gentleman remains behind, just long enough to give
Edgar (and the audience) the latest news on the war front: the two
armies are approaching, and will soon join battle. Gloucester
renews his prayer for strength to endure until it pleases the gods to
'take [his] breath from [him]'. Edgar applauds his prayer: 'Well
pray you, father'. This form of address was appropriate from a
younger man to an older—although, of course, it has a different
meaning for Edgar who, still refusing to disclose his identity,
prepares to lead Gloucester to safety.

Once again we have had a brief interval between the distinct,
but closely related, episodes in this most complex scene; and once
again the apparent calm is shattered. Oswald, on his way to deliver
Goneril's letter to Edmund, comes by chance—a 'happy' chance
as he sees it—upon Gloucester, 'a publish'd traitor' whose death
would certainly 'raise [Oswald's] fortunes'. Although he showed
himself a coward when Kent abused him (in *Act 2*, Scene 2), he is
not afraid to draw his sword on a blind old man.

Gloucester welcomes the thought of death, but Edgar once

more saves his father's life. Assuming the character of a peasant, and speaking with a stage 'rustic' dialect, he fights and kills Oswald. Just before he dies, Oswald—still loyal to his mistress's command—entrusts Goneril's letter to the man who has given him a fatal wound. Edgar has recognized Oswald for who and what he is—'a serviceable villain'—but regrets that it was *he* who had to kill him. He is reluctant, but compelled by necessity, to read private correspondence.

From the letter to Edmund he learns that Goneril is inciting Edmund to murder her husband, Albany, and bribing him with the promise of marriage—he can 'supply [Albany's] place'. This comes as a complete and shocking surprise to Edgar, who hastily buries the body of Oswald 'in the sands'. Shakespeare must have forgotten that his characters are *not* on the beach—or perhaps he has convinced himself by his own rhetoric, just as Edgar has persuaded Gloucester that they are at the foot of Dover cliff!

Gloucester knows only that Oswald is dead and that there is no more threat to his own life—or (as he understands it) no relief from his suffering. He begins to envy King Lear for the insanity which at least makes him oblivious to all other sorrows. Edgar interrupts his lamentation, and hurries his father off to hide from the fighting which is now imminent. A drum signals the approach of the opposing armies.

Scene 7   Kent has revealed himself to Cordelia, and receives her gratitude as, with the Doctor, they wait to see whether Lear, when he recovers consciousness, will be himself again. Cordelia invokes the gods and prays for their aid to restore her father to health. Lear is carried in, wearing fresh clothes (which will manifest the change in his condition), and the Doctor calls for music (which always, in Shakespeare's plays, denotes harmony and reconciliation). Kent and the Doctor stand back, whilst Cordelia advances to greet her father with a kiss. It is one of Shakespeare's most magical moments.

Softly ('her voice was ever soft, Gentle and low'—5, 3, 271), Cordelia talks to her father, willing him back from the dark recesses of his tortured mind. Lear gradually returns to consciousness. At first he is confused—only a pinprick can convince him that he is really alive.

When Cordelia speaks, courteously and respectfully, he does not know who she is—although he feels he *ought* to know her. He looks around, and sees a strange place; when he looks down at himself, he sees unfamiliar clothing. But there is a glimmer of recognition when he looks up again and sees the 'lady'—his 'child', his own Cordelia. She weeps, with tears of joy. But with the dawning recognition there comes also into Lear's mind the recollection of something hurtful in the past. He cannot remember just what it was—and the Doctor counsels Cordelia to proceed slowly and with caution.

To the Doctor, naturally, Lear is a patient, and he speaks with some clinical detachment; but to Cordelia he is not only her beloved father but also a king, as the formality of her address shows: 'Will't please your highness walk?' Lear, no longer the autocratic, seemingly omnipotent majesty who cast off his youngest daughter, now meekly obeys her and asks her forbearance: 'You must bear with me. Pray you now, forget and forgive: I am old and foolish'.

When Cordelia has taken her father inside, Kent and the Gentleman exchange news. Their fairly casual, prose, conversation eases the transition from the gentle, tender 'recognition' scene with all its sensitive emotions. Kent confirms what the Gentleman has heard (and so reminds the audience) that Cornwall is dead and that his troops are being led by Edmund. The Gentleman tells the man whom he still knows only in his disguise as 'Caius' that 'They say that Edgar, his [i.e. Gloucester's] banished son, is with the Earl of Kent in Germany'. Kent must smile at this, at the same time as he anticipates the coming battle which will, somehow, make an end to his life's work.

Act 5

Scene 1 War is imminent. But Albany's forces have not yet arrived and Edmund (who is leading Cornwall's troops now that the duke is dead) is getting impatient. He has not received Goneril's letter—because, as Regan suggests, the messenger 'is certainly miscarried': we know (as Regan does not) that Oswald has been killed by Edgar, who now has possession of the letter.

Regan questions Edmund closely about his relationship with her sister, and asks if they have ever slept together. Edmund denies this, but Regan is still doubtful and enjoins Edmund, 'Be not familiar with her'. This Edmund seems to promise, scoffing at Goneril and 'the duke her husband'. Just at this moment the two enter, leading their army. When she sees Regan and Edmund conferring together, Goneril's suspicions are aroused and, in an 'aside', she declares her real feelings to the audience: 'I had rather lose the battle than that sister Should loosen him and me'.

Albany has the information that King Lear has joined forces with Cordelia, taking with him a number of protesters who are rebelling against the severity of the new regime. Albany states his own position—but the five lines (from 'Where I could not be honest' to 'speak nobly') are omitted from the Folio text and not easily intelligible in the Quarto text. He seems to be saying that he will fight against the King of France *only* because he is morally bound to defend his country against a foreign invasion and *not* because France's support is giving encouragement to Lear and those who are with him.

A council of war is summoned. For a moment it looks as though Goneril will stay behind to speak with Edmund—but Regan makes sure that this will not be allowed! They all leave together, but Albany's attention is caught by a poor man. We recognize Edgar, still disguised in the 'best 'parel' that had been provided by Gloucester's servant (in *Act 4*, Scene 1).

Edgar produces a letter, which we know is the letter written by Goneril to Edmund, inciting him to the murder of Albany. He will not stay until Albany has read the contents of the letter, but promises to return after the battle when he will demonstrate the truth about them. Edgar visualizes a medieval tournament (and we remember that Edmund, like any medieval knight, has been given their favours by both Goneril and Regan—in *Act 4*, Scenes 2 and 5).

Edmund now comes to call Albany to make his arrangements for the battle. Alone on the stage, Edmund takes the audience into his confidence. He enjoys the comedy of his predicament, and the audience too can laugh when he asks 'Which of them shall I take? Both? one? or neither?'. But audience sympathy soon dissolves into horror at his cold-blooded contemplation of the murder of Albany and the frustration of 'the mercy Which he [Albany] intends to Lear and to Cordelia'. Edmund is ambitious to rule over the whole kingdom: nothing is going to stand in his way!

We know, however, that Albany will read the letter from Goneril and learn the truth about Edmund. And Edgar is standing in the wings ready, 'When time shall serve', to play his part in the action.

Scene 2   For the present, Edgar must place his father under the shelter of a tree whilst the quickest battle in all Shakespeare's plays is fought out off-stage. Only the trumpets and drums are heard, sounding the '*Alarum*' and beating the '*retreat*'—calling the troops to engage in fighting, then signalling an end to their hostilities. Shakespeare is not interested in this battle, only in its outcome.

Edgar leaves his father with the injunction to 'pray that right may thrive' and the cheerful promise to return and 'bring [him] comfort'. This is more proleptic irony, anticipating Edgar's almost immediate return with the devastating news that the prayer has not been heard: 'King Lear hath lost, he and his daughter [are] ta'en'. Gloucester is sunk in depression, but Edgar has a philosophy to counter every disaster: 'Ripeness is all'—the important thing is not to seek death, nor to avoid it, but to be ready to accept when it comes. Gloucester gives his assent to this, and father and son withdraw to leave the stage clear for Edmund's conquering army with its two captives.

Scene 3   Cordelia is brave, but worried for her father's sake. Lear himself, however, is quite carefree; he can conceive of no greater happiness than being in prison with Cordelia, where she will enjoy his fatherly love and will grant him her forgiveness. With serene detachment they will survey the agitations of life at court, and endure beyond the fluctuating powers of the 'great ones'. Edmund brusquely orders their removal, and Lear seems to welcome his command. But Cordelia weeps. She knows that this paradisial prison existence will never be more than imaginary, and she sheds tears for the harsh reality which is to come.

When the king and his daughter have left, under strict guard, Edmund calls a captain to him and entrusts the man with a grim task. The captain welcomes his mission (although he does not yet know what it is): he sees it as a means to preferment—but the audience heard Edmund's words at the end of Scene 1!

Albany, coming in with Goneril and Regan, praises Edmund for the valour he has shown in the battle and requests him to yield up his prisoners, Lear and Cordelia. Edmund explains that he has sent them to a place of safety, because he was afraid that the sight of 'the old and miserable king' and his daughter might have such an effect on the hearts of ordinary people—'the common bosom' —that even the soldiers would rebel against their leaders. Furthermore, he adds, this is neither the time nor the place to deal with 'The question of Cordelia and her father'.

Albany is infuriated by the manner of this speech, and he is quick to reprimand Edmund for his presumption: 'I hold you but a subject of this war, Not as a brother'. Regan springs to Edmund's defence, pointing out that he has been acting on her behalf and consequently has every right to be considered as a brother by Albany.

Goneril makes the rejoinder that Edmund does not need Regan's favour: he is quite distinguished enough in himself. But with the position that she has given him, Regan retorts, Edmund is equal to the highest in the land. Albany remarks that Edmund could be no more than this if he were Regan's husband. Her reply to this is enigmatic—but Goneril understands what is meant (and so does the audience).

Goneril is ready for a fight, but Regan is feeling unwell. Refusing to be drawn into a quarrel, she startles them all—including Edmund—with a public declaration: 'Witness the world, that I create thee here My lord and master'. Goneril protests. Albany tells her she has no right to object.

Edmund equally denies Albany's right to interfere—and then Albany (with a contemptuous sarcasm that he has never shown until now) proceeds to denounce his wife and her lover. He accuses Edmund of treachery, and throws down his glove in token of a challenge. Edmund repudiates this allegation and declares himself ready to defend his honour. Albany calls for a herald, informing Edmund that all his troops have already been disbanded.

All this time Regan's sickness has been growing worse; and, in an 'aside', Goneril has betrayed herself to the audience: she has poisoned her sister.

The Herald reads out the formal allegation and (in accordance with the rules of chivalry—and with Edgar's instructions in Scene 1) the trumpet is sounded three times. At the third sound there is a responding call, and Edgar appears, his identity now disguised by the full armour that he wears. He declines to identify himself (as would be more proper in such a combat), but he asserts his nobility and his right to make such a challenge. He then reiterates, with additions, the terms of Albany's indictment, summing them up in the insult that Edmund is 'A most toad-spotted traitor'. All this Edmund denies as 'hell-hated lies', and he takes up the challenge—even though, technically, he could refuse to fight an adversary whose name and chivalric status were unknown.

Edmund falls under his brother's sword. Albany cries out to save his life, hoping to get a full confession and explanation from him. His attention, however, is diverted to Goneril and her exclamations. He holds a paper in front of her, and she recognizes her own letter to Edmund, in which she had urged him to murder Albany. In desperation, she rushes from the scene.

Edmund, knowing he is close to death, acknowledges his guilt and asks to know the identity of the knight who has killed him, forgiving him for his death. Edgar at last reveals himself and extends his forgiveness to the brother who had so cruelly wronged him. Both brothers seem to be at last united in their philosophy of retributive justice: their father paid for his sin of adultery when he lost his sight through the treachery of Edmund, and now Edgar, in retaliation, has taken Edmund's life.

The amazed Albany questions Edgar eagerly—where has he been hiding? How did he know what had happened to his father? Edgar tells 'a brief tale', recounting what the audience already knows, and adding one thing more: Gloucester is dead. When at last Edgar revealed himself to his father, the surprise was too great a shock to the old man's heart and it killed him: but he died 'smilingly'. Edmund, too, is moved by this story, and hints that he may be able to do something to help secure (what now seems almost certain) a happy outcome for all their troubles.

Edgar goes on with his story, describing his meeting with a man who had given him a full account of Lear and his misadventures before, overcome with his own emotion, he had collapsed. That man, of course, was Kent. But Edgar had been forced to leave him, unconscious, when he heard the trumpets sound and knew that he was called to fight with his brother.

More excitement! There is a cry for help from a Gentleman, who waves a knife dripping with blood. Goneril, having confessed to the poisoning of her sister, has killed herself. Albany demands to see the bodies, and Kent—who has revived from his momentary faintness and managed to catch up with the action—asks to see King Lear.

In all this agitation, the king has been forgotten—Cordelia, too! But there is yet another interruption when the bodies of Goneril and Regan are produced. Edmund looks on them and realizes that they have both died for love of *him*. He resolves to do what is probably the one good deed in his life. Someone must run to the castle to save the lives of Lear and Cordelia!

Albany cries out in panic, but Edgar keeps his head and insists on more specific instructions before sending an officer. Edmund confesses that he has given orders to the captain (lines 29–39) to hang Cordelia, making it appear as though she had taken her own life (which was indeed the case in most of Shakespeare's sources—see Appendix, p. 135). Albany expresses a prayer for Cordelia's safety: 'The gods defend her!' Edmund is carried out; he will die off-stage.

From the other side of the stage Lear enters, with the body of Cordelia in his arms. He cannot believe what his eyes tell him is all too true, and he searches desperately for any sign of life—a breath, a murmur. The old man ('I am a very foolish, fond old man, Fourscore and upward'—*4*, 7, 60) has found a new strength in this final calamity, and he can even boast of having killed the captain when he was hanging Cordelia. Albany's officer, who arrived just too late to save Cordelia, can confirm Lear's boast: ''Tis true, my lords, he did'.

Kent tries to attract Lear's notice and gain recognition for his service as 'Caius', but the king cannot understand and will not concentrate—not even when he is told of the deaths of Goneril and Regan. All that matters to him now is this lady—his child—Cordelia! And he must be granted a short space of time to grieve over her body.

Meanwhile Albany receives news of Edmund's death, which he dismisses as 'but a trifle here'. He resigns all his power back to Lear—'this old majesty'—and speaks lines that would seem to bring to an end the action of the play:

> All friends shall taste
> The wages of their virtue, and all foes
> The cup of their deservings.

But this play has still more.

All eyes are turned to the sorrowing Lear, lamenting his lifeless daughter who will never return to him:

> Never, never, never, never, never!

The first word is like a stone dropped down a deep, seemingly bottomless, well, and setting off endless reverberations. The pentameter is simply perfect, bearing in its simplicity all the sorrow and weight of this great play. Lear feels again his former sense of suffocation, and struggles to loosen his clothing—'Pray you, undo this button'. Some slight—and probably imagined—movement excites him and he turns back to Cordelia. The excitement, however, is too much for him—just as his own conflicting emotions were too strong for Gloucester in Edgar's narrative of his father's death. King Lear is dying.

Edgar would try to revive him but Kent knows that such effort would be pointless and heartless. Lear's sufferings are now at an end—and Kent is ready to follow after his master. Albany, after giving orders for the removal of the dead king and his daughter, withdraws and leaves Kent and Edgar in the fore-front of the stage. Kent too retires. Only Edgar is left to draw the play to a close: there is no comfort, but there is peace at the last.

Usually Shakespeare's plays are warmly, even rapturously, applauded as soon as the last curtain falls (or some other signal is given for the closure of the action). But I have never seen a performance of *King Lear* where the ending was not greeted with a hushed and awed silence.

Date and Text

King Lear was written between 1603 and 1606. The title-page of the first edition refers to a performance before the king on Boxing Day, 1606; and Shakespeare could have got his knowledge of Samuel Harsnett's work only after the publication of his *Declaration of Egregious Popishe Impostures* in 1604[3]. The play's First Quarto is dated 1608. Like most quarto plays, it was a cheap, hurried publication—perhaps rushed to the press without proper permission from the theatrical company or (least of all) the author. There are many obvious errors—misunderstandings, misreadings, mishearings; verse printed as prose—and prose, just as misleadingly, printed as verse. A second quarto (also dated 1608 but actually published in 1619) tried to tidy things up—and added fresh errors. Then, in 1623, there was the First Folio, the complete (almost) collection of Shakespeare's plays.

The Folio is a rich, elegant volume which is generally well-printed. The new edition added a few extra lines (including the Fool's prophecy at the end of *Act 3*, Scene 2) to *King Lear*, and purged the Quarto text of many errors. It also omitted some three hundred lines (among them the words from the horrified servants after the blinding of Gloucester in *Act 3*, Scene 7). Was this the work of Shakespeare, his second thoughts on *King Lear*? Perhaps only he could have made some of the corrections—but perhaps some other hand or hands made other alterations (maybe for reasons of censorship, or just to shorten a very long play). Some modern critics believe that there are *two* plays of *King Lear*, both—almost equally—the work of Shakespeare. Others (of whom I am one) dispute the argument: there is just not enough evidence on *either* side.

The present edition uses the Arden text prepared in 1950 (revised 1980) by the greatest of twentieth-century *Lear* scholars, Professor Kenneth Muir. Where substantial passages were omitted in either the Quarto or the Folio texts, these are marked ('*om.* Q', '*om.* F') in the Notes. Appendix A, 'Quarto and Folio', prints some of the disputed passages as 'parallel texts'.

---

[3] See Appendix, p. 141.

Shakespeare's Verse

Underlying *King Lear*, as the groundrock of which the play is made, is the iambic pentameter line which forms the blank verse used by most English dramatists writing in the sixteenth and early seventeenth centuries. It is a very flexible medium, capable—like the human speaking voice—of an infinite variety of tones. Basically the lines, which are unrhymed, are ten syllables long. The syllables have alternating stresses, just like normal English speech; and they divide into five 'feet' to make up the iambic pentameter.

King Lear initiates the rhythm when, following the prose conversation of Kent and Gloucester, he enters in full majesty, summoning all his court to hear his declared intentions:

> **Lear**
> Meantíme, we sháll expréss our dárker púrpose.   35
> Give mé the máp there. Know thát we háve divíded
> In thrée our kíngdom; and 'tís our fást intént
> To sháke all cáres and búsiness fróm our áge,
> Conférring thém on yóunger stréngths, while wé
> Unbúrthen'd cráwl toward déath. Our són of Córnwall,   40
> And yóu, our nó less lóving són of Álbany,
> We háve this hóur a cónstant wíll to públish
> Our dáughters' séveral dówers, that fúture strífe
> May bé prevénted nów . . .
>   . . . Tell mé, my daúghters . . .
> Which óf you sháll we sáy doth lóve us móst?   50

The rhythm is easily shared by other speakers. Lear's elder daughters join with their father in a smooth, dignified interchange—and even the youngest, Cordelia, does not disturb the harmony with her whispered 'aside':

> **Goneril**
> Sir, I lóve you móre than wórd can wiéld the mátter;
> Dearér than eýesight, spáce and líbertý;   55
> Beyónd what cán be válued, rích or ráre . . .
> **Lear**
> Of áll these bóunds, even fróm this líne to thís,

With shádowy fórests ánd with chámpains rích'd,
With plénteous rívers ánd wide-skírted méads,
We máke thee lády . . .   65
                    . . . What sáys our sécond dáughter?
Our déarest Régan, wífe of Córnwall?

   Regan
Í am máde of thát self métal ás my síster,
And prize me át her wórth. In my true héart
I find she námes my véry déed of lóve;   70
Onlý she cómes too shórt: that Í proféss . . .
                    . . . I ám alóne felícitáte
In yóur dear híghness' lóve.

   Cordelia [*Aside*]
                              Then póor Cordélia!   75
And yét not só; since Í am súre my lóve's
More pónderous thán my tóngue.

   Lear [*who is answering Regan*]
To thée and thíne, heréditáry éver,
Remáin this ámple sháre of oúr fair kíngdom . . .

He turns to Cordelia—and now the verse begins to tremble and
falter, *as his favourite daughter holds firm* against *him*:

                              . . . Nów, our jóy,
Althóugh our lást, and léast; to whóse young lóve
The vínes of Fránce and mílk of Búrgundy
Strive tó be ínteréss'd; what cán you sáy to dráw
A thírd more ópulent thán your sísters? Spéak.   85

   Cordelia
Nothíng, my lórd.

   Lear
Nóthing?

   Cordelia
Nóthing.

   Lear
Nothíng will cóme of nóthing: spéak agáin.

   Cordelia
Unháppy thát I ám, I cánnot héave   90
My héart intó my móuth: I lóve your májesty
Accórding tó my bónd; no móre or léss . . .

Cordelia re-asserts the pentameter: no line could be more regular
than line 90. But the play's harmony has been disrupted, and it
will not easily be restored.

   Now tempers break out as passions rise. Kent attempts to

restrain his king, and he is given his answer. Albany and Cornwall offer to rescue the situation. Lines are shared as characters fight for and with their words:

> **Kent**
> My lífe I néver héld but ás a páwn
> To wáge agáinst thine énemies; nor féar to lóse it,   155
> Thy sáfety béing mótive.
>   **Lear**
>   Oút of my síght!
>   **Kent**
> See bétter, Léar; and lét me stíll remáin
> The trúe blank óf thine éye.
>   **Lear**
> Now, bý Apóllo, —
>   **Kent**
>   Now bý Apóllo, kíng,   159
> Thou swéar'st thy góds in váin.
>   **Lear**
>   O, vással! míscreánt!
>   *Laying his hand upon his sword.*
>   **Albany, Cornwall**
> Dear sír, forbéar.

With its alternating stresses as regular as day and night, the blank verse is staunch to the end of the play, but it is often disturbed—just as day and night are both disturbed in *King Lear*. Days are darkened and blackened by natural phenomena—and by the deeds of men: restless nights are shot through with thunder and cruelly fractured by lightning. At the very end, only Edgar is left in command, and he assumes control with the formal regularity of his quatrain:

> **Edgar**
> The wéight of thís sad tíme we múst obéy;
> Speak whát we féel, not whát we oúght to sáy.
> The éldest háth seen móst: we thát are yoúng
> Shall néver sée so múch, nor líve so lóng.

                                                          (5, 3, 322–5)

Characters in the play

King Lear	*King of Britain*
Goneril **Regan** **Cordelia**	*daughters of* King Lear
The Duke of Albany **The Duke of Cornwall**	*husband to* Goneril *husband to* Regan
The King of France **The Duke of Burgundy**	*suitors to* Cordelia
The Earl of Kent	*counsellor at* King Lear's *court*
The Earl of Gloucester **Edgar** **Edmund**	*nobleman at* King Lear's *court* *sons of* Gloucester
The Fool	*jester to* King Lear
Curan	*a courtier,* Cornwall's *messenger*
Oswald	*steward of* Goneril's *household*
Gentleman **Gentleman** **Old Man** **Doctor** **Officer** **Herald**	*attendant on* King Lear *attendant on* Cordelia *tenant of the* Earl of Gloucester *employed by* Edmund

Knights attending on King Lear, Officers, Messengers, Soldiers and Servants.

Scene: Britain.

Act I

Act I Scene I

Gloucester and Kent speak of the division of the kingdom, and Kent meets Edmund, the bastard son of the Earl of Gloucester. King Lear announces his intention of dividing the kingdom into three parts, and giving one part to each of his daughters. The largest share will be given to the daughter who can say that she loves him the most. Goneril is the first to speak, and she is duly rewarded. Regan speaks next, and is given her share of the kingdom. But when Lear turns to his favourite daughter, Cordelia, who is the youngest of the three, he is very disappointed. Cordelia refuses to flatter Lear as her sisters have done. In a rage, Lear disowns Cordelia, and distributes her land between Goneril and Regan. Kent remonstrates with the king; and Lear banishes him from the kingdom. Cordelia's two suitors are called in, and Lear offers his daughter in marriage to the Duke of Burgundy. But Cordelia now has no dowry, and Burgundy rejects King Lear's offer. The King of France, however, asks to know the reason for Lear's displeasure. When he learns the truth, he takes Cordelia as his wife, and they leave for France. Goneril and Regan exchange a few words together.

1–32 Kent and Gloucester chat in an easy, colloquial prose, which gives way to a formal blank verse when the king begins to speak.
1 *more affected*: rather preferred.
2 *Albany*: Brute, the first king of Britain, gave to his younger son Albanus the territory north of the river Humber, which was thereafter called Albanius or Albany.
5 *values*: esteems.
5–6 *equalities . . . moiety*: their shares (which are meant to be equal) are in fact

Scene I

King Lear's *palace*
Enter Kent, Gloucester, *and* Edmund

Kent

I thought the king had more affected the Duke of Albany than Cornwall.

Gloucester

It did always seem so to us; but now, in the division of the kingdom, it appears not which of the dukes he
5   values most; for equalities are so weigh'd that curiosity in neither can make choice of either's moiety.

Kent

Is not this your son, my lord?

Gloucester

His breeding, sir, hath been at my charge: I have so often blush'd to acknowledge him, that now I am
10 braz'd to't.

Kent

I cannot conceive you.

Gloucester

Sir, this young fellow's mother could; whereupon she grew round-womb'd, and had, indeed, sir, a son for her cradle ere she had a husband for her bed. Do you
15 smell a fault?

Kent

I cannot wish the fault undone, the issue of it being so proper.

Gloucester

But I have a son, sir, by order of law, some year elder than this, who yet is no dearer in my account: though
20 this knave came something saucily to the world before he was sent for, yet was his mother fair; there was good sport at his making, and the whoreson

so evenly balanced that no amount of careful scrutiny ('curiosity') in comparing them could make either duke prefer the other's part ('moiety').

8 *breeding . . . charge*: they said I was his father; *or*, I've paid for his upbringing.

10 *braz'd to't*: brazen (= no longer embarrassed) about it.

11 *conceive you*: understand your meaning; Gloucester makes a pun with 'conceive' (= become pregnant) in the next line.

15 *smell a fault*: find anything wrong in this.

16 *issue . . . proper*: since it has had such a fine result.

18 *by order of law*: legitimately.
   some year: about a year.

19 *no dearer in my account*: worth no more in my estimation.

20 *knave*: lad.
   something: somewhat.

22 *whoreson*: little bastard—Gloucester's tone is rough but affectionate.

28 *services*: respectful duty.

29 *sue*: do what I can.

30 *study deserving*: make every effort to earn your good opinion.

31 *out*: out of the country.

32s.d. *Sennet*: A trumpet fanfare heralds the king's entrance.
   coronet: crown—an emblem for the kingdom; the stage property will be used at line 138.

must be acknowledged. Do you know this noble gentleman, Edmund?

Edmund

25 No, my lord.

Gloucester

My lord of Kent: remember him hereafter as my honourable friend.

Edmund

My services to your lordship.

Kent

I must love you, and sue to know you better.

Edmund

30 Sir, I shall study deserving.

Gloucester

He hath been out nine years, and away he shall again. The king is coming.

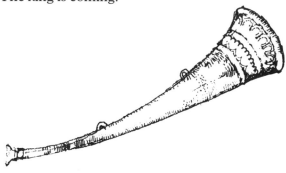

Sennet. Enter one bearing a coronet, King Lear, Cornwall, Albany, Goneril, Regan, Cordelia, *and* Attendants

Lear

Attend the lords of France and Burgundy, Gloucester.

Gloucester

I shall, my liege.

[*Exeunt* Gloucester *and* Edmund

Lear

35 Meantime, we shall express our darker purpose.
Give me the map there. Know that we have divided
In three our kingdom; and 'tis our fast intent
To shake all cares and business from our age,
Conferring them on younger strengths, while we

33 *Attend*: escort into the royal presence.

35 *we*: Lear speaks with the 'royal plural'.
   express our darker purpose: explain my secret intention (i.e. to reward his daughters for their declarations of love—and give the best portion to Cordelia): the division of the kingdom will not be straightforward.

37 *fast*: fixed, unalterable.

40 *son*: i.e. son-in-law.

42 *constant will*: firm purpose.
to publish: to make known.
43 *daughters' several dowers*: the different
dowries of each daughter.
44 *prevented*: forestalled.
45 *Great*: noble.
46 *Long . . . sojourn*: have stayed here a long
time in their courtship of Cordelia.

49 *Interest*: possession.

51–2 Lear will give most generously to the
daughter who can claim ('challenge') it
by what she deserves (her 'merit') as well
as by her natural right.

54 *more . . . matter*: more than words can
say.
55 *space and liberty*: freedom, and the ability
to enjoy it.
57 *grace*: favour, happiness.

59 *unable*: inadequate.

63 *shadowy*: shady.
champains: open plains.
rich'd: enriched.
64 *wide-skirted meads*: extensive meadows.
65 *lady*: queen, ruler.
66 *Be this perpetual*: in perpetuity; Lear
intends to divide the kingdom for ever.
68 *self mettle*: exactly the same nature; Regan
makes a pun with 'metal'.
69 *prize me at her worth*: put exactly the same
value on myself.
70 *she names . . . love*: she tells you just what
my love is (as though she produced the
same 'deed' = legal document).
71 *comes too short*: does not go far enough.
that: in that.
73 *the most . . . sense*: the most perfect
human being (to be 'square' is to be
perfectly fitting, harmonious in every
way).
74 *alone felicitate*: only really made joyful.

40 Unburthen'd crawl toward death. Our son of Cornwall,
And you, our no less loving son of Albany,
We have this hour a constant will to publish
Our daughters' several dowers, that future strife
May be prevented now. The princes, France and
    Burgundy,
45 Great rivals in our youngest daughter's love,
Long in our court have made their amorous sojourn,
And here are to be answer'd. Tell me, my daughters,
(Since now we will divest us both of rule,
Interest of territory, cares of state),
50 Which of you shall we say doth love us most?
That we our largest bounty may extend
Where nature doth with merit challenge. Goneril,
Our eldest-born, speak first.
        Goneril
Sir, I love you more than word can wield the matter;
55 Dearer than eye-sight, space and liberty;
Beyond what can be valued rich or rare;
No less than life, with grace, health, beauty, honour;
As much as child e'er lov'd, or father found;
A love that makes breath poor and speech unable;
60 Beyond all manner of so much I love you.
        Cordelia
[*Aside*] What shall Cordelia speak? Love, and be silent.
        Lear
Of all these bounds, even from this line to this,
With shadowy forests and with champains rich'd
With plenteous rivers and wide-skirted meads,
65 We make thee lady: to thine and Albany's issues
Be this perpetual. What says our second daughter
Our dearest Regan, wife of Cornwall?
        Regan
I am made of that self mettle as my sister,
And prize me at her worth. In my true heart
70 I find she names my very deed of love;
Only she comes too short: that I profess
Myself an enemy to all other joys
Which the most precious square of sense possesses,
And find I am alone felicitate
75 In your dear highness' love.
        Cordelia
[*Aside*]   Then poor Cordelia!

And yet not so; since I am sure my love's
More ponderous than my tongue.
    Lear
To thee and thine, hereditary ever,
Remain this ample third of our fair kingdom,
80 No less in space, validity, and pleasure,
Than that conferr'd on Goneril. Now, our joy,
Although our last, and least; to whose young love
The vines of France and milk of Burgundy
Strive to be interess'd; what can you say to draw
85 A third more opulent than your sisters? Speak.
    Cordelia
Nothing, my lord.
    Lear
Nothing?
    Cordelia
Nothing.
    Lear
Nothing will come of nothing: speak again.
    Cordelia
90 Unhappy that I am, I cannot heave
My heart into my mouth: I love your majesty
According to my bond; no more nor less.
    Lear
How, how, Cordelia! Mend your speech a little,
Lest you may mar your fortunes.
    Cordelia
                Good my lord,
95 You have begot me, bred me, lov'd me: I
Return those duties back as are right fit,
Obey you, love you, and most honour you.
Why have my sisters husbands, if they say
They love you all? Happily, when I shall wed,
100 That lord whose hand must take my plight shall carry
Half my love with him, half my care and duty:
Sure I shall never marry like my sisters,
To love my father all.
    Lear
But goes thy heart with this?
    Cordelia
                Ay, my good lord.
    Lear
105 So young, and so untender?

77 *more . . . tongue*: more weighty than my tongue can express.
78 *hereditary ever*: see line 66.
80 *validity*: value.
82 *last, and least*: youngest child, who would legally be entitled to only the smallest portion.
83 *vines*: vineyards.
  milk: pasture-land (for grazing dairy herds).
84 *interess'd*: concerned with.
89 *Nothing will come of nothing*: Lear quotes a common Latin proverb, *ex nihilo nihil fit*.
92 *bond*: bounden duty.
95 *bred me*: fathered me; see line 8.
96 *right fit*: in the proper proportions.
99 *Happily*: when it happens that.
100 *plight*: troth-plight, pledge of marriage.
103 *all*: with all their hearts.
104 *goes . . . this?*: do you really mean all this?

107 *thy . . . dower*: you can take this honesty
for your (only) dowry.

109 *mysteries*: secret rites.
Hecate: In classical mythology, Hecate
was goddess of the underworld and of
witchcraft.

110–11 *operation . . . be*: influences of the
planets which affect our lives and deaths.

113 *Propinquity . . . blood*: blood relationship
and the obligations of kinship.

115 *from this*: from this time.
barbarous Scythian: The inhabitants of
Scythia (= modern Russia) were
traditionally thought to be savage.

116 *makes . . . messes*: chops up into food the
parents—or children—of his own
breeding.

117 *To . . . appetite*: in mere gluttony.

119 *sometime*: former; Lear renounces
Cordelia.

121 *dragon*: Lear personifies himself as the
heraldic beast of Wales, a red lion
rampant, which is borne on the arms of
all British monarchs.
wrath: i.e. the object of his wrath.

122 *set my rest*: settle everything I had (Lear
uses a gambler's phrase).

123 *kind nursery*: tender loving care.

124 *So . . . peace*: may I find peace only in my
grave.

125 *Who stirs?*: Lear calls for some action
from the courtiers.

128 *Let pride . . . marry her*: let her pride
(which she calls plain-speaking—see line
107) be her dowry and find a husband for
her.

129 *jointly*: both together.

130 *Pre-eminence*: first position.
all . . . effects: all the magnificent
accompaniments.

131 *troop with majesty*: are associated with
kingship.
monthly course: month by month.

132 *With reservation*: Lear uses a legal term
to make an exception; he will give up
everything *except* the hundred knights.

133 *sustain'd*: supported.

133–4 *our abode . . . due turn*: stay with each
of you in turn.

Cordelia
So young, my lord, and true.

Lear
Let it be so; thy truth then be thy dower:
For, by the sacred radiance of the sun,
The mysteries of Hecate and the night,
110 By all the operation of the orbs
From whom we do exist and cease to be,
Here I disclaim all my paternal care,
Propinquity and property of blood,
And as a stranger to my heart and me
115 Hold thee from this for ever. The barbarous Scythian,
Or he that makes his generation messes
To gorge his appetite, shall to my bosom
Be as well neighbour'd, pitied, and reliev'd,
As thou my sometime daughter.

Kent
Good my liege,—

Lear
120 Peace, Kent!
Come not between the dragon and his wrath.
I lov'd her most, and thought to set my rest
On her kind nursery. Hence, and avoid my sight!

So be my grave my peace, as here I give
125 Her father's heart from her! Call France. Who stirs?
Call Burgundy. Cornwall and Albany,
With my two daughters' dowers digest the third;
Let pride, which she calls plainness, marry her.
I do invest you jointly with my power,
130 Pre-eminence, and all the large effects
That troop with majesty. Ourself, by monthly course,
With reservation of an hundred knights
By you to be sustain'd, shall our abode
Make with you by due turn. Only we shall retain

135 *name and all th'addition to*: title and
    proper ceremonious treatment due to.
    sway: government.
137 *Revenue*: The word is stressed on the
    second syllable—'Revénue'.
138 *Royal Lear*: Kent addresses King Lear
    with proper formality.
142 *make . . . shaft*: get away from the arrow,
    or, let go of the arrow.
143 *fork*: two-pointed arrowhead.

144–5 *unmannerly . . . mad*: Kent is prepared
    to speak bluntly when he sees the king
    acting so rashly.
146 *thou*: This form of the second person
    ('you') is an intimate address, which was
    used only with equals or inferiors.
    dread: fear.
147 *plainness*: plain speaking.
148 *Reserve thy state*: keep hold of everything
    you have.
149 *in thy best consideration*: when you have
    thought things over carefully.
150 *answer . . . judgment*: I'll stake my life on
    this opinion.
152–3 Kent seems to be offering an opposite
    sentence for the proverbial saying,
    'empty vessels make most sound'.
153 *Reverb*: re-echo; the word is
    Shakespeare's own coinage from
    'reverberate'.
154 *held*: valued.
    pawn: the stake in a wager.
155 *wage*: gamble, risk.
156 *thy . . . motive*: for your sake.
157 *still*: always.
158 *true blank*: the white spot in the centre of
    a target; if Lear would fix his sights on
    Kent, his intentions would not misfire.
159 *Apollo*: Lear swears by the Roman sun-
    god—an indication that the play is set in
    a pre-Christian world.
160 *miscreant*: misbeliever; Kent has denied
    Lear's god.

135 The name and all th'addition to a king; the sway,
    Revenue, execution of the rest,
    Beloved sons, be yours: which to confirm,
    This coronet part between you.
        Kent
                                    Royal Lear,
    Whom I have ever honour'd as my king,
140 Lov'd as my father, as my master follow'd,
    As my great patron thought on in my prayers,—
        Lear
    The bow is bent and drawn; make from the shaft.
        Kent
    Let it fall rather, though the fork invade
    The region of my heart: be Kent unmannerly,
145 When Lear is mad. What would'st thou do, old man?
    Think'st thou that duty shall have dread to speak
    When power to flattery bows? To plainness honour's
        bound
    When majesty falls to folly. Reserve thy state;
    And, in thy best consideration, check
150 This hideous rashness: answer my life my judgment,
    Thy youngest daughter does not love thee least;
    Nor are those empty-hearted whose low sounds
    Reverb no hollowness.
        Lear
                            Kent, on thy life, no more.
        Kent
    My life I never held but as a pawn
155 To wage against thine enemies; nor fear to lose it,
    Thy safety being motive.
        Lear
                                    Out of my sight!
        Kent
    See better, Lear; and let me still remain
    The true blank of thine eye.
        Lear
    Now, by Apollo,—
        Kent
                            Now, by Apollo, king,
160 Thou swear'st thy gods in vain.
        Lear
                            O, vassal! miscreant!

    Laying his hand upon his sword

164 *vent*: utter.
165 *recreant*: traitor, one who is false to his allegiance.

167 *That*: seeing that.
168 *durst never yet*: have never yet dared to do.
strain'd: unnatural.
169 'To intervene between the sentence and its execution.'
171 *Our . . .good*: since my power is confirmed.
172 *for provision*: to get all that you need.

176 *trunk*: body.
177 *moment is thy death*: you will die immediately.
Jupiter: The king of the Roman gods was also, in ancient times, worshipped in Britain; Lear's oaths help to establish the pre-Christian setting of the play.
179 *sith*: since.
180–86 Kent's rhyming couplets bring the episode to a close, summing up the situation and pointing the moral.

183 *approve*: confirm.
184 *effects*: deeds.
186 *shape his old course*: carry on in his usual manner—i.e. of speaking plainly.

187s.d. *Flourish*: A trumpet-call heralds the approach of the King of France and the Duke of Burgundy.

189 *address toward*: address our remarks to.
190 *rivall'd*: competed.

Albany, Cornwall
Dear sir, forbear.
Kent
Kill thy physician, and the fee bestow
Upon the foul disease. Revoke thy gift;
Or, whilst I can vent clamour from my throat,
165 I'll tell thee thou dost evil.
Lear
⠀⠀⠀⠀⠀⠀⠀⠀⠀⠀Hear me, recreant!
On thine allegiance, hear me!
That thou hast sought to make us break our vow,
Which we durst never yet, and with strain'd pride
To come betwixt our sentence and our power,
170 Which nor our nature nor our place can bear,
Our potency made good, take thy reward.
Five days we do allot thee for provision
To shield thee from disasters of the world;
And on the sixth to turn thy hated back
175 Upon our kingdom: if on the tenth day following
Thy banish'd trunk be found in our dominions,
The moment is thy death. Away! By Jupiter,
This shall not be revok'd.
Kent
Fare thee well, king; sith thus thou wilt appear,
180 Freedom lives hence, and banishment is here.
[*To* Cordelia] The gods to their dear shelter take thee, maid,
That justly think'st and hast most rightly said!
[*To* Goneril *and* Regan] And your large speeches may your deeds approve,
That good effects may spring from words of love.
185 Thus Kent, O princes, bids you all adieu!
He'll shape his old course in a country new.
⠀⠀⠀⠀⠀⠀⠀⠀⠀⠀⠀⠀⠀⠀⠀⠀⠀⠀[*Exit*

Flourish. Enter Gloucester, *with* France, Burgundy, *and* Attendants

Gloucester
Here's France and Burgundy, my noble lord.
Lear
My lord of Burgundy,
We first address toward you, who with this king
190 Hath rivall'd for our daughter. What, in the least,

191 *present dower with her*: for her immediate dowry.

194 *tender*: offer.

195 *so*: i.e. dearly, highly valued.
197 *little-seeming substance*: The phrase is difficult to explain. Lear is offering Cordelia to Burgundy just as she is, without any addition to her person, and she does not appear to be very valuable; *but* 'little-seeming' could also mean 'unpretentious'.
198 *piec'd*: joined.
199 *fitly like*: be pleasing and seem suitable.
201 *infirmities*: disadvantages.
   owes: owns.
202 *new-adopted . . . hate*: whom I have just begun to hate.
203 *Dower'd with our curse*: given my curse for her only dowry.
   stranger'd: made a stranger.
205 *Election . . . conditions*: I cannot reach a decision on such terms.

207 *tell*: describe, count up.
   For: as for.
208 *make . . . stray*: stray so far.
209 *To match*: as to expect you to marry.
210 'To look in some different direction for a wife who is more deserving of you.'

213 *best object*: main object of your love, favourite.
214 *argument*: subject.
   balm: comfort.
215 *trice*: instant.
216 *dismantle*: strip off.
217 *folds of favour*: layers of your affection.
218–19 *such . . . monsters it*: so unnatural as to be monstrous.
219–20 *your . . . taint*: your former love must be discredited.

Will you require in present dower with her,
Or cease your quest of love?

Burgundy
                                    Most royal majesty,
I crave no more than hath your highness offer'd,
Nor will you tender less.

Lear
                                    Right noble Burgundy,
195 When she was dear to us we did hold her so,
But now her price is fallen. Sir, there she stands:
If aught within that little-seeming substance,
Or all of it, with our displeasure piec'd,
And nothing more, may fitly like your grace,
200 She's there, and she is yours.

Burgundy
                                    I know no answer.

Lear
Will you, with those infirmities she owes,
Unfriended, new-adopted to our hate,
Dower'd with our curse and stranger'd with our oath,
Take her, or leave her?

Burgundy
                                    Pardon me, royal sir;
205 Election makes not up in such conditions.

Lear
Then leave her, sir; for, by the power that made me,
I tell you all her wealth. [*To* France] For you, great king,
I would not from your love make such a stray
To match you where I hate; therefore beseech you
210 T'avert your liking a more worthier way
Than on a wretch whom Nature is asham'd
Almost t'acknowledge hers.

France
                                    This is most strange,
That she, whom even but now was your best object,
The argument of your praise, balm of your age,
215 The best, the dearest, should in this trice of time
Commit a thing so monstrous, to dismantle
So many folds of favour. Sure, her offence
Must be of such unnatural degree
That monsters it, or your fore-vouch'd affection
220 Fall into taint; which to believe of her,

221 *a faith ... miracle*: it would take a miracle
to make me believe this.

223 *If for*: even though.
want: lack.
224 *purpose not*: without meaning to do.
226 *vicious blot*: vice, moral stain.
227 *dishonour'd*: dishonourable.

229 *for which*: for want of which.
230 *still-soliciting*: always looking out for
something.

232 *lost*: ruined.

234 *but*: no more than.
tardiness in nature: natural reticence.
235 *leaves the history unspoke*: does not talk
about.
237 *What ... to*: i.e. will you have?
238 *regards*: considerations.
238–9 *stand ... point*: have nothing to do
with the real issue.

247 *respect ... his love*: what he really cares
about is status and money.

Must be a faith that reason without miracle
Should never plant in me.
Cordelia   I yet beseech your majesty,
(If for I want that glib and oily art
To speak and purpose not, since what I well intend,
225 I'll do't before I speak), that you make known
It is no vicious blot, murther or foulness,
No unchaste action, or dishonour'd step,
That hath depriv'd me of your grace and favour,
But even for want of that for which I am richer,
230 A still-soliciting eye, and such a tongue
That I am glad I have not, though not to have it
Hath lost me in your liking.
Lear   Better thou
Hadst not been born than not t'have pleased me better.
France
Is it but this? a tardiness in nature
235 Which often leaves the history unspoke
That it intends to do? My lord of Burgundy,
What say you to the lady? Love's not love
When it is mingled with regards that stand
Aloof from th'entire point. Will you have her?
240 She is herself a dowry.
Burgundy   Royal king,
Give but that portion which yourself propos'd,
And here I take Cordelia by the hand,
Duchess of Burgundy.
Lear
Nothing: I have sworn; I am firm.
Burgundy
245 I am sorry, then, you have so lost a father
That you must lose a husband.
Cordelia   Peace be with Burgundy!
Since that respect and fortunes are his love,
I shall not be his wife.
France
Fairest Cordelia, that art most rich, being poor;
250 Most choice, forsaken; and most lov'd, despis'd!
Thee and thy virtues here I seize upon:

253 *from . . . neglect*: because Cordelia has been cruelly neglected by the gods.

255 *chance*: lot.

257 *wat'rish*: Burgundy is a land with many streams and rivers—but France's adjective also serves to accuse the duke of weakness.
258 *unpriz'd*: unappreciated (by her father).
259 *though unkind*: although they have behaved unnaturally.
260 'You are losing this place in order to find a better one somewhere else.'

264 *benison*: blessing.

267 *The jewels*: you, who are the jewels.
wash'd eyes: tears in my eyes (*and perhaps also* 'clearer sight').
270 *as they are named*: for what they are.
271 *professed bosoms*: the love which you claim to have.
272 *within his grace*: in favour with him.
273 *prefer*: recommend.
277 *At Fortune's alms*: as a charitable hand-out.
obedience scanted: failed in your obedience (as a daughter).
277–280 Here again—as in lines 180–86—the rhymed couplets serve to close the episode and to point a moral.
278 'And deserve to be shown the same lack of affection (by your husband) that you have shown (to your father).'

Be it lawful I take up what's cast away.
Gods, gods! 'tis strange that from their cold'st neglect
My love should kindle to inflam'd respect.
255 Thy dowerless daughter, king, thrown to my chance,
Is queen of us, of ours, and our fair France:
Not all the dukes of wat'rish Burgundy
Can buy this unpriz'd precious maid of me.
Bid them farewell, Cordelia, though unkind:
260 Thou losest here, a better where to find.

Lear
Thou hast her, France; let her be thine, for we
Have no such daughter, nor shall ever see
That face of hers again; therefore be gone
Without our grace, our love, our benison.
265 Come, noble Burgundy.
[*Flourish. Exeunt* Lear, Burgundy, Cornwall,
Albany, Gloucester, *and* Attendants

France
Bid farewell to your sisters.

Cordelia
The jewels of our father, with wash'd eyes
Cordelia leaves you: I know you what you are;
And like a sister am most loth to call
270 Your faults as they are named. Love well our father:
To your professed bosoms I commit him:
But yet, alas! stood I within his grace,
I would prefer him to a better place.
So farewell to you both.

Regan
275 Prescribe not us our duty.

Goneril
Let your study
Be to content your lord, who hath receiv'd you
At Fortune's alms; you have obedience scanted,
And well are worth the want that you have wanted.

279 *plighted*: folded up, concealed.
280 *Who*: i.e. Time.

Cordelia
Time shall unfold what plighted cunning hides;
280 Who covers faults, at last with shame derides.
Well may you prosper!
France
                              Come, my fair Cordelia.
                    [*Exeunt* France *and* Cordelia
Goneril
Sister, it is not little I have to say of what most nearly
appertains to us both. I think our father will hence
to-night.

282–304 A complete change of pace and
        mood is marked by the use of cold,
        unemotional prose.
283 *will hence*: will go hence.

Regan
285 That's most certain, and with you; next month with us.
Goneril
You see how full of changes his age is; the observation
we have made of it hath not been little: he always
lov'd our sister most; and with what poor judgment
he hath now cast her off appears too grossly.

289 *grossly*: obviously.

Regan
290 'Tis the infirmity of his age; yet he hath ever but
slenderly known himself.
Goneril
The best and soundest of his time hath been but rash;
then must we look from his age, to receive not alone
the imperfections of long-engraffed condition, but
295 therewithal the unruly waywardness that infirm and
choleric years bring with them.

292 *rash*: impetuous, hot-headed.
293 *look*: expect.
294 *long-engraffed condition*: deeply-rooted
        nature.

Regan
Such unconstant starts are we like to have from him
as this of Kent's banishment.

297 *unconstant starts*: sudden impulses.

Goneril
There is further compliment of leave-taking between
300 France and him. Pray you, let us hit together: if our
father carry authority with such disposition as he
bears, this last surrender of his will but offend us.

299 *compliment*: formality.
300 *hit together*: agree with each other.
301–2 *carry . . . bears*: continues to act with
        such authority.
302 *this last surrender*: this power he has just
        given up to us.
        offend us: become a problem for us.
304 *do*: i.e. not just *think* about it.
        i'th'heat: right now, strike while the iron
        is hot.

Regan
We shall further think of it.
Goneril
We must do something, and i'th'heat.
                                              [*Exeunt*

Act 1 Scene 2

Edmund tells how bitterly he resents his
brother Edgar, and hints at a scheme which
will injure him. He lets his father, Gloucester,
see a letter from which it appears that Edgar is
plotting against their father's life. Gloucester,
distressed, trusts Edmund to find out the
truth. When the brothers meet together,
Edmund advises Edgar to avoid Gloucester's
presence.

 1 *Thou . . . goddess*: Edmund seems to be
   cutting himself off from society and all
   the observances of civilization.
2–3 *Wherefore . . . custom*: why should I be
   affected (as though by an illness) by
   these pestilent customs.
 4 *The . . . nations*: fine distinctions made by
   national laws.
   deprive me: keep me from my rightful
   position in society.
 5 *moonshines*: months.
 6 *Lag of*: behind, younger than.
   base: Bastards were sometimes called
   'base sons'.
 7 *dimensions*: proportions.
   compact: put together.
 8 *generous*: gentlemanly.
   my shape as true: my appearance as much
   like my father's.
 9 *honest madam's issue*: i.e. Edgar—the
   child of Gloucester's lawful wife.
11 *lusty*: both 'lustful' and 'lusty'.
   stealth of nature: stolen natural pleasures.
12 *More composition*: a fuller mixture of
   different qualities.
   fierce quality: energy.
13 *a dull . . . bed*: i.e. as the result of a long
   marriage.
14 *fops*: weaklings.
15 *Got*: begotten.
17 *to*: for.
18 *legitimate*: legitimate son.
19 *speed*: prosper.
20 *invention*: ability to tell lies.
21 *top*: surpass.
23 *in choler parted*: departed in a rage. The
   play does not show this—but perhaps
   Cordelia's new husband was enraged on
   her behalf.
24 *to-night*: last night.
   prescrib'd his power: told just what he can
   do.

Scene 2

The Earl of Gloucester's *castle*
Enter Edmund, *with a letter.*

   Edmund
Thou, Nature, art my goddess; to thy law
My services are bound. Wherefore should I
Stand in the plague of custom, and permit
The curiosity of nations to deprive me,
For that I am some twelve or fourteen moonshines   5
Lag of a brother? Why bastard? Wherefore base?
When my dimensions are as well compact,
My mind as generous, and my shape as true,
As honest madam's issue? Why brand they us
With base? with baseness? bastardy? base, base?   10
Who in the lusty stealth of nature take
More composition and fierce quality
Than doth, within a dull, stale, tired bed,
Go to th'creating a whole tribe of fops,
Got 'tween asleep and wake? Well then,   15
Legitimate Edgar, I must have your land:
Our father's love is to the bastard Edmund
As to th'legitimate. Fine word, 'legitimate'!
Well, my legitimate, if this letter speed,
And my invention thrive, Edmund the base   20
Shall top th'legitimate—: I grow, I prosper;
Now, gods, stand up for bastards!

Enter Gloucester

   Gloucester
Kent banish'd thus! And France in choler parted!
And the king gone to-night! prescrib'd his power!
Confin'd to exhibition! All this done   25
Upon the gad!—Edmund, how now! What news?
   Edmund
So please your lordship, none.

Putting up the letter

   Gloucester
Why so earnestly seek you to put up that letter?
   Edmund
I know no news, my lord.

25 *Confin'd to exhibition*: restricted to a small allowance.

26 *Upon the gad*: suddenly (as though pricked by a goad).

27s.d. *Putting up*: putting away in his pocket.

28 *earnestly*: eagerly.

32 *dispatch*: haste.

36 *pardon me*: excuse me for not showing it to you.

37 *not all o'erread*: not finished reading.

38 *o'erlooking*: inspection.

41 *to blame*: at fault, offensive.

44 *essay or taste*: trial or test.

45 *This ... age*: This idea that we must respect old people. By using the word 'policy', the writer of the letter seems to imply that this is some kind of a trick.

46 *bitter ... times*: spoils the best years of our lives.

47 *relish*: enjoy.

47–8 *to find ... tyranny*: to think that it is futile and foolish to be tyrannized by an old man.

48–9 *who ... suffer'd*: who does not rule because he has any power, but only because we allow ourselves to be ruled.

58 *casement*: window.
closet: study.

59 *character*: handwriting.

60 *matter*: substance, content.

Gloucester

30 What paper were you reading?

Edmund

Nothing, my lord.

Gloucester

No? What needed then that terrible dispatch of it into your pocket? The quality of nothing hath not such need to hide itself. Let's see: come; if it be

35 nothing, I shall not need spectacles.

Edmund

I beseech you, sir, pardon me; it is a letter from my brother that I have not all o'erread, and for so much as I have perus'd, I find it not fit for your o'erlooking.

Gloucester

Give me the letter, sir.

Edmund

40 I shall offend, either to detain or give it. The contents, as in part I understand them, are to blame.

Gloucester

Let's see, let's see.

Edmund

I hope, for my brother's justification, he wrote this but as an essay or taste of my virtue. [*Gives the letter*

Gloucester

45 [*Reads*] *This policy and reverence of age makes the world bitter to the best of our times; keeps our fortunes from us till our oldness cannot relish them. I begin to find an idle and fond bondage in the oppression of aged tyranny, who sways, not as it hath power, but as it is suffer'd. Come to*

50 *me, that of this I may speak more. If our father would sleep till I wak'd him, you should enjoy half his revenue for ever, and live the beloved of your brother,* EDGAR.— Hum! Conspiracy! 'Sleep till I wak'd him, you should enjoy half his revenue.' My son Edgar! Had he a hand

55 to write this? a heart and brain to breed it in? When came you to this? Who brought it?

Edmund

It was not brought me, my lord; there's the cunning of it; I found it thrown in at the casement of my closet.

Gloucester

You know the character to be your brother's?

Edmund

60 If the matter were good, my lord, I durst swear it

were his; but, in respect of that, I would fain think it
were not.

Gloucester

It is his.

Edmund

65 It is his hand, my lord; but I hope his heart is not in
the contents.

Gloucester

Has he never before sounded you in this business?

Edmund

Never, my lord. But I have heard him oft maintain it
to be fit that, sons at perfect age, and fathers declin'd,
the father should be as ward to the son, and the son
70 manage his revenue.

Gloucester

O villain, villain! His very opinion in the letter!
Abhorred villain! Unnatural, detested, brutish villain!
worse than brutish! Go, sirrah, seek him; I'll apprehend him. Abominable villain! Where is he?

Edmund

75 I do not well know, my lord. If it shall please you to
suspend your indignation against my brother till you
can derive from him better testimony of his intent, you
should run a certain course; where, if you violently
proceed against him, mistaking his purpose, it would
80 make a great gap in your own honour, and shake in
pieces the heart of his obedience. I dare pawn down my
life for him, that he hath writ this to feel my affection to
your honour, and to no other pretence of danger.

Gloucester

Think you so?

Edmund

85 If your honour judge it meet, I will place you where
you shall hear us confer of this, and by an auricular
assurance have your satisfaction; and that without
any further delay than this very evening.

Gloucester

He cannot be such a monster—

Edmund

90 Nor is not, sure.

Gloucester

—to his father, that so tenderly and entirely loves
him. Heaven and earth! Edmund, seek him out; wind

66 *sounded you*: tried to find out your opinion.

68 *sons . . . declin'd*: when the sons have grown up and their fathers are getting old.
69 *as ward to*: under the guardianship of.
70 *manage his revenue*: take control of his income.
71 *his very opinion*: exactly the same idea.
72 *detested*: detestable.

78 *run a certain course*: take the safe way. *where*: whereas.
80 *gap*: breach.
81 *pawn down*: stake.
82 *feel*: test.
83 *to . . . danger*: with no more dangerous intention.

86 *auricular assurance*: hearing for yourself.

92–3 *wind me into him*: worm your way into his confidence; used in this way, 'me' simply intensifies the sense of 'wind'.

93 *frame*: arrange, manage.

94–5 *unstate . . . resolution*: give anything— his own 'state', or social position—to have this situation properly resolved.

96 *presently*: immediately.
convey: handle.

98 *late*: recent; Shakespeare's first audiences might remember actual eclipses of the sun and the moon in 1605.
portend: Gloucester, like many Elizabethans, believes that there is a close correlation between the natural world and the world of human society, and that disturbances in the former always foretell trouble in the latter.

99 *the wisdom of Nature*: those who know about such natural phenomena.
reason: explain.

100 *thus and thus*: in different ways.

101 *the sequent effects*: what follows.
falls off: declines, revolts.

102 *mutinies*: riots.

103 *bond*: see *I, I, 92*.

104 *this villain of mine*: Gloucester's description of Edgar seems to comprehend two senses of 'villain'—*both* evil-doer *and* base-born peasant.
the prediction: i.e. the prediction made by the 'late eclipses'.

105 *falls . . . nature*: goes against nature; Gloucester takes his metaphor from the game of bowls.

107 *hollowness*: emptiness, falseness.

108 *disquietly*: disturbingly.

112 *excellent foppery*: marvellous stupidity.

113 *sick in fortune*: have a bit of bad luck.
surfeits: over-indulgence.

114 *guilty of*: responsible for.

115 *on*: by.

116 *by heavenly compulsion*: because the stars made us to be like that.

117 *by spherical predominance*: according to the ruling planets.

119–20 *divine . . . on*: supernatural compulsion.

120 *admirable evasion*: brilliant way of evading responsibility.
whoremaster: lecherous.

121 *goatish*: lascivious; the goat is the classical archetype of lust.

122 *compounded*: mated.

---

me into him, I pray you: frame the business after your own wisdom. I would unstate myself to be in a due
95 resolution.

Edmund

I will seek him, sir, presently; convey the business as I shall find means, and acquaint you withal.

Gloucester

These late eclipses in the sun and moon portend no good to us: though the wisdom of Nature can reason it
100 thus and thus, yet Nature finds itself scourg'd by the sequent effects. Love cools, friendship falls off, brothers divide: in cities, mutinies; in countries, discord; in palaces, treason; and the bond crack'd 'twixt son and father. This villain of mine comes under the prediction;
105 there's son against father: the king falls from bias of nature; there's father against child. We have seen the best of our time: machinations, hollowness, treachery, and all ruinous disorders follow us disquietly to our
110 graves. Find out this villain, Edmund; it shall lose thee nothing: do it carefully. And the noble and true-hearted Kent banish'd! his offence, honesty! 'Tis strange.

[*Exit*

Edmund

This is the excellent foppery of the world, that, when we are sick in fortune, often the surfeits of our own behaviour, we make guilty of our disasters the sun, the
115 moon, and stars; as if we were villains on necessity, fools by heavenly compulsion, knaves, thieves, and treachers by spherical predominance, drunkards, liars, and adulterers by an enforc'd obedience of planetary influence; and all that we are evil in, by a divine
120 thrusting on. An admirable evasion of whoremaster man, to lay his goatish disposition to the charge of a star! My father compounded with my mother under

123 *the dragon's tail*: Chaucer, in his *Treatise upon the Astrolabe*, describes this among 'the wicked planets'.
my nativity: I was born.
Ursa major: the constellation of the Great Bear, in which Mars is predominant but shares influence with Venus, thus producing temperaments that are both warlike and lascivious.
124 *Fut*: by God's foot—i.e. what rubbish.
126 *my bastardizing*: when I was made a bastard.
127 *pat*: just like that—promptly.
the catastrophe of the old comedy: the ending of old-fashioned plays; Edmund recognizes the theatricality of the situation.
128 *cue . . . melancholy*: Edmund continues his theatrical metaphor, assuming—to impress his brother—the character of a man who is very worried; '*villainous*' is an intensifier (= very), but has obvious ironies here.
129 *Tom o'Bedlam*: Tom the mad beggar—the name given to lunatics discharged from the Bethlehem Hospital for the insane (see *Act 2*, Scene 3).
130 *divisions*: conflicts; the word has also a musical sense—and perhaps this leads Edmund to hum or whistle a few notes—'*Fa, sol, la, mi*'—in assumed nonchalance.
135 *busy yourself with*: take any notice; Edgar has no time for popular superstitions.
136 *succeed unhappily*: happen by unfortunate chance.
137–43 *as . . . astronomical*: These lines are omitted in the Folio text of *King Lear*—perhaps to avoid political censorship; see p. xli.
138 *ancient amities*: friendships of long standing.
140 *diffidences*: suspicions.
141 *dissipation of cohorts*: armies breaking up.
nuptial breaches: broken marriages.
143 *sectary astronomical*: believer in astronomy.

the dragon's tail, and my nativity was under *Ursa major*; so that it follows I am rough and lecherous. Fut! I
125 should have been that I am had the maidenliest star in the firmament twinkled on my bastardizing. Edgar—

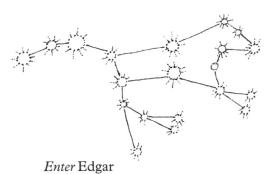

Enter Edgar

and pat he comes, like the catastrophe of the old comedy: my cue is villainous melancholy, with a sigh like Tom o' Bedlam. O! these eclipses do portend
130 these divisions. *Fa, sol, la, mi.*

Edgar

How now, brother Edmund! What serious contemplation are you in?

Edmund

I am thinking, brother, of a prediction I read this other day, what should follow these eclipses.

Edgar

135 Do you busy yourself with that?

Edmund

I promise you, the effects he writes of succeed unhappily; as of unnaturalness between the child and the parent; death, dearth, dissolutions of ancient amities; divisions in state; menaces and maledictions against
140 king and nobles; needless diffidences, banishment of friends, dissipation of cohorts, nuptial breaches, and I know not what.

Edgar

How long have you been a sectary astronomical?

Edmund

When saw you my father last?

Edgar

145 The night gone by.

Edmund

Spake you with him?

Edgar

Ay, two hours together.

Edmund

Parted you in good terms? Found you no displeasure in him by word nor countenance?

Edgar

150 None at all.

Edmund

Bethink yourself wherein you may have offended him; and at my entreaty forbear his presence until some little time hath qualified the heat of his displeasure, which at this instant so rageth in him that with the
155 mischief of your person it would scarcely allay.

Edgar

Some villain hath done me wrong.

Edmund

That's my fear. I pray you have a continent forbearance till the speed of his rage goes slower, and as I say, retire with me to my lodging, from whence I will
160 fitly bring you to hear my lord speak. Pray ye, go; there's my key. If you do stir abroad, go arm'd.

Edgar

Arm'd, brother!

Edmund

Brother, I advise you to the best. I am no honest man if there be any good meaning toward you; I have told
165 you what I have seen and heard; but faintly—nothing like the image and horror of it! Pray you, away.

Edgar

Shall I hear from you anon?

Edmund

I do serve you in this business.   [*Exit* Edgar
A credulous father, and a brother noble,
170 Whose nature is so far from doing harms
That he suspects none; on whose foolish honesty
My practices ride easy! I see the business.
Let me, if not by birth, have lands by wit:
All with me's meet that I can fashion fit.   [*Exit*

152 *forbear his presence*: keep away from him.
153 *qualified*: moderated.

155 *mischief . . . allay*: it would hardly be satisfied by doing physical harm to you.

157–8 *have a continent forbearance*: keep your feelings under control and keep away from him.

160 *fitly*: at a good moment.
161 *abroad*: outside.

164 *meaning*: intention.
    toward: concerning.
165 *but faintly*: i.e. I have only given you a hint of it.
166 *image and horror*: the real, horrible, truth.
167 *anon*: very soon.

172 *practices*: intrigues, deceptions.
    ride easy: work well.
    the business: how things will work out.

173 *wit*: cleverness.
174 *All . . . fit*: I'll use anything I can to suit my own purposes.

Act 1 Scene 3

Some time has elapsed. Lear is now staying with Goneril (as he had planned to do in Scene 1), but Goneril is already dissatisfied with the arrangement. She gives new instructions to her servants. This short scene prepares us to see the major changes of Scene 4, and to understand Goneril's harshness.

1 *chiding*: scolding.
4 *By day and night*: Goneril perhaps means 'every hour of the day and night', *or* she perhaps swears an oath similar to her father's swearing at *1, 1, 108–9*.
5 *flashes*: bursts out.
  crime: offence.
6 *sets . . . odds*: upsets everybody.

10 *come slack*: fall short.
11 *answer*: be responsible for.

13 *weary negligence*: casual disobedience.
14 *I'd . . . question*: I want the subject (of the servants' behaviour) to be raised in discussion.
15 *distaste*: does not like.
  to: go to.
16 *in that*: in this matter.
17–21 *Not . . . abus'd*: om. F.
17 *Idle*: foolish.
18 *manage those authorities*: use those powers.
21 *With checks as flatteries*: with rebukes as well as with praises.
  when . . . abus'd: when we see that they— the old men—are deluded.

24 *grows of*: develops from.
25 *I would . . . occasions*: I want to use this to give me opportunities.
26 *straight*: immediately.
27 *hold my very course*: do exactly the same as I do.

Scene 3

The Duke of Albany's *palace.*
Enter Goneril, *and* Oswald, *her Steward*

Goneril
Did my father strike my gentleman for chiding of his fool?

Oswald
Ay, madam.

Goneril
By day and night, he wrongs me; every hour
5 He flashes into one gross crime or other,
That sets us all at odds: I'll not endure it:
His knights grow riotous, and himself upbraids us
On every trifle. When he returns from hunting
I will not speak with him; say I am sick:
10 If you come slack of former services,
You shall do well; the fault of it I'll answer.

Oswald
He's coming, madam; I hear him.

[Horns within

Goneril
Put on what weary negligence you please,
You and your fellows; I'd have it come to question:
15 If he distaste it, let him to my sister,
Whose mind and mine, I know, in that are one,
Not to be over-rul'd. Idle old man,
That still would manage those authorities
That he hath given away! Now, by my life,
20 Old fools are babes again, and must be us'd
With checks as flatteries, when they are seen abus'd.
Remember what I have said.

Oswald
                              Well, madam.

Goneril
And let his knights have colder looks among you;
What grows of it, no matter; advise your fellows so:
25 I would breed from hence occasions, and I shall,
That I may speak: I'll write straight to my sister
To hold my very course. Prepare for dinner.

[Exeunt

Act 1 Scene 4

Kent has disguised himself, and now applies to Lear for a job. When Oswald, Goneril's servant, is disrespectful in speaking to the king, Kent strikes him. The Fool comments on Lear's folly in giving away his crown. Goneril complains to her father about the behaviour of his knights, and insists that their number must be reduced. Lear pronounces a terrible curse on his eldest daughter. He leaves Goneril's house and sets off to make his home with Regan. Goneril's husband, Albany, reproaches her; but Goneril is unrepentant. She sends a letter to her sister.

2 *defuse*: disguise.
2–3 *my good . . . issue*: I may be able to carry out my good intentions properly.
4 *raz'd my likeness*: altered my appearance; Kent has perhaps shaved off ('raz'd') his beard.
   banish'd Kent: Kent makes sure that the audience can recognize his character in the new disguise.
6 *So may it come*: with any luck it will happen that.
7 *full of labours*: very useful.
7s.d. *Horns within*: The sound of horns, offstage, indicates the king's return from hunting.
8 *Let . . . jot*: Don't keep me waiting for one moment; Lear is obviously not an easy guest to entertain.

11 *What . . . profess?*: What do you claim to be? Lear means simply 'What is your job?', but Kent's answer is less direct.
   would'st thou: do you want.
12 *seem*: appear.
14 *converse*: consort, keep company with.
15 *fear judgement*: i.e. the final judgement on his life, made by some divine judge.
   cannot choose: cannot do anything else.
16 *eat no fish:* This seems to be a joke—but its meaning is not clear.

18 *as poor as the king*: Kent is risking the king's displeasure with this joke, but Lear responds with good humour.

Scene 4

The Duke of Albany's *palace*
Enter Kent, *disguised*

Kent
If but as well I other accents borrow,
That can my speech defuse, my good intent
May carry through itself to that full issue
For which I raz'd my likeness. Now, banish'd Kent,
5 If thou canst serve where thou dost stand condemn'd,
So may it come, thy master, whom thou lov'st,
Shall find thee full of labours.

Horns within. Enter Lear, Knights, *and*
Attendants

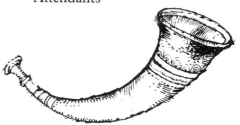

Lear
Let me not stay a jot for dinner: go, get it ready.
                                        [*Exit an* Attendant
How now! what art thou?
Kent
10 A man, sir.
Lear
What dost thou profess? What would'st thou with us?
Kent
I do profess to be no less than I seem; to serve him truly that will put me in trust; to love him that is honest; to converse with him that is wise, and says
15 little; to fear judgement; to fight when I cannot choose; and to eat no fish.
Lear
What art thou?
Kent
A very honest-hearted fellow, and as poor as the king.
Lear
If thou be'st as poor for a subject as he is for a king,
20 thou art poor enough. What would'st thou?

Kent
Service.
Lear
Who would'st thou serve?
Kent
You.
Lear
Dost thou know me, fellow?
Kent

25   No, sir; but you have that in your countenance which
I would fain call master.
Lear
What's that?
Kent
Authority.
Lear
What services canst thou do?
Kent

30   I can keep honest counsel, ride, run, mar a curious
tale in telling it, and deliver a plain message bluntly;
that which ordinary men are fit for, I am qualified in,
and the best of me is diligence.
Lear
How old art thou?
Kent

35   Not so young, sir, to love a woman for singing, nor so
old to dote on her for anything; I have years on my
back forty-eight.
Lear
Follow me; thou shalt serve me; if I like thee no worse
after dinner I will not part from thee yet. Dinner, ho!

40   dinner! Where's my knave? my fool? Go you and call
my fool hither.
                                                    [*Exit an* Attendant

                          Enter Oswald

You, you, sirrah, where's my daughter?
Oswald
So please you—   [*Exit
Lear
What says the fellow there? Call the clotpoll back.
                                                    [*Exit a* Knight

45   Where's my fool, ho? I think the world's asleep.

25 *countenance*: bearing, manner.
26 *would fain*: would like to.

30 *honest counsel*: an honourable secret.
curious: complicated; Kent seems to be
saying that he cannot tell fanciful
stories—i.e. he speaks only the plain
truth.

35 *to love*: as to love.

40 *knave*: boy.

43 *So please you*: Oswald is treating Lear
with the 'weary negligence'
recommended by Goneril in *1*, 3, 13.
44 *clotpoll*: blockhead.

Enter Knight

How now! where's that mongrel?

Knight

He says, my lord, your daughter is not well.

Lear

Why came not the slave back to me when I call'd him?

Knight

50 Sir, he answered me in the roundest manner, he would not.

Lear

He would not!

Knight

My lord, I know not what the matter is; but, to my judgment, your highness is not entertain'd with that
55 ceremonious affection as you were wont; there's a great abatement of kindness appears as well in the general dependents as in the duke himself also and your daughter.

Lear

Ha! say'st thou so?

Knight

60 I beseech you, pardon me, my lord, if I be mistaken; for my duty cannot be silent when I think your highness wrong'd.

Lear

Thou but rememb'rest me of mine own conception: I have perceived a most faint neglect of late; which I
65 have rather blamed as mine own jealous curiosity than as a very pretence and purpose of unkindness: I will look further into't. But where's my fool? I have not seen him this two days.

Knight

Since my young lady's going into France, sir, the fool
70 hath much pined away.

Lear

No more of that; I have noted it well. Go you, and tell my daughter I would speak with her.

[*Exit an* Attendant

Go you, call hither my fool.

[*Exit an* Attendant

---

50 *roundest*: rudest.

53–58 The knight chooses his words carefully to avoid giving offence to his master.
54 *entertain'd*: treated.
55 *ceremonious affection*: the ceremony (due to a king) and the affection (due to a father).
wont: accustomed to.
56 *abatement*: decrease.
57 *general dependents*: the servants in general.

63 *thou . . . conception*: you are only reminding me of what I thought myself.
64 *most faint*: hardly noticeable.
65–6 *mine own . . . kindness*: I put it down to my own worries about whether they were treating me properly.
66 *very pretence and purpose*: actual intention.
68 *this*: these.

70 *hath much pined away*: has been very distressed.

Enter Oswald

O you sir, you! Come you hither, sir.
75 Who am I, sir?
Oswald
My lady's father.
Lear
'My lady's father'! my lord's knave: you whoreson
dog! you slave! you cur!
Oswald
I am none of these, my lord; I beseech your pardon.
Lear
80 Do you bandy looks with me, you rascal?

Striking him

Oswald
I'll not be strucken, my lord.
Kent
Nor tripp'd neither, you base foot-ball player.

Tripping up his heels

Lear
I thank thee, fellow; thou serv'st me, and I'll love thee.
Kent
Come, sir, arise, away! I'll teach you differences:
85 away, away! If you will measure your lubber's length
again, tarry; but away! Go to; have you wisdom? [*Exit
Oswald*] So.
Lear
Now, my friendly knave, I thank thee: there's earnest
of thy service.

Gives Kent *money*
Enter Fool

Fool
90 Let me hire him too: here's my coxcomb.

Offers Kent *his cap*

Lear
How now, my pretty knave! how dost thou?
Fool
Sirrah, you were best take my coxcomb.
Kent
Why, fool?

77 *whoreson*: mis-begotten.

80 *bandy*: exchange; the metaphor is from
the game of tennis, where the players
'bandy' the ball from one to another.

81 *strucken*: struck; Oswald refuses to be
Lear's tennis-ball.
82 *tripp'd*: Kent kicks Oswald, and suggests
that he is better suited to a different
game—tennis was played only by
aristocrats, but football was a game for
servants.

84 *teach you differences*: make you learn your
position.
85 *measure . . . length*: be thrown to the
ground again like the clumsy lout that
you are.
86 *tarry*: stay here.
wisdom: any sense.
87 *So*: that's right.
88 *earnest*: earnest-money—a small sum
paid to secure a contract.

90 *coxcomb*: fool's cap; the professional
jester wore the head and neck of a cock
in his cap.

92 *Sirrah*: The fool uses a form of 'sir' which
is normally addressed to inferiors.
you were best: you had better.

95 *and*: if.
   smile as the wind sits: take the winning side.
96 *catch cold*: be out of favour.
97 *on's*: of his.
97–8 *did ... will*: The fool asserts that by disinheriting Cordelia, Lear has in fact done her a favour—she is now Queen of France.
99 *nuncle*: mine uncle; the affectionate, childish abbreviation emphasizes the fool's simple dependence on Lear.
100 *Would*: I wish.
102 *living*: property.
103 *beg ... daughters*: ask your daughters to give you another one (so Lear will be twice a fool).
104 *whip*: The fool was allowed to take considerable liberties in his jesting, but he would be whipped if he went too far.
105–6 *Truth's ... fire*: Truth is like a dog, that must be whipped and sent to his kennel, whilst the fawning pet—'Brach' was a common name for bitch hounds—can live indoors, however much it smells.
107 'That pains me.' Lear may be referring to something the fool has said, or meditating on his own situation; a 'gall' is a rubbed sore.
111 *Have ... showest*: don't display everything you possess.
112 *Speak ... knowest*: don't tell everything you know.
113 *Lend ... owest*: lend less than you own.
114 *Ride ... goest*: ride more than you walk.
115 *Learn ... trowest*: don't believe all that they tell you.
116 *Set ... throwest*: don't put all that you win on a single throw (of the dice).
118 *keep in-a-door*: stay at home.
119–20 *And ... score*: i.e. you will do better than most people.

Fool

Why? for taking one's part that's out of favour. Nay, 95
and thou canst not smile as the wind sits, thou'lt
catch cold shortly: there, take my coxcomb. Why, this
fellow has banish'd two on's daughters, and did the
third a blessing against his will: if thou follow him thou
must needs wear my coxcomb. How now, nuncle!
Would I had two coxcombs and two daughters! 100

Lear

Why, my boy?

Fool

If I gave them all my living, I'd keep my coxcombs
myself. There's mine; beg another of thy daughters.

Lear

Take heed, sirrah; the whip.

Fool

Truth's a dog must to kennel; he must be whipp'd out 105
when the lady's Brach may stand by th'fire and stink.

Lear

A pestilent gall to me!

Fool

Sirrah, I'll teach thee a speech.

Lear

Do.

Fool

Mark it, nuncle: 110

        Have more than thou showest,
        Speak less than thou knowest,
        Lend less than thou owest,
        Ride more than thou goest,
        Learn more than thou trowest, 115
        Set less than thou throwest;
        Leave thy drink and thy whore,
        And keep in-a-door,
        And thou shalt have more
        Than two tens to a score. 120

122 *breath of an unfee'd lawyer*: A lawyer will
    not plead a case unless he is paid.
125 *nothing . . . nothing*: nothing can only be
    multiplied into nothing; see *1*, 1, 89.

126–7 *so much . . . comes to*: i.e. nothing; Lear
    has no 'land'—property—now.

128 *bitter*: sarcastic.

132–47 These lines ('That . . . snatching')
    are only printed in the Quarto text; they
    were perhaps omitted from the Folio
    because of the 'monopoly' reference in
    line 145.
134–35 *place . . . stand*: you take his place
    (because, of course, there was no 'lord'
    who 'counsell'd' Lear to give away his
    kingdom).
137 *presently*: immediately.
138 *motley*: fool's costume.
139 *there*: The fool points to Lear.

141–2 *that . . . with*: i.e. Lear was born a fool.

143 *not altogether fool*: not entirely a fool; but
    the fool answers as though Kent's words
    meant 'one who possesses all the folly
    there is'.
145 *monopoly out*: sole rights (in folly). There
    was much contemporary disquiet about
    the freedom with which James I granted
    monopolies to his courtiers.

149 *What . . . be?*: Lear gives a 'feed' to his
    fool.

Kent
This is nothing, fool.
Fool
Then 'tis like the breath of an unfee'd lawyer; you
gave me nothing for't. Can you make no use of
nothing, nuncle?
Lear
125 Why no, boy; nothing can be made out of nothing.
Fool
[*To* Kent] Prithee, tell him, so much the rent of his
land comes to: he will not believe a fool.
Lear
A bitter fool!
Fool
Dost thou know the difference, my boy, between a
130 bitter fool and a sweet one?
Lear
No, lad; teach me.
Fool
    That lord that counsell'd thee
        To give away thy land,
    Come place him here by me,
135   Do thou for him stand:
    The sweet and bitter fool
        Will presently appear;
    The one in motley here,
        The other found out there.
Lear
140 Dost thou call me fool, boy?
Fool
All thy other titles thou hast given away; that thou
wast born with.
Kent
This is not altogether fool, my lord.
Fool
No, faith, lords and great men will not let me; if I had
145 a monopoly out, they would have part on't: and
ladies too, they will not let me have all the fool to
myself; they'll be snatching. Nuncle, give me an egg,
and I'll give thee two crowns.
Lear
What two crowns shall they be?

151 *meat*: i.e. the yolk.
152 *clovest*: split.
153 *thou . . . dirt*: The fool refers to one of
     Aesop's fables about a man who, for fear
     of overloading the beast, carried his ass
     to the market.
155 *like myself*: i.e. like a fool.
156 *so*: true.
157–60 *Fools . . . apish*: Fools have never
     been so much out of favour as they are at
     the present time, when wise men have
     become so silly: instead of using their
     intelligence, they imitate (ape) the fools.
162 *used it*: made a habit of it.

167 *bo-peep*: a children's game which involves
     covering the eyes and pretending not to
     see.
172 *kin*: relationship.

177 *pared*: peeled.

179 *what . . . on*: why are you looking like
     that; a 'frontlet' was a band worn round
     the forehead.

182–3 *an O without a figure*: a zero with no
     other number before it to give it value—
     i.e. nothing.

Fool

150 Why, after I have cut the egg i'th'middle and eat up
the meat, the two crowns of the egg. When thou
clovest thy crown i'th'middle, and gav'st away both
parts, thou bor'st thine ass on thy back o'er the dirt:
thou hadst little wit in thy bald crown when thou
155 gav'st thy golden one away. If I speak like myself in
this, let him be whipp'd that first finds it so.

    Fools have ne'er less grace in a year;
      For wise men are grown foppish,
    And know not how their wits to wear,
160   *Their manners are so apish.*

Lear

When were you wont to be so full of songs, sirrah?

Fool

I have used it, nuncle, e'er since thou mad'st thy
daughters thy mothers; for when thou gav'st them the
rod and putt'st down thine own breeches,

165   *Then they for sudden joy did weep,*
      And I for sorrow sung,
    That such a king should play bo-peep,
      And go the fools among.

Prithee, nuncle, keep a schoolmaster that can teach
170 thy fool to lie: I would fain learn to lie.

Lear

And you lie, sirrah, we'll have you whipp'd.

Fool

I marvel what kin thou and thy daughters are: they'll
have me whipp'd for speaking true, thou'lt have me
whipp'd for lying; and sometimes I am whipp'd for
175 holding my peace. I had rather be any kind o'thing
than a fool; and yet I would not be thee, nuncle; thou
hast pared thy wit o'both sides, and left nothing
i'th'middle: here comes one o'the parings.

Enter Goneril

Lear

How now, daughter! what makes that frontlet on?
180 You are too much of late i'th'frown.

Fool

Thou wast a pretty fellow when thou hadst no need to
care for her frowning; now thou art an O without a
figure. I am better than thou art now; I am a fool, thou

186 *Mum, Mum*: softly, softly.
    'He who gives everything away (*nor...
    nor* = neither ... nor) because he is tired
    of it all, will one day want it back.'
189 *sheal'd peascod*: shelled peapod.
190 *all-licens'd fool*: see note to line 104.
191 *other*: others.
192 *carp*: find fault with things.
193 *rank*: gross.
195 *safe redress*: sure remedy.
196 *too late*: only recently.
197 *put it on*: encourage it.
198 *By your allowance*: by giving your
    permission.
198–203 *which ... proceeding*: Goneril's
    speech is curiously involved in its syntax;
    she seems to be saying to her father 'If
    you are encouraging this misbehaviour
    ('course'), you are making a mistake
    ('fault') which cannot go unnoticed
    (''scape censure'); and I shall have to
    find remedies for the misbehaviour—
    even though in my desire for a healthy
    state of affairs ('wholesome weal') I
    might have to adopt measures whose
    effects ('working') are displeasing to you,
    and which at any other time would be
    wrong of me ('else were shame'); but
    when it is seen how necessary this is, it
    will be called a sensible course of action'.
205–6 *The ... young*: Cuckoos, which are
    quite large birds, lay their eggs in the
    nests of smaller birds—which then have
    to rear the young cuckoo. The fool's
    couplet sounds like proverbial wisdom.
206 *it*: its.

207 *darkling*: in the dark.

209 *I would*: I wish.
210 *are fraught*: have plenty.
211 *dispositions*: states of mind.
213 *May ... horse?*: May not a fool see that
    something is wrong when a daughter
    gives orders to her father.
214 *Whoop ... thee*: This must be the refrain
    of a song—which is now lost; 'Jug' is a
    nickname for 'Joan'.

art nothing. [*To* Goneril] Yes, forsooth, I will hold my
185 tongue; so your face bids me, though you say nothing.
        Mum, Mum:
        He that keeps nor crust nor crumb,
        Weary of all, shall want some.
That's a sheal'd peascod [*Pointing to* Lear]
    Goneril
190 Not only, sir, this your all-licens'd fool,
But other of your insolent retinue
Do hourly carp and quarrel, breaking forth
In rank and not-to-be-endured riots. Sir,
I had thought, by making this well known unto you,
195 To have found a safe redress; but now grow fearful,
By what yourself too late have spoke and done,
That you protect this course, and put it on
By your allowance; which if you should, the fault
Would not 'scape censure, nor the redresses sleep,
200 Which, in the tender of a wholesome weal,
Might in their working do you that offence,
Which else were shame, that then necessity
Will call discreet proceeding.
    Fool
For you know, nuncle,
205   The hedge-sparrow fed the cuckoo so long,
        That it's had it head bit off by it young.

So out went the candle, and we were left darkling.
    Lear
Are you our daughter?
    Goneril
I would you would make use of your good wisdom,
210 Whereof I know you are fraught; and put away
These dispositions which of late transport you
From what you rightly are.
    Fool
May not an ass know when a cart draws the horse?
Whoop, Jug! I love thee.

Lear

215 Does any here know me? This is not Lear:
Does Lear walk thus? speak thus? Where are his eyes?
Either his notion weakens, his discernings
Are lethargied—Ha! waking? 'tis not so.
Who is it that can tell me who I am?

Fool

220 Lear's shadow.

Lear

I would learn that; for by the marks of sovereignty,
knowledge, and reason, I should be false persuaded I
had daughters.

Fool

Which they will make an obedient father.

Lear

225 Your name, fair gentlewoman?

Goneril

This admiration, sir, is much o'th'savour
Of other your new pranks. I do beseech you
To understand my purposes aright:
As you are old and reverend, should be wise.
230 Here do you keep a hundred knights and squires;
Men so disorder'd, so debosh'd, and bold,
That this our court, infected with their manners,
Shows like a riotous inn: epicurism and lust
Makes it more like a tavern or a brothel
235 Than a grac'd palace. The shame itself doth speak
For instant remedy; be then desir'd
By her, that else will take the thing she begs,
A little to disquantity your train;
And the remainders, that shall still depend,
240 To be such men as may besort your age,
Which know themselves and you.

Lear

                              Darkness and devils!
Saddle my horses; call my train together.
Degenerate bastard! I'll not trouble thee:
Yet have I left a daughter.

Goneril

245 You strike my people, and your disorder'd rabble
Make servants of their betters.

Enter Albany

217 *notion*: mind.
discernings: understanding.
218 *lethargied*: slowed down.
waking?: am I awake?
'tis not so: I can't believe this—I must be
dreaming.
221–24 *I would . . . father*: *om*. F.

222 *false persuaded*: falsely led to believe.

226 *admiration*: pretence of amazement.
o'th'savour: of the same kind.
227 *other your*: others of your.
pranks: childish tricks.
228 *my purposes*: what I mean.
229 *should*: you should.
231 *disorder'd*: disorderly.
debosh'd: debauched.
233 *Shows*: looks like.
epicurism: gluttony.

235 *grac'd*: graced with the royal presence.
236 *desir'd*: requested.
238 *disquantity*: reduce the size of.
239 *remainders . . . depend*: those who remain
as your followers.
240 *besort*: be suitable for.
241 'Who know their own places, and
understand what you need.'

Lear
Woe, that too late repents; O sir, are you come?
Is it your will? Speak, sir. Prepare my horses.
Ingratitude, thou marble-hearted fiend,
250 More hideous, when thou show'st thee in a child,
Than the sea-monster.
Albany
                  Pray sir, be patient.
Lear
[*To* Goneril] Detested kite, thou liest!
My train are men of choice and rarest parts,
That all particulars of duty know,
255 And in the most exact regard support
The worships of their name. O most small fault,
How ugly didst thou in Cordelia show!
Which, like an engine, wrench'd my frame of nature
From the fix'd place, drew from my heart all love,
260 And added to the gall. O Lear, Lear, Lear!
Beat at this gate, that let thy folly in, [*Striking his head*]
And thy dear judgement out! Go, go, my people.
                  [*Exeunt* Kent *and* Knights
Albany
My lord, I am guiltless, as I am ignorant
Of what hath moved you.
Lear
             It may be so, my lord.
265 Hear, Nature, hear! dear goddess, hear!
Suspend thy purpose, if thou didst intend
To make this creature fruitful!
Into her womb convey sterility!
Dry up in her the organs of increase,
270 And from her derogate body never spring
A babe to honour her! If she must teem,
Create her child of spleen, that it may live
And be a thwart disnatur'd torment to her!
Let it stamp wrinkles in her brow of youth,
275 With cadent tears fret channels in her cheeks,
Turn all her mother's pains and benefits
To laughter and contempt, that she may feel
How sharper than a serpent's tooth it is
To have a thankless child! Away, away!   [*Exit*
Albany
280 Now, gods that we adore, whereof comes this?

247 *Woe, that too late repents*: woe unto him that repents when it is too late.
251 *the sea-monster*: any sea-monster.
252 *kite*: carrion-bird.
253 *choice and rarest parts*: chosen for their very special abilities.
254 'Who know exactly what is expected of them.'
255–6 *And . . . name*: And are most careful to live up to their reputations.
258–9 *Which . . . place*: Lear seems to be saying that Cordelia's behaviour, like some kind of powerful instrument ('engine'), has thrown his whole being out of order.

270 *derogate*: dishonoured.
271 *teem*: bear children.
272 *spleen*: evil temper.
273 *thwart*: perverse.
    disnatur'd: unnatural.
275 *cadent*: falling.
    fret: wear away.
276 *her . . . benefits*: the cares and joys that a mother should have.
277 *To . . . contempt*: into a source for other people's laughter and contempt.
278 *a serpent's tooth*: a snake's bite.
280 *gods*: by all the gods.

282–3 *let . . . gives it*: let him have his mood ('disposition') since he's in his dotage.

Goneril
Never afflict yourself to know more of it:
But let his disposition have that scope
As dotage gives it.

Enter Lear

284 *fifty of my followers*: It is dramatically effective that Lear should lose half his attendants so suddenly ('at a clap')— although it is difficult to explain when the dismissal could have taken place.
285 *Within a fortnight*: Lear has been staying with Goneril for less than two weeks.

Lear
What! fifty of my followers at a clap;
285 Within a fortnight!
          Albany
                              What's the matter, sir?
          Lear
I'll tell thee. [*To* Goneril] Life and death! I am asham'd
That thou hast power to shake my manhood thus,
That these hot tears, which break from me perforce,
Should make thee worth them. Blasts and fogs upon
          thee!

290 *untented woundings*: wounds too deep to be cleansed by a 'tent'—a roll of lint which could be used for either probing or dressing a wound.
291 *fond*: foolish.
292 *Beweep*: if you weep for.
293 *loose*: let fall.
294 *temper*: soften.
296 *kind and comfortable*: offering comfort as a daughter should.

299 *shape*: appearance—i.e. as a king.

290 Th'untented woundings of a father's curse
Pierce every sense about thee! Old fond eyes,
Beweep this cause again, I'll pluck ye out,
And cast you, with the waters that you loose,
To temper clay. Yea, is't come to this?
295 Ha, let it be so! I have another daughter,
Who, I am sure, is kind and comfortable:
When she shall hear this of thee, with her nails
She'll flay thy wolvish visage. Thou shalt find
That I'll resume the shape which thou dost think
300 I have cast off for ever.   [*Exit*
          Goneril
Do you mark that?
          Albany
I cannot be so partial, Goneril,
To the great love I bear you,—
          Goneril
Pray you, content. What, Oswald, ho!
305 [*To the* Fool] You, sir, more knave than fool, after
          your master.
          Fool
Nuncle Lear, nuncle Lear! tarry, take the fool with
thee.
          A fox, when one has caught her,
          And such a daughter,
310 *Should sure*: should certainly be sent.
310   Should sure to the slaughter,

311 *halter*: hangman's noose; the word was
pronounced (with 'after') to rhyme with
'caught her', 'daughter' and 'slaughter'.

313–24 *This man . . . th'unfitness*: om. Q.

315 *At point*: armed and ready.
316 *buzz*: rumour.
317 *enguard*: protect.
318 *in mercy*: at his mercy.

320 *still*: always.
321 *Not . . . taken*: rather than be in constant
fear for my own safety.
322 *writ*: written to.

327 *away to horse*: ride off quickly.
328 *particular*: personal.

330 *compact*: strengthen, confirm.

> If my cap would buy a halter;
> So the fool follows after.   [*Exit*
>
> **Goneril**
> This man hath had good counsel. A hundred knights!
> 'Tis politic and safe to let him keep
> 315 At point a hundred knights; yes, that on every dream,
> Each buzz, each fancy, each complaint, dislike,
> He may enguard his dotage with their powers,
> And hold our lives in mercy. Oswald, I say!
>
> **Albany**
> Well, you may fear too far.
>
> **Goneril**
>   Safer than trust too far.
> 320 Let me still take away the harms I fear,
> Not fear still to be taken: I know his heart.
> What he hath utter'd I have writ my sister;
> If she sustain him and his hundred knights,
> When I have show'd th'unfitness,—
>
> *Enter* Oswald
>
>   How now, Oswald!
> 325 What, have you writ that letter to my sister?
>
> **Oswald**
> Ay, madam.
>
> **Goneril**
> Take you some company, and away to horse:
> Inform her full of my particular fear;
> And thereto add such reasons of your own
> 330 As may compact it more. Get you gone,
> And hasten your return.   [*Exit* Oswald

No, no, my lord,
This milky gentleness and course of yours
Though I condemn not, yet, under pardon,
You are much more attax'd for want of wisdom
335 Than prais'd for harmful mildness.
Albany
How far your eyes may pierce I cannot tell:
Striving to better, oft we mar what's well.
Goneril
Nay, then—
Albany
Well, well; th'event.

[*Exeunt*

Scene 5

A courtyard in front of
Albany's *palace*

Lear
Go you before to Gloucester with these letters.
Acquaint my daughter no further with any thing you
know than comes from her demand out of the letter. If
your diligence be not speedy I shall be there afore you.
Kent
5 I will not sleep, my lord, till I have delivered your
letter.
Fool
If a man's brains were in's heels, were't not in danger
of kibes?
Lear
Ay, boy.
Fool
10 Then, I prithee, be merry; thy wit shall not go slip-
shod.
Lear
Ha, ha, ha!
Fool
Shalt see thy other daughter will use thee kindly; for
though she's as like this as a crab's like an apple, yet I
15 can tell what I can tell.

Act I Scene 5

Lear gives Kent a letter to take to Regan. The fool tries to make Lear laugh, but his jokes are bitter to the king.

1 *before*: ahead.
Gloucester: See Commentary, p. xviii.
these letters: this letter.
2–3 *Acquaint . . . letter*: don't tell her anything more than she might ask after reading the letter; Lear already seems wary of Regan.

8 *kibes*: chilblains.

10 *slip-shod*: in slippers.

13 *kindly*: The fool intends two senses of the word, *both* 'affectionately' *and* 'after her own nature'.
14 *she's as like this*: in appearance Regan is as much like Goneril.
crab: crab-apple—which looks like a sweet apple but tastes sour.

332 *This . . . yours*: your mild and gentle course of action.
333 *under pardon*: if you don't mind me saying so.
334 *attax'd for*: charged with.
335 *harmful mildness*: a leniency that could be dangerous.

339 *th'event*: let's see what will happen.

18 *on's*: of his.

20 *side's nose*: side of his nose.

22 *her*: Lear is thinking of Cordelia.

27 *put's head*: put his head.

29 *I will . . . nature*: I will cease to be a loving father.
32   *seven stars*: the Pleiades.
     mo: more.
     pretty: neat.

35 *To take't again*: Lear may be thinking that he will reclaim his kingdom; *or* perhaps he is referring to the reduction in the number of his attendants.
perforce: by force.

Lear
What canst tell, boy?

Fool
She will taste as like this as a crab does to a crab. Thou canst tell why one's nose stands i'th'middle on's face?

Lear
No.

Fool
20   Why, to keep one's eyes of either side's nose, that what a man cannot smell out, he may spy into.

Lear
I did her wrong,—

Fool
Canst tell how an oyster makes his shell?

Lear
No.

Fool
25   Nor I neither; but I can tell why a snail has a house.

Lear
Why?

Fool
Why, to put's head in; not to give it away to his daughters, and leave his horns without a case.

Lear
I will forget my nature. So kind a father! Be my
30   horses ready?

Fool
Thy asses are gone about 'em. The reason why the seven stars are no mo than seven is a pretty reason.

Lear
Because they are not eight?

Fool
Yes, indeed: thou would'st make a good fool.

Lear
35   To take't again perforce! Monster Ingratitude!

Fool
If thou wert my fool, nuncle, I'd have thee beaten for being old before thy time.

Lear
How's that?

Fool
Thou should'st not have been old till thou hadst been
40   wise.

41 *mad*: This is the first hint that Lear's sanity is threatened.
42 *in temper*: well balanced.

Lear

O! let me not be mad, not mad, sweet heaven;
Keep me in temper; I would not be mad!

Enter Gentleman

How now! Are the horses ready?

Gentleman

Ready, my lord.

Lear

45 Come, boy.

Fool

46–7 *She . . . shorter*: The fool's couplet, warning of impending disaster, is addressed to the audience.
47 *maid*: virgin.

She that's a maid now, and laughs at my departure,
Shall not be a maid long, unless things be cut shorter.

[*Exeunt*

Act 2

Act 2 Scene 1

Edmund learns that Regan and her husband, the Duke of Cornwall, are coming to visit the Earl of Gloucester. There are rumours of war. Gloucester has set a guard to spy on Edgar, and when Edgar comes on to the scene, Edmund warns his brother to fly from their father's wrath. Hearing Gloucester's approach, Edmund draws his sword and wounds his own arm; he tells his father that he was hurt by Edgar. Gloucester tells Cornwall and Regan of what he believes to be Edgar's murderous intentions and Edmund's filial loyalty. Cornwall takes Edmund into his service, and a full-scale search is instigated to capture Edgar. Regan tells Gloucester that she and her husband have come to ask his advice about Lear.

1 *Save thee*: May God save you (a common Elizabethan greeting).
6 *news abroad*: talk going around.
7 *ear-bussing*: ear-kissing, whispering.
8 *arguments*: topics of conversation.
10 *toward*: threatened; this is the first of the many suggestions that the two dukes intend to fight (presumably for each other's share of the kingdom).

15 'This is going to work well with my schemes.'
17 *of a queasy question*: of a sensitive ('queasy' = likely to vomit) nature; Edmund must handle the matter very delicately.
18 *Briefness . . . work*: let me have quick action and good luck.

Scene 1

The Earl of Gloucester's *castle*
Enter Edmund *and* Curan, *meeting*

Edmund
Save thee, Curan.
    Curan
And you, sir. I have been with your father, and given him notice that the Duke of Cornwall and Regan his duchess will be here with him this night.
    Edmund
5 How comes that?
    Curan
Nay, I know not. You have heard of the news abroad? I mean the whisper'd ones, for they are yet but ear-bussing arguments.
    Edmund
Not I: pray you, what are they?
    Curan
10 Have you heard of no likely wars toward, 'twixt the Dukes of Cornwall and Albany?
    Edmund
Not a word.
    Curan
You may do then, in time. Fare you well, sir.   [*Exit*
    Edmund
The duke be here to-night! The better! best!
15 This weaves itself perforce into my business.
My father hath set guard to take my brother;
And I have one thing, of a queasy question,
Which I must act. Briefness and Fortune, work!
Brother, a word; descend: brother, I say!

Enter Edgar

20 *watches*: is still awake.
21 *Intelligence is given*: someone has told
   him.

24 *i'th'haste*: in great haste.

26 *Upon his party*: on his side.
27 *Advise yourself*: think of what you have
   been saying.
   on't: of it.

29 *In cunning*: as part of the deception.
30 *quit you well*: give a good account of
   yourself (in seeming to fight).
31 *Yield*: Edmund now speaks loudly, so
   that he will be overheard.
33–4 *beget . . . endeavour*: make it appear
   that I have had to fight fiercely.
34–5 *drunkards . . . sport*: Edmund
   overcomes his natural reluctance to
   wound his own body by reminding
   himself of the way that young gallants,
   under the influence of drink, would stab
   themselves in order to drink the health of
   a mistress in blood mingled with wine.

38 *charms*: spells; Edmund plays on
   Gloucester's superstitious nature.
38–9 *conjuring . . . mistress*: invoking the
   moon to look favourably upon him.

40 *I bleed*: Edmund must make time for
   Edgar to escape; when he indicates 'this
   way' (line 41), he probably points in the
   wrong direction.

43 *murther*: murder; this is Shakespeare's
   preferred form of the word.
44 *revenging*: avenging.
45 *parricides*: those who murder their
   fathers.
   bend: aim.
47 *in fine*: to put it briefly.
48 *loathly opposite*: bitterly opposed.
49 *in fell motion*: with a deadly thrust.

20 My father watches: O sir, fly this place!
Intelligence is given where you are hid;
You have now the good advantage of the night.
Have you not spoken 'gainst the Duke of Cornwall?
He's coming hither, now, i'th'night, i'th'haste,
25 And Regan with him; have you nothing said
Upon his party 'gainst the Duke of Albany?
Advise yourself.
   Edgar
                    I am sure on't, not a word.
   Edmund
I hear my father coming; pardon me;
In cunning I must draw my sword upon you;
30 Draw; seem to defend yourself; now quit you well.
Yield! Come before my father! Light ho! here!
Fly, brother. Torches! torches! So, farewell. [*Exit* Edgar
Some blood drawn on me would beget opinion
                    Wounds his arm
Of my more fierce endeavour: I have seen drunkards
35 Do more than this in sport. Father! father!
Stop, stop! No help?

                    Enter Gloucester, *and* Servants *with torches*

   Gloucester
                    Now, Edmund, where's the villain?
   Edmund
Here stood he in the dark, his sharp sword out,
Mumbling of wicked charms, conjuring the moon
To stand auspicious mistress.
   Gloucester
                                   But where is he?
   Edmund
40 Look, sir, I bleed.
   Gloucester
                    Where is the villain, Edmund?
   Edmund
Fled this way, sir, when by no means he could—
   Gloucester
Pursue him, ho! Go after.   [*Exeunt some* Servants
                              'By no means' what?
   Edmund
Persuade me to the murther of your lordship;
But that I told him, the revenging gods

50 *prepared*: unsheathed.
   charges home: makes a direct attack on.
51 *unprovided*: unprotected.
   lanch'd: pierced, wounded.
52 *best alarum'd spirits*: courage aroused (as
   though by an alarum—a trumpet-call to
   battle).
53 *Bold . . . right*: made brave by the justice
   of the cause.
54 *gasted*: scared.
55 *Full*: quite.
   Let him fly far: however far he flies.
57 *And . . . dispatch*: and when he is found,
   kill him.
58 *My worthy arch and patron*: the most
   honourable and best patron that I have—
   i.e. his over-lord.
61 *the stake*: any place of execution (not
   necessarily the stake, where criminals
   were burned to death).
62 'Anyone who hides him shall die.'
64 *pight*: fully determined (past participle of
   pitch).
   curst: angry.
65 *discover him*: reveal his secret plans.
66 *unpossessing*: owning nothing, beggarly; a
   bastard son had no legal rights of
   inheritance.
67–9 'If I wanted to oppose you, would
   anything that you say be believed
   ('faith'd') because of the placing
   ('reposal') of any trust in you, or your
   own virtue or merit?'
70–1 *produce . . . character*: bring evidence
   in my own writing—which is what
   Edmund did in *Act 1, Scene 2*.
71 *I'ld turn it all*: I would blame it all.
72 *practice*: treacherous scheme.
73 'And you must think everyone is very
   stupid.'
74 *If . . . thought*: if they don't think.
   profits of my death: what you will gain if I
   die.
75 *pregnant*: conceivable, understandable.
   potential spirits: powerful motives.
76 *seek it*: try to get me put to death.
77 *strange*: unnatural.
   fast'ned: hardened.
78 *got*: begot, fathered.
78 s.d. *Tucket*: trumpet-call; Gloucester
   recognizes Cornwall's personal signal.
79 *All ports I'll bar*: I'll close all the sea-ports.
   'scape: escape.
80 *grant me that*: allow me to do that.

45 'Gainst parricides did all the thunder bend;
    Spoke with how manifold and strong a bond
    The child was bound to th'father; sir, in fine,
    Seeing how loathly opposite I stood
    To his unnatural purpose, in fell motion,
50 With his prepared sword he charges home
    My unprovided body, lanch'd mine arm:
    And when he saw my best alarum'd spirits
    Bold in the quarrel's right, roused to th'encounter,
    Or whether gasted by the noise I made,
55 Full suddenly he fled.
        Gloucester
                        Let him fly far:
    Not in this land shall he remain uncaught;
    And found—dispatch. The noble duke my master,
    My worthy arch and patron, comes to-night:
    By his authority I will proclaim it
60 That he which finds him shall deserve our thanks,
    Bringing the murderous coward to the stake;
    He that conceals him, death.
        Edmund
    When I dissuaded him from his intent,
    And found him pight to do it, with curst speech
65 I threaten'd to discover him: he replied,
    'Thou unpossessing bastard! dost thou think,
    If I would stand against thee, would the reposal
    Of any trust, virtue, or worth in thee
    Make thy words faith'd? No: what I should deny,—
70 As this I would; ay, though thou didst produce
    My very character—I'ld turn it all
    To thy suggestion, plot, and damned practice:
    And thou must make a dullard of the world,
    If they not thought the profits of my death
75 Were very pregnant and potential spirits
    To make thee seek it.'
        Gloucester
                        O strange and fast'ned villain!
    Would he deny his letter, said he? I never got him.

                                    [*Tucket within*

    Hark! the duke's trumpets. I know not why he comes.
    All ports I'll bar; the villain shall not 'scape;
80 The duke must grant me that: besides his picture

83 *natural boy*: Gloucester praises
Edmund's natural filial loyalty, making a
play on another sense of the words (=
illegitimate son).
work the means: make legal arrangements.
84 *capable*: able to inherit.

86 *I can call but now*: was only just now.

87 *too short*: is inadequate.

91 *nam'd*: In the Christian church, the
godparent may pronounce the infant's
name in the ceremony of baptism—but
the action of *King Lear* takes place in a
pre-Christian world.

94 *tended upon*: attended on, served.

96 *consort*: company; the stress is on the
second syllable.
97 *though*: if.
ill affected: disloyal.
98–9 'They are the ones who have incited
him to kill his father so that he will be
able to spend and squander all his
income.'
100 *this present*: this very.

105 *child-like office*: filial duty.

106 *bewray his practice*: reveal his plot.
107 *apprehend*: arrest.

I will send far and near, that all the kingdom
May have due note of him; and of my land,
Loyal and natural boy, I'll work the means
To make thee capable.

Enter Cornwall, Regan, *and* Attendants

Cornwall
85 How now, my noble friend! Since I came hither,
Which I can call but now, I have heard strange news.
Regan
If it be true, all vengeance comes too short
Which can pursue th'offender. How dost, my lord?
Gloucester
O, madam, my old heart is crack'd, it's crack'd!
Regan
90 What, did my father's godson seek your life?
He whom my father nam'd, your Edgar?
Gloucester
O lady, lady, shame would have it hid!
Regan
Was he not companion with the riotous knights
That tended upon my father?
Gloucester
95 I know not, madam; 'tis too bad, too bad.
Edmund
Yes, madam, he was of that consort.
Regan
No marvel then though he were ill affected;
'Tis they have put him on the old man's death,
To have th'expense and waste of his revenues.
100 I have this present evening from my sister
Been well inform'd of them, and with such cautions
That if they come to sojourn at my house,
I'll not be there.
Cornwall
                              Nor I, assure thee, Regan.
Edmund, I hear that you have shown your father
105 A child-like office.
Edmund
                              It was my duty, sir.
Gloucester
He did bewray his practice; and receiv'd
This hurt you see, striving to apprehend him.

110 *Be . . . harm*: give you cause to fear that
     he might do harm.
110–11 *make . . . please*: use all my resources
     to do whatever you think necessary.
111 *For you*: as for you personally.
112–13 *Whose . . . itself*: Whose virtuous
     obedience in this matter has so much to
     recommend it.
113 *ours*: in my service; the Duke of Cornwall
     is using the royal plural.
114 *Natures . . . trust*: such very trustworthy
     characters.
118 *Thus*: Regan, interrupting her husband,
     takes control of the situation.
     out of season: at an unexpected time
     (probably it is winter).
     threading . . . night: Travelling in the
     dark—perhaps riding through forests—
     needs as much care as threading a
     needle.
119 *Occasions*: matters.
     prize: importance.
122 *differences*: quarrels.
     best . . . fit: thought it would be best to
     answer away from home (so that Lear
     cannot take up residence with Regan
     until she has been able to talk to her
     sister).
123 *several*: different.
124 *attend dispatch*: are waiting to be sent
     back (with replies).
126 *Your needful counsel*: your much-needed
     advice.
127 *craves the instant use*: needs to be done
     immediately.

Cornwall
Is he pursued?
Gloucester
                                    Ay, my good lord.
Cornwall
If he be taken he shall never more
110 Be fear'd of doing harm; make your own purpose
How in my strength you please. For you, Edmund,
Whose virtue and obedience doth this instant
So much commend itself, you shall be ours:
Natures of such deep trust we shall much need;
115 You we first seize on.
Edmund
                         I shall serve you, sir,
Truly, however else.
Gloucester
                    For him I thank your grace.
Cornwall
You know not why we came to visit you,—
Regan
Thus out of season, threading dark-ey'd night:
Occasions, noble Gloucester, of some prize,
120 Wherein we must have use of your advice.
Our father he hath writ, so hath our sister,
Of differences, which I best thought it fit
To answer from our home; the several messengers
From hence attend dispatch. Our good old friend,
125 Lay comforts to your bosom, and bestow
Your needful counsel to our businesses,
Which craves the instant use.
Gloucester
                              I serve you, madam.
Your graces are right welcome.
                                   [*Flourish. Exeunt*

Act 2 Scene 2

Kent encounters Oswald again and attacks him—at first verbally and then with his sword—for obeying Goneril when she quarrelled with Lear. Oswald's cries bring Edmund to the scene, closely followed by Cornwall, Regan, and Gloucester. Kent denounces Oswald, but Cornwall is more impressed by Oswald's plea of innocence and punishes Kent by locking his legs in the stocks. Gloucester is sympathetic, but he can do nothing. When Kent is alone, he produces a letter from Cordelia. In both Quarto and Folio editions, the text of this scene is often corrupt—and the meanings of many lines are obscure.

os.d. *severally*: separately; the two characters probably come from different sides of the stage.
1 *Good dawning*: Oswald's greeting sounds affected, especially as it is still dark—see line 29.
art of this house?: do you belong to this household, are you a servant here?
3 *set*: stable.
4 *I'th'mire*: in the mud.
5 *if . . . me*: i.e. if you would be so kind; but Kent pretends to understand literally.
8 *If . . . pinfold*: if you were where I would like to have you—i.e. in my power; Kent's meaning is plain enough, although 'Lipsbury' is unknown (perhaps Kent is saying 'Lip-town', meaning 'between my teeth'). A 'pinfold' is a pen for stray cattle.
10 *use*: speak to.
13–22 *A knave . . . addition*: Kent abuses Oswald by pointing out the realities which underlie his pretensions.
13 *eater of broken meats*: one who lives on scraps, left-over food.
14 *three-suited*: owning only the three suits of clothes that were given annually to servants.
hundred-pound: cheap; the expression can carry this meaning only because James I sold knighthoods for a hundred pounds.
15 *worsted-stocking*: wearing stockings made of cheap woollen material; a gentleman's stockings were made of silk.
lily-livered: cowardly—with a white (bloodless) liver.
16 *action-taking*: one who goes to law

Scene 2

Before Gloucester's *castle*
Enter Kent *and* Oswald, *severally*

Oswald
Good dawning to thee, friend: art of this house?
Kent
Ay.
Oswald
Where may we set our horses?
Kent
I'th'mire.
Oswald
5 Prithee, if thou lov'st me, tell me.
Kent
I love thee not.
Oswald
Why, then I care not for thee.
Kent
If I had thee in Lipsbury pinfold, I would make thee care for me.
Oswald
10 Why dost thou use me thus? I know thee not.
Kent
Fellow, I know thee.
Oswald
What dost thou know me for?
Kent
A knave, a rascal, an eater of broken meats; a base, proud, shallow, beggarly, three-suited, hundred-
15 pound, filthy worsted-stocking knave; a lily-livered, action-taking, whoreson, glass-gazing, super-service-able, finical rogue; one-trunk-inheriting slave; one that wouldst be a bawd in way of good service, and art nothing but the composition of a knave, beggar,
20 coward, pandar, and the son and heir of a mongrel bitch: one whom I will beat into clamorous whining if thou deni'st the least syllable of thy addition.
Oswald
Why, what a monstrous fellow art thou, thus to rail on one that is neither known of thee nor knows thee!
Kent
25 What a brazen-fac'd varlet art thou, to deny thou

(instead of fighting) about an injury.
glass-gazing: vain, admiring himself in
the mirror.
super-serviceable: over-officious.
17 *finical*: fussy.
one-trunk-inheriting: with all his
possessions in a single trunk.
18 *be a bawd . . . service*: do anything for
money.
19 *composition*: compound.
20 *pandar*: go-between.
heir: inheriting the characteristics.
22 *addition*: the titles I've given you.
25 *varlet*: rascal.
29 *sop*: bread or cake soaked in liquid.
Kent's reference is unclear; perhaps he
threatens to beat Oswald until he is
soaked in his own blood and leave him to
lie in the moonshine.
30 *cullionly*: wretched.
barber-monger: one who goes often to the
barber's shop.
33 *Vanity the puppet*: The Lady Vanity was a
regular character in the Morality Plays
and the puppet-shows.
35 *carbonado*: score meat (as though for
grilling).
35–6 *come your ways*: come along now.
38 *neat*: fancy.

42 *With you*: Kent now tries to make
Edmund fight, taunting him as an
impudent youth ('goodman boy'), and
offering to initiate him ('I'll flesh ye')
into the adult world.

48 *your difference*: subject of your quarrel.

knowest me! Is it two days since I tripp'd up thy heels
and beat thee before the king? Draw, you rogue; for
though it be night, yet the moon shines: I'll make a
sop o'th'moonshine of you.   [*Drawing his sword*
30 You whoreson cullionly barber-monger, draw.

Oswald

Away! I have nothing to do with thee.

Kent

Draw, you rascal; you come with letters against the
king, and take Vanity the puppet's part against the
royalty of her father. Draw, you rogue, or I'll so
35 carbonado your shanks: draw, you rascal; come your
ways.

Oswald

Help, ho! murther! help!

Kent

Strike, you slave; stand, rogue, stand; you neat slave,
strike. [*Beats him*]

Oswald

40 Help, ho! murther! murther!

Enter Edmund, *with his rapier drawn*

Edmund

How now! What's the matter? Part!

Kent

With you, goodman boy, if you please: come, I'll
flesh ye; come on, young master.

Enter Cornwall, Regan, Gloucester, *and*
Servants

Gloucester

Weapons! arms! What's the matter here?

Cornwall

45 Keep peace, upon your lives:
He dies that strikes again. What is the matter?

Regan

The messengers from our sister and the king.

Cornwall

What is your difference? speak.

Oswald

I am scarce in breath, my lord.

Kent

50 No marvel, you have so bestirr'd your valour.

51 *disclaims in thee*: refuses to own you.
51–2 *a tailor made thee*: you're just a tailor's dummy.
56 *o'th'trade*: at the job.
58–9 *at suit*: in pity of.
60 *Thou . . . unnecessary letter*: The letter Z was often ignored in dictionaries of this period, and said to be unnecessary because its functions could be served by the letter S; Kent declares Oswald to be similarly superfluous to society.
62 *unbolted*: thoroughgoing, unsifted—like lime whose lumps must be trodden out to make mortar.
63 *jakes*: lavatory.
wagtail: The epithet suggests that Oswald bobs up and down like this little bird.
65 *beastly*: bestial, uncivilized.
reverence: respect.
66 *a privilege*: i.e. to overstep the bounds.
68 *wear a sword*: In Shakespeare's day, only gentlemen were allowed to carry swords.
70–1 *bite . . . unloose*: bite apart those knots which are too tightly fastened ('intrince') ever to be untied.
71 *smooth*: flatter.
72 *rebel*: i.e. against reason, which should control the passions.
73 *Bring oil to fire*: pour oil on the flames.
74 *Renege*: deny.
75 *halcyon beaks*: It was a popular belief that the dead kingfisher, hung up by the neck, would always turn its beak into the prevailing wind.
75 *gale and vary*: varying wind.
77 *epileptic visage*: The adjective has no particular meaning; Oswald's face shows his confusion and distress.
78 *Smoile*: smile. Both Quarto and Folio texts have this unusual spelling, and some editors suggest that the disguised Kent is assuming a rustic dialect.
as I were a fool: as though I were some professional jester.
79–80 *Goose . . . Camelot*: Kent's line of associations is not clear: geese are proverbially foolish birds; 'Sarum (= Salisbury) plain' is near Winchester, which was sometimes identified with 'Camelot'—the home of King Arthur; and a syphilitic swelling was called the 'Winchester goose' because there were so many brothels on land owned in

You cowardly rascal, nature disclaims in thee: a tailor made thee.

Cornwall

Thou art a strange fellow; a tailor make a man?

Kent

A tailor, sir: a stone-cutter or a painter could not have
55 made him so ill, though they had been but two years o'th'trade.

Cornwall

Speak yet, how grew your quarrel?

Oswald

This ancient ruffian, sir, whose life I have spar'd at suit of his grey beard,—

Kent

60 Thou whoreson zed! thou unnecessary letter! My lord, if you will give me leave, I will tread this unbolted villain into mortar, and daub the wall of a jakes with him. Spare my grey beard, you wagtail?

Cornwall

Peace, sirrah!
65 You beastly knave, know you no reverence?

Kent

Yes, sir; but anger hath a privilege.

Cornwall

Why art thou angry?

Kent

That such a slave as this should wear a sword,
Who wears no honesty. Such smiling rogues as these,
70 Like rats, oft bite the holy cords a-twain
Which are too intrince t'unloose; smooth every passion
That in the natures of their lords rebel;
Bring oil to fire, snow to their colder moods;
Renege, affirm, and turn their halcyon beaks
75 With every gale and vary of their masters,
Knowing nought, like dogs, but following.
A plague upon your epileptic visage!
Smoile you my speeches, as I were a fool?
Goose, if I had you upon Sarum plain,
80 I'd drive ye cackling home to Camelot.

Cornwall

What! art thou mad, old fellow?

Gloucester

How fell you out? say that.

Southwark which was part of the diocese
of Winchester. Any or all—or none—of
these references could have gone into the
making of Kent's lines.

86 *likes*: pleases.

87 *perchance*: perhaps.

92 *affect*: put on.

93–4 *constrains . . . nature*: forces the
fashion ('garb') of his speech to be
absolutely unnatural.

94 *his*: its.

96 'If people will put up with his rudeness,
that's fine; if not—then he says he is only
speaking the truth.'

97 *this plainness*: what they claim as
'speaking the truth'.

98 *Harbour*: conceal.

99 *silly-ducking observants*: obsequious
courtiers making silly bows.

100 *stretch . . . nicely*: make great efforts to
carry out their duties with precision.

102–4 *Under . . . front*: Kent now speaks with
exaggerated courtly diction, addressing
Cornwall as though he were some
celestial body whose position in the sky
('aspect') would have as much power
('influence') as the sun.

104 *Phoebus*: Phoebus Apollo, the classical
god of the sun, who was depicted with a
crown of flames on his forehead ('front').

105 *dialect*: manner of speaking.
discommend: disapprove of.

106–7 *that . . . knave*: anyone who ever
deceived you by speaking in a plain
manner was a complete villain.

108–9 *I will not . . . to't*: Kent's speech is not
easy to explain; he is perhaps saying, 'I
will never be a villain, even though I
make you so annoyed with me that you
say I am one'.

112 *very late*: quite recently.

Kent
No contraries hold more antipathy
Than I and such a knave.

Cornwall
85 Why dost thou call him knave? What is his fault?

Kent
His countenance likes me not.

Cornwall
No more, perchance, does mine, nor his, nor hers.

Kent
Sir, 'tis my occupation to be plain:
I have seen better faces in my time
90 Than stands on any shoulder that I see
Before me at this instant.

Cornwall
                              This is some fellow,
Who, having been prais'd for bluntness, doth affect
A saucy roughness, and constrains the garb
Quite from his nature: he cannot flatter, he,
95 An honest mind and plain, he must speak truth:
And they will take it, so; if not, he's plain.
These kind of knaves I know, which in this plainness
Harbour more craft and more corrupter ends
Than twenty silly-ducking observants,
100 That stretch their duties nicely.

Kent
Sir, in good faith, in sincere verity,
Under th'allowance of your great aspect,
Whose influence, like the wreath of radiant fire
On flick'ring Phoebus' front,—

Cornwall
                              What mean'st by this?

Kent
105 To go out of my dialect, which you discommend so
much. I know, sir, I am no flatterer: he that beguil'd
you in a plain accent was a plain knave; which for my
part I will not be, though I should win your displeasure to entreat me to't.

Cornwall
110 What was th'offence you gave him?

Oswald
I never gave him any:
It pleas'd the king his master very late

113 *upon his misconstruction*: because of something he did not understand.

114 *compact . . . displeasure*: in league with the king and wanting to encourage him in his bad temper.

115 *being down . . . rail'd*: when I was on the floor, he insulted me.

116 *put upon . . . man*: pretended to be so brave.

117 *worthied him*: made him seem a hero.

118 *For . . . subdu'd*: for attacking someone who had already had to humble himself.

119 *fleshment . . . exploit*: excitement of doing this terrible deed (Oswald speaks ironically).

120 *Drew*: drew his sword.

120–1 *None . . . fool*: every one of these cowardly rogues wants you to believe that, in comparison with him, Ajax (a mighty Greek warrior) is nothing but a fool.

121 *stocks*: Confinement in the stocks was a humiliating punishment, used mainly for petty misdemeanours—see lines 138–40.

122 *ancient . . . braggart*: Kent, being old, should be worthy of respect: but he is a villain and a braggart. Cornwall enjoys his oxymorons.

127 'To the Crown, and to Lear as a person.'

128 *stocking*: putting in the stocks.

132 *should not*: ought not to.

133 *colour*: description.

134 *bring away*: bring here.

137 *check*: rebuke.

138 *contemned'st*: most contemptible.

139 *trespasses*: faults.

141–2 'That you show so little esteem for him that you can treat his messenger like this.'

142 *answer*: be responsible for.

149 *Will not be rubb'd*: will not let anything get in his way; in the game of bowls, a *rub* is anything that impedes the bowl's course.

To strike at me, upon his misconstruction;
When he, compact, and flattering his displeasure,
115 Tripp'd me behind; being down, insulted, rail'd,
And put upon him such a deal of man,
That worthied him, got praises of the king
For him attempting who was self-subdu'd;
And, in the fleshment of this dread exploit,
120 Drew on me here again.

    Kent
                None of these rogues and cowards
But Ajax is their fool.

    Cornwall
                Fetch forth the stocks!
You stubborn ancient knave, you reverend braggart,
We'll teach you.

    Kent
                Sir, I am too old to learn.
Call not your stocks for me; I serve the king,
125 On whose employment I was sent to you;
You shall do small respect, show too bold malice
Against the grace and person of my master,
Stocking his messenger.

    Cornwall
                Fetch forth the stocks!
As I have life and honour, there shall he sit till noon.

    Regan
130 Till noon! till night, my lord; and all night too.

    Kent
Why madam, if I were your father's dog,
You should not use me so!

    Regan
                Sir, being his knave, I will.

    Cornwall
This is a fellow of the self-same colour
Our sister speaks of. Come, bring away the stocks.

Stocks brought out

    Gloucester
135 Let me beseech your grace not to do so.
His fault is much, and the good king his master
Will check him for't: your purpos'd low correction
Is such as basest and contemned'st wretches
For pilf'rings and most common trespasses

150 *watch'd*: be awake all night.

151 *whistle*: i.e. pass as well as I can.

152 *out at heels*: become threadbare (like worn-out stockings).

153 *Give*: may God give.

154 'The duke is at fault here, and this will not be well received.'

155 *approve . . . saw*: prove the old saying to be true.

156–7 *out of . . . sun*: A more common form of the 'saw' is 'out of the frying-pan into the fire'.

158 Kent welcomes the rising sun, which gives light to the earth beneath it ('this under globe').

159 *comfortable*: reassuring, giving comfort.

160–1 *Nothing . . . misery*: when you are really desperate, you have to believe in miracles.

163 *obscured course*: what I am doing in this disguise.

163–5 *and . . . remedies*: The sense of the passage (whose text is probably corrupt) seems to be: 'In time Cordelia will rescue us from this terribly abnormal state of affairs ('enormous state') and give us back what we have lost.' Kent may have difficulty in reading the letter because it is still dark and he is very tired.

165 *o'erwatch'd*: exhausted through loss of sleep.

166 *vantage*: opportunity (of falling asleep).

168 *Fortune*: The goddess Fortune was depicted with a wheel, whose turning brought good or bad luck.

140 Are punish'd with: the king must take it ill,
That he, so slightly valued in his messenger,
Should have him thus restrained.

Cornwall
                          I'll answer that.

Regan
My sister may receive it much more worse
To have her gentleman abus'd, assaulted,
145 For following her affairs. Put in his legs.

Kent is put in the stocks

Cornwall
Come, my lord, away.
                   [*Exeunt all but* Gloucester *and* Kent

Gloucester
I am sorry for thee, friend; 'tis the duke's pleasure,
Whose disposition, all the world well knows,
Will not be rubb'd nor stopp'd: I'll entreat for thee.

Kent
150 Pray, do not, sir. I have watch'd and travell'd hard;
Some time I shall sleep out, the rest I'll whistle.
A good man's fortune may grow out at heels:
Give you good morrow!

Gloucester
The duke's to blame in this; 'twill be ill taken.   [*Exit*

Kent
155 Good king, that must approve the common saw,
Thou out of heaven's benediction com'st
To the warm sun!
Approach, thou beacon to this under globe,
That by thy comfortable beams I may
160 Peruse this letter. Nothing almost sees miracles,
But misery: I know 'tis from Cordelia,
Who hath most fortunately been inform'd
Of my obscured course; and shall find time
From this enormous state, seeking to give
165 Losses their remedies. All weary and o'erwatch'd,
Take vantage, heavy eyes, not to behold
This shameful lodging.
Fortune, good night; smile once more; turn thy wheel!

He sleeps

Act 2 Scene 3

Edgar, in order to escape the search-party, is disguising himself as a mad beggar.

1 *proclaim'd*: proclaimed an outlaw.
2 *by the . . . tree*: by good fortune there was a hollow tree (in which he could hide).
3 *No port is free*: see 2, 1, 79.
5 *attend my taking*: wait to capture me.
   Whiles I may 'scape: As long as I can escape capture.
6 *am bethought*: I have got the idea.
7 *shape*: appearance.
8 *in contempt of man*: to show how contemptible a creature man really is.
10 *elf*: tangle; neglected hair, matted and knotted, was called 'elf-locks', and elves were blamed for its appearance.

11 *presented nakedness*: exposing my nakedness.
   outface: brave, confront.
13 *country*: countryside.
   proof: example.
14 *Bedlam beggars*: former inmates of the Bethlehem Hospital for the insane, who had licences to beg; see p. 141.
15 *numb'd and mortified*: frozen and dead to all pain.
16 *pricks*: skewers.
17 *object*: spectacle.
   low: lowly, humble.
18 *pelting*: paltry.
   sheep-cotes: shepherds' cottages.
19 *bans*: curses.
20 *Poor . . . Tom*: Edgar practises his beggar's call; 'Turlygod' has never been satisfactorily explained.
21 'At least I can have some identity (as Poor Tom); I can no longer be Edgar.'

Scene 3

Outside Gloucester's *castle*
Enter Edgar

Edgar
I heard myself proclaim'd;
And by the happy hollow of a tree
Escap'd the hunt. No port is free; no place,
That guard, and most unusual vigilance,
5 Does not attend my taking. Whiles I may 'scape,
I will preserve myself; and am bethought
To take the basest and most poorest shape
That ever penury, in contempt of man,
Brought near to beast; my face I'll grime with filth,
10 Blanket my loins, elf all my hairs in knots,
And with presented nakedness outface
The winds and persecutions of the sky.
The country gives me proof and precedent
Of Bedlam beggars, who, with roaring voices,
15 Strike in their numb'd and mortified bare arms
Pins, wooden pricks, nails, sprigs of rosemary;
And with this horrible object, from low farms,
Poor pelting villages, sheep-cotes, and mills,
Sometime with lunatic bans, sometime with prayers,
20 Enforce their charity. Poor Turlygod! Poor Tom!
That's something yet: Edgar I nothing am.

[*Exit*

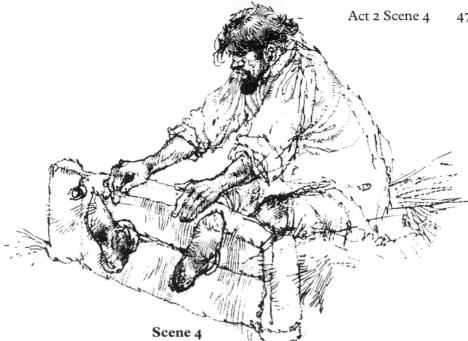

Lear, accompanied by the fool, arrives at
Gloucester's house, where he finds Kent in
the stocks and hears how he has been treated.
Lear goes to find Regan, leaving the fool and
Kent to talk about their situation until the
king returns with Gloucester, who tells him
that Regan is refusing to see her father. At first
Lear excuses her, but soon his anger increases
and he demands her presence. Regan and
Cornwall come out to meet Lear, and Kent is
released from the stocks. Lear describes
Goneril's unkindness and his curse on her.
Suddenly Goneril herself arrives, and the two
sisters join to oppose their father. They try to
force him to reduce his train of attendants so
that he will be completely dependent on his
daughters. A distant storm is heard.
Maddened, Lear rushes from the stage, taking
Kent and the fool with him. Gloucester
follows them, but returns to tell how the king
has disappeared into the stormy night.
Cornwall commands Gloucester to lock all
the gates.

3–4 *no purpose . . . remove*: they (Regan
and Cornwall) had no intention of
moving to any other place.

6 *Mak'st . . . pastime*: are you sitting in the
stocks for fun.

Scene 4

Gloucester's *castle*. Kent *in the stocks*
Enter Lear, Fool, *and* Gentleman

Lear
'Tis strange that they should so depart from home,
And not send back my messenger.

Gentleman
                                        As I learn'd,
The night before there was no purpose in them
Of this remove.

Kent
                                        Hail to thee, noble master!

Lear
5 Ha!
Mak'st thou this shame thy pastime?

Kent
                                        No, my lord.

Fool
Ha, ha, he wears cruel garters! Horses are tied by the
heads, dogs and bears by th'neck, monkeys by th'loins,
and men by th'legs: when a man's over-lusty at legs
10 then he wears wooden nether-stocks.

Lear
What's he that hath so much thy place mistook
To set thee here?

7 *cruel garters*: i.e. the stocks; the fool
makes a pun with 'crewel' (= thin
worsted yarn).
9 *over-lusty at legs*: too much of a
vagabond.
10 *nether-stocks*: stockings.
11 *place*: position as the king's servant.
12 *To*: as to.
13 *son*: son-in-law.

20 *Jupiter*: king of the Roman gods.

21 *Juno*: Jupiter's queen.

23 'To do such a flagrant insult where they
ought to show respect.'
24 *Resolve me*: explain to me.
all modest haste: as quickly as you
reasonably can.
26 *Coming from us*: since you came as a royal
messenger.

27 *commend*: deliver.

28–9 *the place . . . kneeling*: the kneeling
position which showed my respect.
29 *reeking post*: sweating messenger.
30 *Stew'd*: soaked with sweat.
32 *spite of intermission*: i.e. without stopping
to draw breath.
33 *presently*: immediately.
on whose contents: because of something
these letters contained.
34 *meiny*: household, all their servants.
straight took horse: at once got on their
horses.
35–6 *attend . . . answer*: wait until they had
time to answer.
40 *Display'd so saucily*: acted in such an
obviously rude manner.

Kent

It is both he and she,
Your son and daughter.
    Lear
No.
    Kent
15 Yes.
    Lear
No, I say.
    Kent
I say, yea.
    Lear
No, no; they would not.
    Kent
Yes, yes, they have.
    Lear
20 By Jupiter, I swear, no.
    Kent
By Juno, I swear, ay.
    Lear

They durst not do't,
They could not, would not do't; 'tis worse than
   murther,
To do upon respect such violent outrage.
Resolve me, with all modest haste, which way
25 Thou might'st deserve, or they impose, this usage,
Coming from us.
    Kent
My lord, when at their home
I did commend your highness' letters to them,
Ere I was risen from the place that show'd
My duty kneeling, came there a reeking post,
30 Stew'd in his haste, half breathless, panting forth
From Goneril his mistress salutations;
Deliver'd letters, spite of intermission,
Which presently they read: on whose contents
They summon'd up their meiny, straight took horse;
35 Commanded me to follow, and attend
The leisure of their answer; gave me cold looks:
And meeting here the other messenger,
Whose welcome, I perceiv'd, had poison'd mine,
Being the very fellow which of late
40 Display'd so saucily against your highness,

41 *more man than wit*: more courage than
    sense.
    drew: i.e. drew his sword.
42 *rais'd the house*: woke up all the servants.
45 *that way*: i.e. fly south; the flight of the
    wild-geese is a clear sign that winter is
    approaching—and the fool can see that
    the events which Kent has been
    describing are sure indicators of bad
    times to come.
45–53 *Winter's . . . year*: om. Q.
46–9 'When the fathers are poor, then the
    children refuse to see what they need;
    but when fathers keep control of the
    moneybags, then their children show a
    proper affection.'
50–1 'The goddess Fortune is just like any
    prostitute: she will not open her door to a
    poor man.'
52 *dolours*: griefs; the fool makes a pun with
    'dollars' (= English name for some
    continental currency).
    for: on account of, in exchange for.
53 *tell*: speak of, reckon.
54–5 *this mother . . . Hysterica passio*:
    Hysterica Passio, commonly known as
    'the mother', was the name given to an
    affliction characterized by a sense of
    choking and suffocation, starting from
    the heart and rising to the throat; it was
    thought to begin in the womb—Greek
    hysteros—but was not suffered
    exclusively by women.
56 *Thy element's below*: your proper place is
    underneath.
59 *Made*: committed.
61 *How chance*: why is it that.
62 *And*: if.

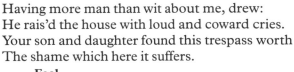

Having more man than wit about me, drew:
He rais'd the house with loud and coward cries.
Your son and daughter found this trespass worth
The shame which here it suffers.
    Fool
45 Winter's not gone yet, if the wild-geese fly that way.
    Fathers that wear rags
        Do make their children blind,
    But fathers that bear bags
        Shall see their children kind.
50   Fortune, that arrant whore,
        Ne'er turns the key to th'poor.
But for all this thou shalt have as many dolours for
thy daughters as thou canst tell in a year.
    Lear
O how this mother swells up toward my heart!
55 *Hysterica passio!* down, thou climbing sorrow!
Thy element's below. Where is this daughter?
    Kent
With the earl, sir; here within.
    Lear
Follow me not; stay here.   [*Exit*
    Gentleman
Made you no more offence but what you speak of?
    Kent
60 None.
How chance the king comes with so small a number?
    Fool
And thou hadst been set i'th'stocks for that question,
thou'dst well deserv'd it.
    Kent
Why, fool?
    Fool
65 We'll set thee to school to an ant, to teach thee there's
no labouring i'th'winter. All that follow their noses are
led by their eyes but blind men; and there's not a nose
among twenty but can smell him that's stinking. Let go
thy hold when a great wheel runs down a hill, lest it
70 break thy neck with following; but the great one that
goes upward, let him draw thee after. When a wise man
gives thee better counsel, give me mine again: I would
have none but knaves follow it, since a fool gives it.

65 *set thee to school*: make you take lessons
   from.
   ant: In Aesop's fable the ant laboured all
   summer to provide for winter; it is now
   the winter of Lear's fortunes, and those
   who worked for him when it was summer
   have deserted him.
66–9 *All that . . . stinking*: all those who go
   straight can see where they are going
   unless they are blind (i.e. they can see
   that Lear is ruined); and the smell of ruin
   is easily detected.
70–1 *the great one that goes upward*: the man
   whose fortunes are rising.
74 *That sir*: any servant.
75 *form*: appearance.
76 *pack*: be off.
78 *tarry*: stay behind.
80–81 'By running away the servant
   ('knave') shows what a fool he is, but this
   fool (who 'will tarry') shows that he is no
   villain ('knave').'
83 *Not . . . fool*: Lear's fool seems to admit
   that Kent is, at least, no 'knave'.
84 *Deny*: refuse.
85 *fetches*: excuses, tricks, pretences.
86 *images*: signs.
   flying off: desertions.
88 *quality*: temperament.
89 *unremovable*: stubborn.

92 *what 'quality'?*: Lear cannot accept that
   Cornwall is a person with his own
   temperament and demands to be
   respected as such.

94–5 *Well . . . man: om*. Q.
98 *commands, tends service*: Lear is
   demanding to see Regan; but both
   Quarto and Folio texts are doubtful at
   this point, and it is not easy to explain
   'tends'. It is unlikely that Lear, in his
   imperative mood, is offering his own
   'service' to his daughter, even ironically.
100 *hot*: hot-tempered.
101 *no, but not yet*: Lear hesitates before
   unleashing his anger.
102 *still*: always.
102–3 *neglect . . . bound*: fail to do all the
   duties which are required of us when we
   are healthy.

That sir which serves and seeks for gain,
    And follows but for form,
Will pack when it begins to rain,
    And leave thee in the storm.
But I will tarry; the fool will stay,
And let the wise man fly:
The knave turns fool that runs away;
    The fool no knave, perdy.

Kent
Where learn'd you this, fool?
Fool
Not i'th'stocks, fool.

Enter Lear, *with* Gloucester

Lear
Deny to speak with me! They are sick! They are weary!
They have travell'd all the night! Mere fetches, ay,
The images of revolt and flying off.
Fetch me a better answer.
Gloucester
                                    My dear lord,
You know the fiery quality of the duke;
How unremovable and fix'd he is
In his own course.
Lear
Vengeance! plague! death! confusion!
'Fiery!' what 'quality'? Why, Gloucester, Gloucester,
I'd speak with the Duke of Cornwall and his wife.
Gloucester
Well, my good lord, I have inform'd them so.
Lear
Inform'd them! Dost thou understand me, man?
Gloucester
Ay, my good lord.
Lear
The king would speak with Cornwall; the dear father
Would with his daughter speak, commands, tends
    service:
Are they inform'd of this? My breath and blood!
'Fiery!' the 'fiery duke'! Tell the hot duke that—
No, but not yet; may be he is not well:
Infirmity doth still neglect all office
Whereto our health is bound; we are not ourselves

Line numbers: 75, 80, 85, 90, 95, 100

104 *oppress'd*: afflicted.
106 *am . . . will*: regret my hasty impulse.
107–8 *to take . . . man*: to mistake this sudden indisposition for the act of a healthy man.
108 *Death on my state*: Lear's anger returns when he sees Kent in the stocks, and he swears by his royal position.
110 *remotion*: removal (i.e. the visit to Gloucester).
111 *practice only*: a deliberate scheme.
Give . . . forth: set my servant free.
112 *and's*: and his.
113 *presently*: this minute.
115 *Till . . . death*: until sleep is utterly destroyed by the noise.
117 *rising*: the suffocation of the 'mother' see note on line 54.
118–21 *as the cockney . . . down*: A 'cockney' could be either a child, a cook, a Londoner, or a pampered woman (or a combination of all these). The ignorant girl did not know that the eels should have been killed before they were put into the pie ('paste'); and when they tried to wriggle out, she rapped ('knapped') them over the heads ('coxcombs') and ordered the playful creatures ('wantons') to lie down. Lear must try to subdue his heart which (like the eels) should have been dead before getting into such a mess.
121–2 *her brother . . . hay*: The girl's simple-minded brother put butter on the hay because he wanted to be kind to his horse—but this was the practice of cheating ostlers, who knew that horses cannot eat greasy hay.

When Nature, being oppress'd, commands the mind
105 To suffer with the body. I'll forbear;
And am fall'n out with my more headier will,
To take the indispos'd and sickly fit
For the sound man. Death on my state! wherefore

Looking on Kent

Should he sit here? This act persuades me
110 That this remotion of the duke and her
Is practice only. Give me my servant forth.
Go tell the duke and's wife I'd speak with them,
Now, presently: bid them come forth and hear me,
Or at their chamber-door I'll beat the drum
115 Till it cry sleep to death.
    Gloucester
I would have all well betwixt you.   [*Exit*
    Lear
O me, my heart, my rising heart! but, down!
    Fool
Cry to it, nuncle, as the cockney did to the eels when she put 'em i'th'paste alive; she knapp'd 'em o'th'
120 coxcombs with a stick, and cried 'Down wantons, down!' 'Twas her brother that, in pure kindness to his horse, buttered his hay.

Enter Gloucester, *with* Cornwall, Regan, *and* Servants

123 *Good morrow*: Lear's greeting is spoken with irony: it is now evening.

    Lear
Good morrow to you both.
    Cornwall
                      Hail to your grace!

Kent *is set at liberty*

Regan

I am glad to see your highness.

Lear

Regan, I think you are; I know what reason

I have to think so: if thou shouldst not be glad,

I would divorce me from thy mother's tomb,

Sepulchring an adult'ress. [*To* Kent] O, are you free?

Some other time for that. [*Exit* Kent]

                         Beloved Regan,

Thy sister's naught: O Regan, she hath tied

Sharp-tooth'd unkindness, like a vulture, here!

Points to his heart

I can scarce speak to thee; thou'lt not believe

With how deprav'd a quality—O Regan!

Regan

I pray you sir, take patience. I have hope

You less know how to value her desert

Than she to scant her duty.

Lear

                         Say? how is that?

Regan

I cannot think my sister in the least

Would fail her obligation. If, sir, perchance

She have restrain'd the riots of your followers,

'Tis on such ground, and to such wholesome end,

As clears her from all blame.

Lear

                         My curses on her!

Regan

O sir, you are old!

Nature in you stands on the very verge

Of her confine: you should be rul'd and led

By some discretion that discerns your state

Better than you yourself. Therefore I pray you

That to our sister you do make return;

Say you have wrong'd her.

Lear

                         Ask her forgiveness?

Do you but mark how this becomes the house:

'Dear daughter, I confess that I am old;

Age is unnecessary: on my knees I beg [*Kneeling*]

That you'll vouchsafe me raiment, bed, and food.'

125

130

135

140

145

150

127–8 *I would divorce . . . adult'ress*: i.e. Lear would not believe that Regan was his own daughter (if she were not pleased to see him), and declare that her mother's tomb was the sepulchre of an adultress.

130 *naught*: utterly worthless.

131 *sharp-tooth'd unkindness*: see *1, 4, 278*. *like a vulture*: Lear may be recalling the myth of Prometheus, whose liver was endlessly devoured by a vulture.

133 *quality*: manner, disposition.

134–6 *I have hope . . . duty*: Regan seems to be saying, 'I hope it is you who do not know how to appreciate Goneril's merits, rather than that she should fall short ('scant') of what is required.'

143–4 *very verge . . . confine*: the utmost limit—i.e. Lear is very near the end of his life.

145 *discretion*: discreet person. *state*: condition (both 'state of mind' and 'social position').

149 *the house*: the royal family.

151 *Age . . . unnecessary*: old people are useless, *or* old people do not need much; Lear speaks ironically.

152 *vouchsafe*: grant. *raiment*: rainment, clothing.

153 *tricks*: rhetorical devices (i.e. Lear's ironies).

155 *abated*: deprived.

158 *stor'd vengeances*: the divine revenge (which Lear invokes at line 189).
159 *ingrateful top*: ungrateful head.
young bones: deform the bones of any child that she might bear.
160 *taking*: blasting, infecting.

163 *fen-suck'd*: drawn up from the fens.
164 *blister her*: blister her face (and so ruin her beauty).

168 *tender-hefted nature*: tender-hearted nature—*or* nature set in a tender—womanly—frame (haft).
172 *bandy*: exchange (see note on *1, 4, 80*).
scant my sizes: reduce my allowance.
173 *oppose the bolt*: bar the door.
175 *offices*: duties.
bond of childhood: a child's duty to her parents.
176 *Effects of courtesy*: to show good manners.
178 *to th'purpose*: get to the point.

179s.d. *Tucket*: the trumpet-call that heralds and identifies a visitor; Regan recognizes her sister's signal.

Regan
Good sir, no more; these are unsightly tricks.
Return you to my sister.
Lear
[*Rising*]   Never, Regan.
155 She hath abated me of half my train;
Look'd black upon me; struck me with her tongue,
Most serpent-like, upon the very heart.
All the stor'd vengeances of heaven fall
On her ingrateful top! Strike her young bones,
160 You taking airs, with lameness!
Cornwall
                                              Fie sir, fie!
Lear
You nimble lightnings, dart your blinding flames
Into her scornful eyes! Infect her beauty,
You fen-suck'd fogs, drawn by the pow'rful sun,
To fall and blister her!
Regan
165 O the blest gods! so will you wish on me,
When the rash mood is on.
Lear
No, Regan, thou shalt never have my curse:
Thy tender-hefted nature shall not give
Thee o'er to harshness: her eyes are fierce, but thine
170 Do comfort and not burn. 'Tis not in thee
To grudge my pleasures, to cut off my train,
To bandy hasty words, to scant my sizes,
And, in conclusion to oppose the bolt
Against my coming in: thou better know'st
175 The offices of nature, bond of childhood,
Effects of courtesy, dues of gratitude;
Thy half o'th'kingdom hast thou not forgot,
Wherein I thee endow'd.
Regan
                                    Good sir, to th'purpose.
Lear
Who put my man i'th'stocks?

Tucket within

Cornwall
                                    What trumpet's that?

180 *approves*: confirms what she said.

182 *whose easy-borrow'd pride*: i.e. Oswald
     wears his 'pride' like borrowed clothes;
     he has done nothing to earn or deserve it.
183 *fickle grace*: unstable—changeable—
     favour.
     follows: serves.

185 *stock'd my servant*: put my servant in the
     stocks.
186 *on't*: of it.
     heavens: Lear invokes his gods.

187 *sway*: rule.
188 *Allow*: approves of.
189 *send down*: i.e. some of the 'stor'd
     vengeances' (see line 158).
190 *beard*: the sign of his age and reverence.

193 *indiscretion finds*: want of judgement finds
     offensive.

194–5 *O sides . . . hold*: Lear wonders why his
     chest does not split open to release his
     breaking heart.

196 *disorders*: misconduct.
197 *advancement*: promotion; Kent deserved
     even more humiliating punishment.

202 *from*: away from.

Regan
180 I know't, my sister's: this approves her letter,
    That she would soon be here.

Enter Oswald

                                    Is your lady come?
Lear
    This is a slave, whose easy-borrow'd pride
    Dwells in the fickle grace of her he follows.
    Out, varlet, from my sight!
Cornwall
                            What means your grace?
Lear
185 Who stock'd my servant? Regan, I have good hope
    Thou didst not know on't. Who comes here?

Enter Goneril

                                        O heavens,
    If you do love old men, if your sweet sway
    Allow obedience, if you yourselves are old,
    Make it your cause; send down and take my part!
190 [*To* Goneril] Art not asham'd to look upon this beard?
    O Regan! will you take her by the hand?
        Goneril
    Why not by th'hand, sir? How have I offended?
    All's not offence that indiscretion finds
    And dotage terms so.
        Lear
                        O sides,you are too tough!
195 Will you yet hold? How came my man i'th'stocks?
        Cornwall
    I set him there, sir; but his own disorders
    Deserv'd much less advancement.
        Lear
                                    You! did you?
        Regan
    I pray you, father, being weak, seem so.
    If, till the expiration of your month,
200 You will return and sojourn with my sister,
    Dismissing half your train, come then to me:
    I am now from home, and out of that provision
    Which shall be needful for your entertainment.

205 *abjure all roofs*: refuse to stay under anybody's roof.
206 *wage*: fight against.
207 *wolf and owl*: predators of the night.
208 *Necessity's sharp pinch*: Lear will choose to feel real need rather than accept Goneril's charity.
209 *hot-blooded*: passionate—in 1, 2, 23 Gloucester remarked that the King of France had left England 'in choler' (= angry).
211 *to knee*: to kneel before.
     squire-like: like a humble body-servant.
212 *afoot*: going on.
213 *sumpter*: packhorse, drudge.
214 *groom*: menial—i.e. Oswald.
     at your choice: as you wish.

221 *embossed*: swollen.

224 *thunder-bearer*: Jupiter, who aims thunderbolts (his 'stor'd vengeances', line 158) at the sinful.
225 *high-judging Jove*: the supreme judge, who reigns on high.

229 *look'd not*: did not expect.

231 'Any reasonable person who hears this passionate talk.'

234 *avouch*: declare it to be true.

236 *sith*: since.
     charge: expense.

Lear
Return to her? and fifty men dismiss'd?
205 No, rather I abjure all roofs, and choose
To wage against the enmity o'th'air;
To be a comrade with the wolf and owl—
Necessity's sharp pinch! Return with her!
Why, the hot-blooded France, that dowerless took
210 Our youngest born, I could as well be brought
To knee his throne, and, squire-like, pension beg
To keep base life afoot. Return with her!
Persuade me rather to be slave and sumpter
To this detested groom. [*Pointing at* Oswald]
Goneril
                            At your choice, sir.
Lear
215 I prithee, daughter, do not make me mad:
I will not trouble thee, my child; farewell.
We'll no more meet, no more see one another;
But yet thou art my flesh, my blood, my daughter;
Or rather a disease that's in my flesh,
220 Which I must needs call mine: thou art a boil,
A plague-sore, or embossed carbuncle,
In my corrupted blood. But I'll not chide thee;
Let shame come when it will, I do not call it;
I do not bid the thunder-bearer shoot,
225 Nor tell tales of thee to high-judging Jove.
Mend when thou canst; be better at thy leisure;
I can be patient; I can stay with Regan,
I and my hundred knights.
Regan
                            Not altogether so;
I look'd not for you yet, nor am provided
230 For your fit welcome. Give ear, sir, to my sister;
For those that mingle reason with your passion
Must be content to think you old, and so—
But she knows what she does.
Lear
                            Is this well spoken?
Regan
I dare avouch it, sir: what! fifty followers?
235 Is it not well? What should you need of more?
Yea, or so many, sith that both charge and danger
Speak 'gainst so great a number? How, in one house,

239 *Hold amity*: remain friendly with each
     other.

242 *chanc'd to slack ye*: if for any reason they
     did not perform their duty properly.

246 *notice*: recognition.

248 *guardians*: stewards.
     depositaries: trustees.
249 *reservation*: saving clause in his deed-of-
     gift (see *1, 1, 132*).
253 *well-favour'd*: good-looking.
259 *follow*: be your servants.
261 *reason not*: do not argue about.
262 *are . . . superfluous*: have something,
     however poor, more than is absolutely
     essential.
263 'If you do not allow to human nature
     more than its natural (i.e. animal)
     needs.'

Should many people, under two commands,
Hold amity? 'Tis hard; almost impossible.
    Goneril
240 Why might not you, my lord, receive attendance
From those that she calls servants, or from mine?
    Regan
Why not, my lord? If then they chanc'd to slack ye
We could control them. If you will come to me,
For now I spy a danger, I entreat you
245 To bring but five-and-twenty; to no more
Will I give place or notice.
    Lear
I gave you all—
    Regan
                                    And in good time you gave it.
    Lear
Made you my guardians, my depositaries,
But kept a reservation to be follow'd
250 With such a number. What! must I come to you
With five-and-twenty? Regan, said you so?
    Regan
And speak't again, my lord; no more with me.
    Lear
Those wicked creatures yet do look well-favour'd
When others are more wicked; not being the worst
255 Stands in some rank of praise. [*To* Goneril] I'll go
     with thee:
Thy fifty yet doth double five-and-twenty,
And thou art twice her love.
    Goneril
                                    Hear me, my lord.
What need you five-and-twenty, ten, or five,
To follow in a house where twice so many
260 Have a command to tend you?
    Regan
                                    What need one?
    Lear
O, reason not the need! our basest beggars
Are in the poorest thing superfluous:
Allow not nature more than nature needs,
Man's life is cheap as beast's. Thou art a lady;
265 If only to go warm were gorgeous,
Why, nature needs not what thou gorgeous wear'st,

265–7 *If . . . warm*: If it were considered gorgeous merely to be warm, you wouldn't need these fashionable clothes you wear because they don't keep you warm.

267 *but, for true need*: Lear is about to explain the differences between real need and fashionable—social—needs; but he breaks off in order to pray for what he is most in need of at the present time.

272 *fool me*: don't make such a fool of me.

273 *tamely*: meekly.

281 *full cause of*: plenty of reasons for.

282 *flaws*: fragments.

283 *or ere*: before.

286 *bestow'd*: accommodated.

287 *blame*: fault.
hath: he has.
put . . . rest: just upset himself.

288 *taste his folly*: find out what his foolishness has done for him.

289 *For his particular*: as far as he himself is concerned.

Which scarcely keeps thee warm. But, for true need,—
You heavens, give me that patience, patience I need!—
You see me here, you gods, a poor old man,
270 As full of grief as age; wretched in both!
If it be you that stirs these daughters' hearts
Against their father, fool me not so much
To bear it tamely; touch me with noble anger,
And let not women's weapons, water-drops,
275 Stain my man's cheeks! No, you unnatural hags,
I will have such revenges on you both
That all the world shall—I will do such things,
What they are, yet I know not, but they shall be
The terrors of the earth. You think I'll weep;
280 No, I'll not weep:
I have full cause of weeping, [*Storm heard at a distance*]
                                                    but this heart
Shall break into a hundred thousand flaws
Or ere I'll weep. O Fool! I shall go mad.
          [*Exeunt* Lear, Gloucester, Gentleman, *and* Fool
     Cornwall
Let us withdraw, 'twill be a storm.
     Regan
285 This house is little: the old man and's people
Cannot be well bestow'd.
     Goneril
'Tis his own blame; hath put himself from rest,
And must needs taste his folly.
     Regan
For his particular, I'll receive him gladly,
290 But not one follower.
     Goneril
                              So am I purpos'd.
Where is my lord of Gloucester?
     Cornwall
Follow'd the old man forth. He is return'd.

                    Enter Gloucester

     Gloucester
The king is in high rage.
     Cornwall
                              Whither is he going?

294 'He is shouting for his horses, but I do not know where he wants to go.'
295 *give him way*: let him go.
he leads himself: insists on having his own way.

299 *do sorely ruffle*: are getting very strong.
300–2 *to wilful men . . . schoolmasters*: headstrong people have to learn their lessons from their own mistakes.
303 *with a desperate train*: by a gang of ruffians; Regan seems to think that all Lear's attendants are still with him.
304 *incense*: provoke.
304–5 *being apt . . . abus'd*: since he is willing to listen to any lies.
305 *wisdom bids fear*: common sense tells us to worry about (for our own sakes).
306 *Shut up your doors*: Despite his own feelings, Gloucester must obey his overlord.

Gloucester
He calls to horse; but will I know not whither.
Cornwall
295 'Tis best to give him way; he leads himself.
Goneril
My lord, entreat him by no means to stay.
Gloucester
Alack, the night comes on, and the bleak winds
Do sorely ruffle! for many miles about
300 There's scarce a bush.
Regan
                 O sir, to wilful men,
The injuries that they themselves procure
Must be their schoolmasters. Shut up your doors;
He is attended with a desperate train,
And what they may incense him to, being apt
305 To have his ear abus'd, wisdom bids fear.
Cornwall
Shut up your doors, my lord; 'tis a wild night:
My Regan counsels well: come out o'th'storm.
                  [Exeunt

Act 3

Act 3 Scene 1

Kent, searching for Lear, meets a Gentleman (one of Lear's original followers) who tells him that the king is out in the storm, accompanied only by his fool. Kent speaks of the quarrel between Albany and Cornwall, and the likelihood of a French invasion. He sends the Gentleman to Dover, giving him a ring to show to Cordelia. But first, they must find King Lear.

2 *minded like*: whose mind is like.
4 *Contending*: struggling against *and* competing.
   fretful elements: raging elements of wind and water.
6 *curled waters*: high waves.
   main: land.
7 *things*: i.e. everything, the whole world.
8 *eyeless*: unseeing.
9 *make nothing of*: show no respect for.
10 *little world of man*: Elizabethans believed that there were many correspondences between the human body (the microcosm) and the great world of the universe (the macrocosm).
   out-storm: create a greater storm than.

Scene 1

The heath
A storm, with thunder and lightning. Enter
Kent *and a* Gentleman, *meeting*

Kent
Who's there, besides foul weather?
   Gentleman
One minded like the weather, most unquietly.
   Kent
I know you. Where's the king?
   Gentleman
Contending with the fretful elements;
5 Bids the wind blow the earth into the sea,
Or swell the curled waters 'bove the main,
That things might change or cease; tears his white hair,
Which the impetuous blasts, with eyeless rage,
Catch in their fury, and make nothing of;
10 Strives in his little world of man to out-storm
The to-and-fro-conflicting wind and rain.
This night, wherein the cub-drawn bear would couch,
The lion and the belly-pinched wolf

11 *to-and-fro-conflicting*: turbulent.
12 *cub-drawn bear*: female bear sucked dry
    by her cubs—and consequently
    ravenously hungry.
    couch: lie in its lair.
13 *belly-pinched*: hungry.
14 *unbonneted*: bare-headed.
15 *bids . . . take all*: The last cry of the
    gambler who stakes everything on his
    final throw of dice.
16–17 *labours . . . injuries*: tries to drive the
    thoughts of his heart-breaking injuries
    out of Lear's mind, *or* tries to exceed the
    injuries by the wild extravagance of his
    jests.
18 *upon . . . note*: because of what I know
    you to be.
19 *Commend*: entrust.
    dear: most important.
    division: disagreement.
22–3 *that . . . high*: that good fortune has set
    in high places.
22–9 *Who have . . . furnishings*: om. Q.
23 *seem no less*: i.e. who look like servants.
24 *speculations*: secret agents.
25 *Intelligent*: giving information about.
26 *snuffs and packings*: quarrels and plots.
27 *hard rein . . . borne*: the way they have
    both been so strict with the king.
29 *furnishings*: outward signs that conceal
    what is really going on.
30–42 *But . . . to you*: om. F.
30 *power*: army.
31 *scatter'd*: unsettled, divided among
    itself—and consequently a ready prey for
    an invader.
32 *have secret feet*: have gained a secret
    foothold.
33 *at point*: ready.
34 *show . . . banner*: declare themselves
    openly (by spreading military banners).
35 *on my credit*: you trust me.
36 *To*: as to.
    speed: hasten.
37 *making just report*: for giving an honest
    account.
38 *bemadding sorrow*: grief which is turning
    him mad.
39 *to plain*: to complain of.
40 *of blood and breeding*: by birth and
    education.
41 *assurance*: reliable information.
42 *office*: service (i.e. the mission to Dover).
45 *out-wall*: outward appearance.

Keep their fur dry, unbonneted he runs,
15 And bids what will take all.
        Kent
                                    But who is with him?
        Gentleman
None but the fool, who labours to out-jest
His heart-strook injuries.
        Kent
                                Sir, I do know you;
And dare, upon the warrant of my note,
Commend a dear thing to you. There is division,
20 Although as yet the face of it is cover'd
With mutual cunning, 'twixt Albany and Cornwall;
Who have—as who have not, that their great stars
Thron'd and set high?—servants, who seem no less,
Which are to France the spies and speculations
25 Intelligent of our state. What hath been seen,
Either in snuffs and packings of the dukes,
Or the hard rein which both of them have borne
Against the old kind king; or something deeper,
Whereof perchance these are but furnishings—
30 But, true it is, from France there comes a power
Into this scatter'd kingdom; who already,
Wise in our negligence, have secret feet
In some of our best ports, and are at point
To show their open banner. Now to you:
35 If on my credit you dare build so far
To make your speed to Dover, you shall find
Some that will thank you, making just report
Of how unnatural and bemadding sorrow
The king hath cause to plain.
40 I am a gentleman of blood and breeding,
And from some knowledge and assurance offer
This office to you.
        Gentleman
I will talk further with you.
        Kent
                                No, do not.
For confirmation that I am much more
45 Than my out-wall, open this purse, and take
What it contains. If you shall, see Cordelia,—
As fear not but you shall,—show her this ring,

48 *fellow*: companion.

And she will tell you who that fellow is
That yet you do not know. Fie on this storm!
50 I will go seek the king.

Gentleman
Give me your hand. Have you no more to say?

Kent
Few words, but, to effect, more than all yet;

52 *to effect*: in importance.
53–4 *in which . . . this*: you take the trouble to go that way, I'll go this.
54 *lights on*: finds.
55 *Holla*: give a shout to.
55s.d. *severally*: in different directions.

That, when we have found the king, in which your pain
That way, I'll this, he that first lights on him
55 Holla the other.

[*Exeunt severally*

Act 3 Scene 2

On another part of the heath, Lear allies himself with the storm and joins his curses with the noise of the thunder. The fool begs him to take shelter, and eventually Kent persuades the old man to go into a nearby 'hovel'.

1 *crack your cheeks*: Lear's image derives from pictures of the winds in the corners of old maps.
2 *cataracts and hurricanoes*: waterspouts from the air and from the sea; Lear is calling down a second Flood.
3 *drown'd the cocks*: submerged the weather-cocks.
4 *thought-executing*: flashing quick as thought.
5 *Vaunt-couriers*: fore-runners, heralds. *oak-cleaving thunderbolts*: thunderbolts that split oaktrees.
7 *thick rotundity of the world*: world's dense roundness.

Scene 2

Storm still
Enter Lear *and* Fool

Lear
Blow, winds, and crack your cheeks! rage! blow!
You cataracts and hurricanoes, spout
Till you have drench'd our steeples, drown'd the cocks!
You sulph'rous and thought-executing fires,
5 Vaunt-couriers of oak-cleaving thunderbolts,
Singe my white head! And thou, all-shaking thunder,
Strike flat the thick rotundity o'th'world!
Crack Nature's moulds, all germens spill at once
That makes ingrateful man!

Fool
10 O nuncle, court holy-water in a dry house is better than this rain-water out o'door. Good nuncle, in, ask thy daughters blessing; here's a night pities neither wise men nor fools.

8 *Nature's moulds*: moulds in which human nature is made.
germens: germs, seeds; Lear wants to destroy the whole race of 'ingrateful man'.
spill: destroy.
9 *ingrateful*: ungrateful.
10 *court holy-water*: flattery, courtly blessing.
12 *ask . . . blessing*: ask your daughters to give you their blessing (but first, Lear would have to admit he had been wrong).
14 *thy bellyful*: as much as you want.
16 *tax*: charge.
18 *subscription*: allegiance.
21 *ministers*: agents willing to serve.
23 *high-engender'd battles*: battalions descending from their lofty positions.
25 *put's*: put his.
head-piece: helmet for his head, *and* head on his shoulders.
27–30 'The man who takes a woman, before he has a house to live in, will find that he will have to share her lice.'
27 *cod-piece*: cover worn in front of the hose to protect the penis—and hence the penis itself.

Lear
Rumble thy bellyful! Spit, fire! spout, rain!
15 Nor rain, wind, thunder, fire, are my daughters:
I tax you not, you elements, with unkindness;
I never gave you kingdom, call'd you children,
You owe me no subscription: then let fall
Your horrible pleasure; here I stand, your slave,
20 A poor, infirm, weak, and despis'd old man.
But yet I call you servile ministers,
That will with two pernicious daughters join
Your high-engender'd battles 'gainst a head
So old and white as this. O, ho! 'tis foul.

Fool
25 He that has a house to put's head in has a good head-piece.

The cod-piece that will house
    Before the head has any,
The head and he shall louse;
    So beggars marry many.
The man that makes his toe
    What he his heart should make,
Shall of a corn cry woe,
    And turn his sleep to wake.

31–4 'The man who cherishes something trivial rather than something precious will never be free from pain and will never be able to rest.'

30

35 For there was never yet fair woman but she made mouths in a glass.

35–6 'Lovely ladies always glance at themselves in the mirror'; this is probably a bit of irrelevant nonsense from the fool.

Enter Kent

Lear
No, I will be the pattern of all patience;
I will say nothing.

37 *pattern*: model.

Kent
Who's there?

40 *Marry*: a common exclamation, deriving from 'by the Virgin Mary'.
grace: the king's person.
cod-piece: The fool's costume sometimes featured an extra large item (see note on line 27).
44 *Gallow*: terrify.
wanderers of the dark: wild beasts.
45 *keep their caves*: stay in their lairs.
46 *bursts*: claps.
48 *carry*: endure.
50 *pudder*: tumult.
51 *Find . . . now*: i.e. by the terror that the sinners must be showing.
53 *of*: by.
54 *perjur'd*: perjuror.
simular: hypocrite.
55 *caitiff*: wretch.
56 *under . . . seeming*: behind a cleverly-planned appearance.
57 *practis'd on*: plotted against.
close pent-up guilts: well-concealed crimes.
58 *Rive . . . continents*: burst out of your hiding-places.
58–9 *cry . . . grace*: plead for mercy to these terrible powers that are hauling you to judgement (as the 'summoners' dragged criminals before the ecclesiastical courts).
59–60 *I am . . . sinning*: Lear marks himself off from those sinners he has just been describing.
61 *Gracious my lord*: my gracious lord.
hard by: very close by.
62 *lend*: afford.
63 *hard house*: cruel household.
64 *rais'd*: built.

Fool
40 Marry, here's grace and a cod-piece, that's a wise man and a fool.
Kent
Alas, sir, are you here! things that love night
Love not such nights as these; the wrathful skies
Gallow the very wanderers of the dark,
45 And make them keep their caves. Since I was man
Such sheets of fire, such bursts of horrid thunder,
Such groans of roaring wind and rain, I never
Remember to have heard; man's nature cannot carry
Th'affliction nor the fear.
Lear
               Let the great gods,
50 That keep this dreadful pudder o'er our heads,
Find out their enemies now. Tremble, thou wretch,
That hast within thee undivulged crimes,
Unwhipp'd of Justice; hide thee, thou bloody hand,
Thou perjur'd, and thou simular of virtue
55 That art incestuous; caitiff, to pieces shake,
That under covert and convenient seeming
Has practis'd on man's life; close pent-up guilts
Rive your concealing continents, and cry
These dreadful summoners grace. I am a man
60 More sinn'd against than sinning.
Kent
               Alack, bare-headed!
Gracious my lord, hard by here is a hovel;
Some friendship will it lend you 'gainst the tempest;
Repose you there while I to this hard house,—
More harder than the stones whereof 'tis rais'd,

65 *Which*: i.e. the people there.
   even but now: only just now.
   demanding after: asking where you were.
66 *Denied . . . in*: refused to let me in.
   force: compel.
67 *scanted*: miserable.

70 *The . . . strange*: necessity has strange power.
72–3 'There is a little part of my heart that is still capable of feeling pity, and I am sorry for you.'
74–7 'If a man has not much sense, he must make the best use of what he has— since every day brings its troubles'; see 'The Fool', p. xii.
78 *True*: Lear seems to acquiesce with the fool's teaching.
   bring: conduct.
79–96 *This . . . time*: om. Q.
79 *brave*: fine.
   courtezan: prostitute; perhaps there is a pun on 'night'/'knight'.
80 *prophecy*: See Commentary, p. xxiii.
81 *more . . . matter*: talk more (about good living) than they practise it.
82 *mar their malt*: spoil their beer.
83 *noblemen . . . tutors*: gentlemen tell tailors how to do their jobs.
84 'Only faithless lovers should be burned (i.e. with the syphilitic pox).'
87 *tongues*: what people say.
88 *cut-purses*: pickpurses.
   throngs: crowds.
89 *usurers*: money-lenders.
   tell . . . field: count their money openly.
90 *do . . . build*: i.e. in sign of repentance.
91 *Albion*: An old name for Britain.
92 *confusion*: stressed with four syllables— 'con-fu-si-on'.
94 *going . . . feet*: feet shall be used for walking.
95 *Merlin*: The magician at the court of King Arthur (6th century AD); the historical Lear lived in the eighth century BC. See p. xxiii.

65 Which even but now, demanding after you,
Denied me to come in,—return and force
Their scanted courtesy.

Lear
                   My wits begin to turn.
Come on, my boy. How dost, my boy? Art cold?
I am cold myself. Where is this straw, my fellow?
70 The art of our necessities is strange,
And can make vile things precious. Come, your hovel.
Poor fool and knave, I have one part in my heart
That's sorry yet for thee.

Fool
He that has and a little tiny wit,
75   *With hey, ho, the wind and the rain,*
Must make content with his fortunes fit,
Though the rain it raineth every day.

Lear
True, boy. Come, bring us to this hovel.
                 [*Exeunt* Lear *and* Kent

Fool
This is a brave night to cool a courtezan.
80 I'll speak a prophecy ere I go:
When priests are more in word than matter;
When brewers mar their malt with water;
When nobles are their tailors' tutors;
No heretics burn'd, but wenches' suitors;
85 When every case in law is right;
No squire in debt, nor no poor knight;
When slanders do not live in tongues;
Nor cut-purses come not to throngs;
When usurers tell their gold i'th'field;
90 And bawds and whores do churches build;
Then shall the realm of Albion
Come to great confusion:
Then comes the time, who lives to see't,
That going shall be us'd with feet.
95 This prophecy Merlin shall make; for I live before his time.
                            [*Exit*

Act 3 Scene 3

Gloucester confides in Edmund—and
Edmund determines to betray his father's
confidence.

2 *pity*: take pity, relieve.

5 *sustain*: care for.

7 *Go to*: it's true.
8 *worse matter*: i.e. the threatened French
   invasion.
9 *spoken*: talked about.
10 *closet*: private room.
11 *home*: fully.
12 *power*: army.
   footed: landed.
   incline to: take the side of.
13 *look him*: seek for him.
   privily: secretly.
14 *maintain talk*: keep in conversation.
   of him: by him.
16 *If I die*: Gloucester at last shows some
   moral strength.
18 *toward*: happening.

19 *forbid thee*: which you are forbidden to
   do.
21 *fair deserving*: action which ought to be
   rewarded.
21–2 *must draw me . . . all*: I shall get
   whatever he loses—and that's
   everything.

Scene 3

Gloucester's *castle*
Enter Gloucester *and* Edmund, *with lights*

Gloucester

Alack, alack! Edmund, I like not this unnatural dealing. When I desir'd their leave that I might pity him,
they took from me the use of mine own house; charg'd
me, on pain of perpetual displeasure, neither to speak
5 of him, entreat for him, or any way sustain him.

Edmund

Most savage and unnatural!

Gloucester

Go to; say you nothing. There is division between the
dukes, and a worse matter than that. I have receiv'd a
letter this night; 'tis dangerous to be spoken; I have
10 lock'd the letter in my closet. These injuries the king
now bears will be revenged home; there is part of a
power already footed; we must incline to the king. I
will look him and privily relieve him; go you and
maintain talk with the duke, that my charity be not of
15 him perceiv'd. If he ask for me, I am ill and gone to
bed. If I die for it, as no less is threatened me, the
king, my old master, must be reliev'd. There is
strange things toward, Edmund; pray you, be careful.
                                                    [*Exit*

Edmund

This courtesy, forbid thee, shall the duke
20 Instantly know; and of that letter too:
This seems a fair deserving, and must draw me
That which my father loses; no less than all:
The younger rises when the old doth fall.
                                                    [*Exit*

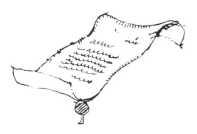

Act 3 Scene 4

Kent has led Lear and the fool to a little shelter. Lear speaks his thoughts about human suffering. The fool is frightened by a madman—who is in fact the disguised Edgar. Edgar keeps up his pretence of madness whilst he is talking to Lear, but this encounter finally drives the king completely out of his mind. Gloucester comes in search of the king, offering him more suitable accommodation. He tells Kent (whom he does not recognize) of his own grief, and then tries to take the king away. Lear, however, refuses to be separated from Poor Tom. At last, the mad king, the disguised beggar, and the fool are all shepherded away to the safety of a nearby farmhouse.

2 *open night*: night in the open air.
4 *Wilt . . . heart?*: Lear wants to remain outside in the storm so that physical discomfort will take his mind off his mental suffering, which will otherwise break his heart.

8 *the greater malady*: i.e his daughters' ingratitude.
  is fix'd: has taken root.
9 *the lesser*: i.e. the storm.
11 *i'th'mouth*: head-on.
  free: at ease.
12 *delicate*: sensitive.
13 *all feeling else*: any other feeling.
14 *beats . . . ingratitude*: i.e. his heart which has been broken by filial ingratitude.

16 *home*: thoroughly.

20 *frank*: generous.

Scene 4

The heath.
Enter Lear, Kent, *and* Fool

Kent
Here is the place, my lord; good my lord, enter:
The tyranny of the open night's too rough
For nature to endure.

Storm still

Lear
                                    Let me alone.
Kent
Good my lord, enter here.
Lear
                                    Wilt break my heart?
Kent
5 I had rather break mine own. Good my lord, enter.
Lear
Thou think'st 'tis much that this contentious storm
Invades us to the skin: so 'tis to thee;
But where the greater malady is fix'd,
The lesser is scarce felt. Thou'ldst shun a bear;
10 But if thy flight lay toward the roaring sea,
Thou'ldst meet the bear i'th'mouth. When the
        mind's free
The body's delicate; this tempest in my mind
Doth from my senses take all feeling else
Save what beats there—filial ingratitude!
15 Is it not as this mouth should tear this hand
For lifting food to't? But I will punish home:
No, I will weep no more. In such a night
To shut me out? Pour on—I will endure!
In such a night as this? O Regan, Goneril!
20 Your old kind father, whose frank heart gave all,—
O that way madness lies! let me shun that;
No more of that.
Kent
                                    Good my lord, enter here.
Lear
Prithee, go in thyself; seek thine own ease:
This tempest will not give me leave to ponder
25 On things would hurt me more. But I'll go in.

26 *houseless poverty*: poor homeless people.
26–7 *In, boy ... sleep*: om. Q.
27 *pray*: Lear is in fact praying *to* the victims (perhaps asking their forgiveness).

29 *bide*: endure.
30 *unfed sides*: starving bodies.
31 *loop'd and window'd raggedness*: rags full of holes and openings (Elizabethan windows were usually unglazed).
33 *take physic, Pomp*: let every proud and pompous man purge himself.
35 *superflux*: superfluous possessions.
36 *and ... just*: show how things can be more fairly distributed.

37–8 *Fathom ... Tom*: om. Q.
37 *Fathom and half*: Edgar calls the depth of the rainwater as though he were a sailor.

39 *spirit*: evil spirit, i.e. devil; it was popularly supposed that those who were mad were possessed by the devil.

53 *halters*: ropes to hang himself; these, with 'knives' and poison ('ratsbane') were traditionally offered by the devil to lead men to despair and suicide.
   pew: gallery.
54 *porridge*: broth.
55 *trotting-horse*: high-stepping horse.
   four-inch'd bridges: tiny bridges used to train horses to lift their feet when trotting.

[*To the* Fool] In, boy; go first. You houseless poverty,—
Nay, get thee in. I'll pray, and then I'll sleep.
                                    [Fool *goes in*
Poor naked wretches, whereso'er you are,
That bide the pelting of this pitiless storm,
30 How shall your houseless heads and unfed sides,
Your loop'd and window'd raggedness, defend you
From seasons such as these? O, I have ta'en
Too little care of this! Take physic, Pomp;
Expose thyself to feel what wretches feel,
35 That thou mayst shake the superflux to them,
And show the heavens more just.

Edgar
[*Within*] Fathom and half, fathom and half!
Poor Tom!

The Fool *runs out from the hovel*

Fool
Come not in here, nuncle; here's a spirit.
40 Help me! help me!

Kent
Give me thy hand. Who's there?

Fool
A spirit, a spirit: he says his name's Poor Tom.

Kent
What art thou that dost grumble there i'th'straw?
Come forth.

Enter Edgar *disguised as a madman*

Edgar
45 Away! the foul fiend follows me! Through the sharp
hawthorn blow the cold winds. Humh! go to thy bed
and warm thee.

Lear
Didst thou give all to thy daughters?
And art thou come to this?

Edgar
50 Who gives any thing to Poor Tom? whom the foul fiend
hath led through fire and through flame, through ford
and whirlpool, o'er bog and quagmire; that hath laid
knives under his pillow, and halters in his pew; set
ratsbane by his porridge; made him proud of heart, to
55 ride on a bay trotting-horse over four-inch'd bridges, to

56 *course . . . traitor*: chases his own shadow
thinking it is a traitor.
bless thy five wits: i.e. common wit,
imagination, fantasy, estimation, and
memory.

57 *Tom's a-cold*: The cry of the Bedlam
beggar.
O . . . do de: The fool is probably
shivering.

58 *star-blasting*: coming under the influence
of an evil star.
taking: infection.

59 *There*: The beggar hunts for lice, and
aims a blow at the imaginary spirit.

61 *pass*: distress.

63 *sham'd*: embarrassed.

64–5 *all . . . faults*: There was a belief that
diseases were stored up in the air until it
was time for them to be poured down to
punish sinners.

65 *light*: alight.

67 *subdu'd nature*: reduced his natural
powers.

69 *discarded*: cast off.

70 *little . . . flesh*: Lear may refer *either* to the
pins and thorns stuck in Poor Tom's
flesh (2, 3, 16), *or* to those in his own
mind—*or* to both.

71 *Judicious*: fitting, well-judged.
begot: bred.

72 *pelican*: The young birds were thought to
devour the flesh of their parents.

course his own shadow for a traitor. Bless thy five wits!
Tom's a-cold. O! do de, do de, do de. Bless thee from
whirlwinds, star-blasting, and taking! Do Poor Tom
some charity, whom the foul fiend vexes. There could I
60 have him now, and there, and there again, and there.

Storm still

Lear
What, has his daughters brought him to this pass!
Couldst thou save nothing? Would'st thou give 'em all?

Fool
Nay, he reserv'd a blanket, else we had been all sham'd.

Lear
Now all the plagues that in the pendulous air
65 Hang fated o'er men's faults light on thy daughters!

Kent
He hath no daughters, sir.

Lear
Death, traitor! nothing could have subdu'd nature
To such a lowness but his unkind daughters.
Is it the fashion that discarded fathers
70 Should have thus little mercy on their flesh?
Judicious punishment! 'twas this flesh begot
Those pelican daughters.

Edgar
Pillicock sat on Pillicock hill:
Alow, alow, loo, loo!

Fool
75 This cold night will turn us all to fools and madmen.

Edgar
Take heed o'th'foul fiend. Obey thy parents; keep thy
word justly; swear not; commit not with man's sworn
spouse; set not thy sweet heart on proud array. Tom's
a-cold.

Lear
80 What hast thou been?

73 *Pillicock*: the word (referring either to a
loved one, or to the penis) was probably
suggested by Lear's 'pelican'.

75 The fool now has the commonsense
line.

76–78 *obey . . . array*: Edgar recites a kind
of catechism.

76–7 *keep thy word justly*: be true to your
word.

77–78 *commit . . . spouse*: do not commit
adultery with one who has promised to
be another man's wife.

78 *proud array*: fine clothing.

81–2 *curl'd my hair*: Edgar claims to have been a courtier, not a common servant.

82 *wore . . . cap*: i.e. favours from his mistress.

83 *act of darkness*: fornication.

85–6 *slept . . . lust*: made lustful plots in my dreams.

87 *dice*: gambling.
 out-paramour'd: had more mistresses than.

88 *the Turk*: the Sultan of Turkey.
 light of ear: ready to believe anything.

89–90 *hog . . . prey*: Edgar accuses himself of all the deadly sins—which were often figured as animals; the dog represents madness through the association with rabies.

90 *creaking*: squeaking (made of new leather).

93 *plackets*: the openings in women's petticoats.
 lenders' books: money-lenders' books.

95 *suum . . . nonny*: He imitates the noise of the wind.

95–6 *Dolphin . . . by*: words of encouragement for a horse.

97 *Thou wert better*: it would be more comfortable for you.
 answer: confront.

98 *extremity*: extreme severity.

100 *worm*: silkworm.
 beast: ox.

101 *cat*: civet-cat, giving musk for perfumes.
 on's: of us.
 sophisticated: adulterated, disguised; the pure humanity of nakedness is adulterated with clothing.

102 *unaccommodated man*: the human creature with none of the 'lendings' of civilization.

103 *forked*: two-legged.

104 *lendings*: clothes lent by animals.
 unbutton here: Lear wishes to identify himself with 'Poor Tom' and the 'poor naked wretches' of line 28.

105 *naughty*: wicked.

106 *a little fire*: The fool catches sight of an approaching torch.

Edgar

A servingman, proud in heart and mind; that curl'd my hair, wore gloves in my cap, serv'd the lust of my mistress' heart, and did the act of darkness with her; swore as many oaths as I spake words, and broke 85 them in the sweet face of heaven; one that slept in the contriving of lust, and wak'd to do it. Wine lov'd I deeply, dice dearly, and in woman out-paramour'd the Turk: false of heart, light of ear, bloody of hand; hog in sloth, fox in stealth, wolf in greediness, dog in 90 madness, lion in prey. Let not the creaking of shoes nor the rustling of silks betray thy poor heart to woman: keep thy foot out of brothels, thy hand out of plackets, thy pen from lenders' books, and defy the foul fiend. Still through the hawthorn blows the cold 95 wind; says suum, mun, hey no nonny. Dolphin my boy, boy; sessa! let him trot by.

Storm still

Lear

Thou wert better in a grave than to answer with thy uncover'd body this extremity of the skies. Is man no more than this? Consider him well. Thou ow'st the 100 worm no silk, the beast no hide, the sheep no wool, the cat no perfume. Ha! here's three on's are sophisticated; thou art the thing itself; unaccommodated man is no more but such a poor, bare, forked animal as thou art. Off, off, you lendings! Come; unbutton here.

Tearing off his clothes

Fool

Prithee, nuncle, be contented; 'tis a naughty night to 105 swim in. Now a little fire in a wild field were like an

109 *Flibbertigibbet*: one of the evil spirits named in Harsnett; see p. 141.
109–110 *curfew . . . first cock*: dusk to dawn; when the first cock crows, all evil spirits must withdraw from the world of the living.
110–11 *the web and the pin*: cataract of the eye.
111 *squinies*: causes squints.
hare-lip: a birth-defect.
112 *white wheat*: almost ripened corn.
112–17 *Swithold . . . aroint thee*: As protection against the spirit, Edgar recites a rhyme describing how St Withold, having gone three times round the weald (= upland plains, the downs; *wold*—'old'—is probably a dialect pronunciation), subdued a demon and her nine followers: he made her promise ('her troth plight') to obey him, and ordered her to be gone ('aroint').

123 *todpole*: tadpole.
wall-newt: lizard.
water: water-newt.
125 *for sallets*: as salads.
ditch-dog: dead dog lying in the ditch.
126 *green mantle*: scum.
standing: stagnant.
127 *tithing*: hamlet containing ten households.
stock-punish'd: set in the stocks for punishment.
128 *three suits*: the serving man's allowance, see note on *2, 2, 14*.
131 *deer*: game.
133 *follower*: familiar spirit, devil.
Smulkin: Another name suggested by Harsnett, like 'Modo' and 'Mahu'.

old lecher's heart; a small spark, all the rest on's body cold. Look! here comes a walking fire.

Enter Gloucester, *with a torch*

Edgar
This is the foul Flibbertigibbet: he begins at curfew, and walks till the first cock; he gives the web and the pin, squinies the eye, and makes the hare-lip; mildews the white wheat, and hurts the poor creature of earth.
Swithold footed thrice the wold;
He met the night-mare, and her nine-fold;
Bid her alight,
And her troth plight,
And aroint thee, witch, aroint thee!

Kent
How fares your grace?

Lear
What's he?

Kent
Who's there? What is't you seek?

Gloucester
What are you there? Your names?

Edgar
Poor Tom; that eats the swimming frog, the toad, the todpole, the wall-newt, and the water; that in the fury of his heart, when the foul fiend rages, eats cow-dung for sallets; swallows the old rat and the ditch-dog; drinks the green mantle of the standing pool; who is whipp'd from tithing to tithing, and stock-punish'd, and imprison'd; who hath had three suits to his back, six shirts to his body,
Horse to ride, and weapons to wear,
But mice and rats and such small deer,
Have been Tom's food for seven long year.
Beware my follower. Peace, Smulkin! peace, thou fiend!

Gloucester
What! hath your grace no better company?

Edgar
The Prince of Darkness is a gentleman; Modo he's called, and Mahu.

138–9 *Our . . . gets it*: nowadays the children hate their parents.

141 *suffer*: bear.

147 *philosopher*: i.e a natural scientist, who might have been able to answer the question of line 148.

150 *learned Theban*: Edgar's blanket now suggests the robes of a Greek scholar from Thebes.
151 *study*: subject of research.
152 *prevent*: avoid.

160 *outlaw'd from my blood*: cast out of my inheritance *and* forced to become an outlaw.
sought my life: tried to kill me.
161 *But lately*: very recently.

164 *cry you mercy*: I beg your pardon.

Gloucester
Our flesh and blood, my lord, is grown so vile,
That it doth hate what gets it.
Edgar
140 Poor Tom's a-cold.
Gloucester
Go in with me. My duty cannot suffer
T'obey in all your daughters' hard commands:
Though their injunction be to bar my doors,
And let this tyrannous night take hold upon you,
145 Yet I have ventured to come seek you out
And bring you where both fire and food is ready.
Lear
First let me talk with this philosopher.
What is the cause of thunder?
Kent
Good my lord, take his offer; go into th'house.
Lear
150 I'll talk a word with this same learned Theban.
What is your study?
Edgar
How to prevent the fiend, and to kill vermin.
Lear
Let me ask you one word in private.
Kent
Importune him once more to go, my lord;
155 His wits begin t'unsettle.
Gloucester
                                    Canst thou blame him?

Storm still

His daughters seek his death. Ah! that good Kent;
He said it would be thus, poor banish'd man!
Thou say'st the king grows mad; I'll tell thee, friend,
I am almost mad myself. I had a son,
160 Now outlaw'd from my blood; he sought my life,
But lately, very late; I lov'd him, friend,
No father his son dearer; true to tell thee,
The grief hath craz'd my wits. What a night's this!
I do beseech your grace,—
Lear
                                    O, cry you mercy, sir!
165 Noble philosopher, your company.

167 Gloucester does not intend to include
     Poor Tom in his rescue mission to the
     king.

168 *With him*: Lear refuses to be separated
     from his new friend.
170 *soothe*: humour.
171 Gloucester still refuses to touch the
     beggar.
173 *Athenian*: philosopher from Athens.
175–77 *Child . . . man*: As the little party
     moves towards Gloucester's castle
     (which is itself a 'dark tower'), the
     nonsense rhyme intensifies the terror.
175 *Child Rowland*: Prince Roland, the
     nephew of Charlemagne, and chivalric
     hero of *The Song of Roland*.
176 *word*: password.
     still: always.
176–77 *Fie . . . man*: These are the Giant's
     words from the story of 'Jack the Giant-
     killer'; it has been suggested that 'British'
     here (instead of the usual 'English') is a
     tribute to King James's unification of the
     realm in 1603.

Edgar
Tom's a-cold.
Gloucester
In, fellow, there, into th'hovel: keep thee warm.
Lear
Come, let's in all.
Kent
                                    This way, my lord.
Lear
                                              With him;
I will keep still with my philosopher.
Kent
170 Good my lord, soothe him; let him take the fellow.
Gloucester
Take him you on.
Kent
Sirrah, come on; go along with us.
Lear
Come, good Athenian.
Gloucester
No words, no words: hush.
Edgar
175   *Child Rowland to the dark tower came,*
         His word was still: Fie, foh, and fum,
         I smell the blood of a British man.

                                    [*Exeunt*

Act 3 Scene 5
Edmund has betrayed his father to Cornwall,
who orders Gloucester's arrest.

2 *how . . . censured*: what people will think.
   nature: my natural feelings as a son.
3 *loyalty*: sense of duty to the ruler.
   something fears me: I am rather
   frightened.
5 *seek his death*: want to kill him.
5–6 *provoking . . . himself*: Cornwall's
   language is deliberately involved; he
   seems to be saying that Edgar was guilty
   of a wickedness ('a reproveable badness')
   which had encouraged him to wish that
   his father should die the kind of death

Scene 5

Gloucester's castle
Enter Cornwall *and* Edmund

Cornwall
I will have my revenge ere I depart his house.
Edmund
How, my lord, I may be censured, that nature thus
gives way to loyalty, something fears me to think of.
Cornwall
I now perceive it was not altogether your brother's evil
5 disposition made him seek his death; but a provoking
merit, set a-work by a reproveable badness in himself.

(i.e. a traitor's death) which Gloucester did in fact deserve ('merit').

8 *just*: righteous (in revealing his father's apparent treachery).
approves: proves him to be.

9 *intelligent party*: spy, providing intelligence.
the advantages: the assistance.

10 *were not*: had not happened.

13 *this paper*: i.e. the letter that Gloucester was reading in Scene 3.
certain: correct.

15 *made . . . Gloucester*: Edmund's plans (see 3, 3, 22) seem to have worked.

17 *apprehension*: arrest.

18 *comforting*: giving assistance (to a known traitor).

19 *persever*: continue; the accent is on the second syllable—'perséver'.

20 *sore*: sharp.

21 *blood*: natural feelings.

Edmund

How malicious is my fortune, that I must repent to be just! This is the letter he spoke of, which approves him an intelligent party to the advantages of France.
10 O heavens! that this treason were not, or not I the detector!

Cornwall

Go with me to the duchess.

Edmund

If the matter of this paper be certain, you have mighty business in hand.

Cornwall

15 True or false, it hath made thee Earl of Gloucester. Seek out where thy father is, that he may be ready for our apprehension.

Edmund

[*Aside*] If I find him comforting the king, it will stuff his suspicion more fully. [*Aloud*] I will persever in my
20 course of loyalty, though the conflict be sore between that and my blood.

Cornwall

I will lay trust upon thee; and thou shalt find a dearer father in my love.

[*Exeunt*

Act 3 Scene 6

Gloucester has brought the king indoors, and leaves him safe with Kent. Now Lear, aided by the fool and the disguised Edgar, holds a mock trial of his daughters, until he falls asleep with exhaustion. Gloucester returns with news of fresh danger, and the sleeping Lear must be carried to safety. Alone for a moment, Edgar drops his disguise.

2 *piece . . . can*: do what I can to make it more comfortable.

4–5 *power . . . impatience*: his mind is totally destroyed because he cannot bear this suffering.

Scene 6

A farmhouse
Enter Gloucester, *and* Kent

Gloucester

Here is better than the open air; take it thankfully. I will piece out the comfort with what addition I can: I will not be long from you.

Kent

All the power of his wits have given way to his impati-
5 ence. The gods reward your kindness!

[*Exit*

Enter Lear, Edgar, *and* Fool

6–7 *Frateretto . . . Darkness*: These are more borrowings from Harsnett; see p. 141.

10 *yeoman*: property-owner without a coat-of-arms.

12–14 *No . . . before him*: *om.* Q.
12–14 *a mad . . . before him*: i.e. because the son will despise his father's humbler status.

15 *a thousand*: i.e. devils.

17–55 *The foul . . . 'scape*: *om.* F.

19 *horse's health*: i.e. trusts the word of a horsedealer about the condition of the animal he is selling.
20 *arraign*: Lear suddenly decides to bring his daughters to trial.
21 *justicer*: justice of the peace.
22 *sapient*: wise.

23 *he*: an imaginary devil.
      eyes: an audience.
25–8 Edgar sings a line from a song where the lover calls his sweetheart to cross the stream ('bourn'); the fool improvises a reply.

30 *nightingale*: i.e. the voice of the fool.
      Hoppedance: a devil.
31 *white*: unsmoked.
      Croak not: stop rumbling.

33 *amaz'd*: dumbfounded.

Edgar
Frateretto calls me, and tells me Nero is an angler in the Lake of Darkness. Pray, innocent, and beware the foul fiend.

Fool
Prithee, nuncle, tell me whether a madman be a
10   gentleman or a yeoman?

Lear
A king, a king!

Fool
No; he's a yeoman that has a gentleman to his son; for he's a mad yeoman that sees his son a gentleman before him.

Lear
15   To have a thousand with red burning spits
Come hizzing in upon 'em—

Edgar
The foul fiend bites my back.

Fool
He's mad that trusts in the tameness of a wolf, a horse's health, a boy's love, or a whore's oath.

Lear
20   It shall be done; I will arraign them straight.
[*To* Edgar] Come, sit thou here, most learned justicer;
[*To the* Fool] Thou, sapient sir, sit here. Now, you she foxes!

Edgar
Look where he stands and glares! Want'st thou eyes at trial, madam?
25   *Come o'er the bourn, Bessy, to me,*—

Fool [*Sings*]
            Her boat hath a leak,
            And she must not speak;
            Why she dares not come over to thee!

Edgar
The foul fiend haunts Poor Tom in the voice of a
30   nightingale. Hoppedance cries in Tom's belly for two white herring. Croak not, black angel; I have no food for thee.

Kent
How do you, sir? Stand you not so amaz'd:
Will you lie down and rest upon the cushions?

35 *their evidence*: those who will give evidence against them.
36 *robed*: Edgar's blanket now has (for Lear) the appearance of judicial robes.
37 *yoke-fellow of equity*: partner in justice.
38 *Bench*: take your seat on the bench.
   o'th'commission: commissioned as a justice.

41–4 *Sleepest . . . harm*: The fragment of a song, similar to 'Little Boy Blue'; the sheep will come to no harm for the short time that the shepherd plays a few notes with his delicate ('minikin') lips.
45 *Purr*: Edgar imitates the sound of a cat.

51 *Cry . . . joint-stool*: sorry, I didn't notice you (literally translated, the words mean 'I beg your pardon, I thought I was only looking at a stool made by a joiner').
52 *warp'd*: distorted.
53 *store*: kind of material.

60 *mar my counterfeiting*: get in the way of my acting (as 'Poor Tom').
62 *Tray, Blanch, and Sweetheart*: the names of pet dogs.
63 *throw his head*: shout at.
   Avaunt: clear off.

Lear
35 I'll see their trial first. Bring in their evidence.
   [*To* Edgar] Thou robed man of justice, take thy place;
   [*To the* Fool] And thou, his yoke-fellow of equity,
   Bench by his side. [*To* Kent] You are o'th'commission,
   Sit you too.
Edgar
40 Let us deal justly.
   Sleepest or wakest thou, jolly shepherd?
   Thy sheep be in the corn;
   And for one blast of thy minikin mouth,
   Thy sheep shall take no harm.
45 Purr, the cat is grey.
Lear
   Arraign her first; 'tis Goneril. I here take my oath before this honourable assembly, she kick'd the poor king her father.
Fool
   Come hither, mistress. Is your name Goneril?
Lear
50 She cannot deny it.
Fool
   Cry you mercy, I took you for a joint-stool.
Lear
   And here's another, whose warp'd looks proclaim
   What store her heart is made on. Stop her there!
   Arms, arms, sword, fire! Corruption in the place!
55 False justicer, why hast thou let her 'scape?
Edgar
   Bless thy five wits!
Kent
   O pity! Sir, where is the patience now
   That you so oft have boasted to retain?
Edgar
   [*Aside*] My tears begin to take his part so much,
60 They mar my counterfeiting.
Lear
   The little dogs and all,
   Tray, Blanch, and Sweetheart, see, they bark at me.
Edgar
   Tom will throw his head at them. Avaunt, you curs!

67 *brach*: hound bitch.
  lym: lymmer, a species of bloodhound so
  called from the *liam* (= leash) by which it
  was led.
68 *Or bobtail . . . trundle-tail*: little terrier dog
  either dock-tailed or with a long
  drooping tail.
70 *For . . . head*: He perhaps puts the
  beggar's horn (see note on line 73) on his
  head and pretends to charge at these
  (imaginary) dogs.
71 *hatch*: half-door.

Be thy mouth or black or white,
Tooth that poisons if it bite;   65
Mastiff, greyhound, mongrel grim,
Hound or spaniel, brach or lym;
Or bobtail tike or trundle-tail;
Tom will make him weep and wail: 70
For, with throwing thus my head,
Dogs leap'd the hatch, and all are fled.

72 *Do de . . . Sessa*: He pretends to make
  sure there are no dogs left.
72–3 *Come . . . market-towns*: This may be a
  call for companions to travel to feasts
  ('wakes') and fairs in the surrounding
  market-towns.
73 *thy horn is dry*: The beggar's plea for
  drink; the Bedlam beggar wore a horn
  round his neck to carry any alms given to
  him. But Edgar means now that he
  cannot play his 'Poor Tom' role any
  longer.
74 *anatomize*: dissect.
74–5 *what . . . heart*: what has happened to
  her heart.
76 *make*: should make.
77 *entertain*: take into service.
  hundred: i.e. the hundred knights.
77–9 *I do not . . . Persian*: The Roman poet
  Horace wrote (*Odes* I, 38) of how he
  disliked the elaborate dress of the
  Persians.
81 *curtains*: Lear imagines he is in his own
  bed.
82 *supper . . . morning*: i.e. we can forget
  about supper for the moment (rest is
  more important than food).

Do de, de, de. Sessa! Come, march to wakes and
fairs and market-towns. Poor Tom, thy horn is dry.
  Lear
Then let them anatomize Regan, see what breeds
about her heart. Is there any cause in nature that   75
make these hard hearts? [*To* Edgar] You, sir, I
entertain for one of my hundred; only I do not like
the fashion of your garments: you will say they are
Persian; but let them be chang'd.
  Kent
Now, good my lord, lie here and rest awhile.   80
  Lear
Make no noise, make no noise; draw the curtains: so,
so. We'll go to supper i'th'morning.
  Fool
And I'll go to bed at noon.

Enter Gloucester

  Gloucester
Come hither, friend: where is the king my master?

83 *And . . . noon*: If supper is to be eaten in
the morning, then the middle of the day
will be the logical time to go to bed: the
world is turned completely upside down.
These are the fool's last words in the
play.
87 *upon*: against.
88 *litter*: a wheeled vehicle, apparently
horse-drawn (see 'drive', line 89).
91 *dally*: delay.
92 *offer*: attempt.
93 *Stand . . . loss*: will certainly be lost.

96 *broken sinews*: racked nerves.
97 *convenience . . . allow*: it isn't convenient.
98 *Stand . . . cure*: are not likely to be healed.
100–13 *When . . . lurk*: om. F.
100–13 *When . . . lurk*: Edgar brings the
scene to a close with formal rhymed
couplets—and his speech emphasizes the
present inter-connectedness of the play's
two plots.
103 *free*: care-free.
happy shows: things that look happy.
104 *o'erskip*: pass over.
105 *bearing fellowship*: endurance is shared.
106 *portable*: endurable.
108 *he . . . fathered*: he has cruel children, just
as I have a cruel father.
109 *Mark the high noises*: take note of what is
happening right at the top (i.e. between
the two dukes).
thyself bewray: reveal yourself, throw off
this disguise.
110 *false opinion*: i.e. Gloucester's mistaken
opinion of his son.
111 *just proof*: proof of your innocence.
repeals: i.e. the sentence of outlawry.
reconciles thee: reinstates you in your
former position of favour.
112 *What will hap*: whatever happens.
safe 'scape: may the king escape safely.
113 *Lurk, lurk*: keep in hiding.

Kent
85 Here, sir; but trouble him not, his wits are gone.
Gloucester
Good friend, I prithee, take him in thy arms;
I have o'erheard a plot of death upon him.
There is a litter ready; lay him in't,
And drive toward Dover, friend, where thou shalt meet
90 Both welcome and protection. Take up thy master:
If thou should'st dally half an hour, his life,
With thine, and all that offer to defend him,
Stand in assured loss. Take up, take up;
And follow me, that will to some provision
95 Give thee quick conduct.
Kent
                              Oppressed nature sleeps.
This rest might yet have balm'd thy broken sinews
Which, if convenience will not allow,
Stand in hard cure. [*To the* Fool] Come, help to bear
        thy master;
Thou must not stay behind.
Gloucester
                              Come, come, away.
        [*Exeunt* Kent, Gloucester, *and the* Fool,
                bearing off the King
Edgar
100 When we our betters see bearing our woes,
We scarcely think our miseries our foes.
Who alone suffers, suffers most i'th'mind,
Leaving free things and happy shows behind;
But then the mind much sufferance doth o'erskip,
105 When grief hath mates, and bearing fellowship.
How light and portable my pain seems now,
When that which makes me bend makes the king bow;
He childed as I father'd! Tom, away!
Mark the high noises, and thyself bewray
110 When false opinion, whose wrong thoughts defile thee,
In thy just proof repeals and reconciles thee.
What will hap more to-night, safe 'scape the king!
Lurk, lurk.

                                        [*Exit*

Act 3 Scene 7

Gloucester has been arrested, and he is brought to face his accusers. Cornwall sends Edmund and Goneril away together. Gloucester is accused of giving aid to Lear, and Cornwall tears Gloucester's eyes out of his head. One of Cornwall's servants, outraged by the cruelty, wounds his master. Gloucester learns the truth about his two sons, and then he is thrown out of the house. Servants go to look for 'the Bedlam'—Gloucester's son, Edgar—who will be able to lead the blind old man towards Dover.

1 *Post speedily*: ride fast.
2 *letter*. The same letter (about Cordelia's return) which Gloucester mentioned to Edmund in *3, 3, 10*, and which Edmund gave to Cornwall in *3, 5, 8*.

6–7 *keep . . . company*: i.e. leave the room with Goneril.
7 *bound*: prepared, obliged.
10 *festinate preparation*: get everything ready very quickly.
   bound to the like: we intend to do the same.
11 *posts*: messengers on horseback.
   intelligent: giving information.
12 *Lord of Gloucester*: i.e. Edmund; Cornwall recognizes Edmund's new status, although Oswald in line 14 still refers to Edmund's father by this title.
16 *Hot questrists*: eager seekers.
18 *boast*: claim.

23 *pass upon his life*: condemn him to death.

Scene 7

Gloucester's *castle*
Enter Cornwall, Regan, Goneril, Edmund, *and* Servants

Cornwall
[*To* Goneril] Post speedily to my lord your husband;
show him this letter: the army of France is landed.
Seek out the traitor Gloucester.
                    [*Exeunt some of the* Servants
    Regan
Hang him instantly.
    Goneril
5 Pluck out his eyes.
    Cornwall
Leave him to my displeasure. Edmund, keep you our
sister company: the revenges we are bound to take
upon your traitorous father are not fit for your
beholding. Advise the duke, where you are going, to a
10 most festinate preparation: we are bound to the like.
Our posts shall be swift and intelligent betwixt us.
Farewell, dear sister; farewell, my Lord of Gloucester.

    Enter Oswald

How now! where's the king?
    Oswald
My Lord of Gloucester hath convey'd him hence:
15 Some five or six and thirty of his knights,
Hot questrists after him, met him at gate;
Who, with some other of the lord's dependants,
Are gone with him toward Dover, where they boast
To have well-armed friends.
    Cornwall
                    Get horses for your mistress.
    Goneril
20 Farewell, sweet lord, and sister.
    Cornwall
Edmund, farewell.
            [*Exeunt* Goneril, Edmund, *and* Oswald
            Go seek the traitor Gloucester,
Pinion him like a thief, bring him before us.
            [*Exeunt other* Servants
Though well we may not pass upon his life

24 *form of justice*: the appearance of a trial.
25 *do a court'sy*: bow, give way; Cornwall will let his wrath take precedence over his rightful power.

27 *Ingrateful fox*: In Cornwall's eyes, Gloucester has acted with ingratitude towards his 'noble arch and patron' (*2, 1, 58*), and been as stealthy as a fox in giving succour to the king.
28 *corky*: sapless, withered.

31 *filthy*: odious.

32 *Unmerciful*: merciless.

34s.d. *plucks his beard*: An outrageous insult.

Without the form of justice, yet our power
25 Shall do a court'sy to our wrath, which men
May blame but not control. Who's there? The traitor?

Enter Servants, *with* Gloucester *prisoner*

Regan
Ingrateful fox! 'tis he.
Cornwall
Bind fast his corky arms.
Gloucester
What means your graces? Good my friends, consider
30 You are my guests: do me no foul play, friends.
Cornwall
Bind him, I say.

Servants bind him

Regan
                                  Hard, hard. O filthy traitor!
Gloucester
Unmerciful lady as you are, I'm none.
Cornwall
To this chair bind him. Villain, thou shalt find—

Regan plucks his beard

Gloucester
By the kind gods, 'tis most ignobly done
35 To pluck me by the beard.
Regan
So white, and such a traitor!

36 *Naughty*: wicked.

38 *quicken*: come to life.
39 *hospitable favours*: the features of your host.
40 *ruffle*: treat with violence.

41 *late*: lately.

42 *Be simple-answer'd*: give a straight answer.

43 *confederacy*: conspiracy.
44 *Late footed*: recently landed.

46 *guessingly set down*: written without certain knowledge.
47 *of a neutral heart*: is not taking sides.

50 *at peril*: on peril of death.
52 'Like a baited bear, I am tied to the stake and must face the pack of dogs ('course') who are attacking me.'

Gloucester
                              Naughty lady,
These hairs, which thou dost ravish from my chin,
Will quicken, and accuse thee: I am your host:
With robbers' hands my hospitable favours
40 You should not ruffle thus. What will you do?
    Cornwall
Come, sir, what letters had you late from France?
    Regan
Be simple-answer'd, for we know the truth.
    Cornwall
And what confederacy have you with the traitors
Late footed in the kingdom?
    Regan
                              To whose hands
45 You have sent the lunatic king: speak.
    Gloucester
I have a letter guessingly set down,
Which came from one that's of a neutral heart,
And not from one oppos'd.
    Cornwall
                              Cunning.
    Regan
                              And false.
    Cornwall
Where hast thou sent the king?
    Gloucester
                              To Dover.
    Regan
50 Wherefore to Dover? Wast thou not charg'd at peril—
    Cornwall
Wherefore to Dover? Let him answer that.
    Gloucester
I am tied to th'stake, and I must stand the course.

55 *anointed flesh*: At the king's coronation his body was anointed with holy oil; it was sacrilegious to harm the royal person.
56 *Rash boarish fangs*: attack like a wild boar.
58 *buoyed up*: risen up.
stelled fires: stars.

59 *holp*: helped.
60 *dearn*: dreadful.
61 *turn the key*: i.e. give them shelter.
62 *All . . . subscribe*: all other cruel creatures show compassion in extraordinary situations.
63 *winged vengeance*: divine vengeance from heaven.
66 'If anyone values his life.'

72 *bid you hold*: tell you to stop.

73 'If you were a man I would pull your beard (see line 33) for this outrage.'

74 *What do you mean?*: how dare you presume to speak.

75 *villain*: servant, peasant (*also* wicked person).

76 *take . . . anger*: risk fighting me in my anger.

Regan
Wherefore to Dover?
Gloucester
                    Because I would not see
Thy cruel nails pluck out his poor old eyes;
55 Nor thy fierce sister in his anointed flesh
Rash boarish fangs. The sea, with such a storm
As his bare head in hell-black night endur'd,
Would have buoy'd up, and quench'd the stelled fires;
Yet, poor old heart, he holp the heavens to rain.
60 If wolves had at thy gate howl'd that dearn time,
Thou should'st have said 'Good porter, turn the key.'
All cruels else subscribe: but I shall see
The winged vengeance overtake such children.
Cornwall
See't shalt thou never. Fellows, hold the chair.
65 Upon these eyes of thine I'll set my foot.
Gloucester
He that will think to live till he be old,
Give me some help! O cruel! O you gods!
Regan
One side will mock another; th'other too.
Cornwall
If you see vengeance,—
First Servant
                    Hold your hand, my lord.
70 I have serv'd you ever since I was a child,
But better service have I never done you
Than now to bid you hold.
Regan
                    How now, you dog!
First Servant
If you did wear a beard upon your chin
I'd shake it on this quarrel.
Regan
                    What do you mean?
Cornwall
75 My villain!

They draw and fight

First Servant
Nay then, come on, and take the chance of anger.

77 *stand up thus*: make such a challenge.

Regan
Give me thy sword. A peasant stand up thus!

Takes a sword and runs at him behind

First Servant
O I am slain! My lord, you have one eye left
To see some mischief on him. Oh!

79 *mischief on him*: that some harm comes to
him.

[*Dies*

Cornwall
80 Lest it see more, prevent it. Out, vile jelly!
Where is thy lustre now?
Gloucester
All dark and comfortless. Where's my son Edmund?
Edmund, enkindle all the sparks of nature
To quit this horrid act.
Regan
                                    Out, treacherous villain!
85 Thou call'st on him that hates thee; it was he
That made the overture of thy treasons to us,
Who is too good to pity thee.
Gloucester
O my follies! Then Edgar was abus'd.
Kind gods, forgive me that, and prosper him!
Regan
90 Go thrust him out at gates, and let him smell
His way to Dover.   [*Exit one with* Gloucester
                    How is't, my lord. How look you?
Cornwall
I have receiv'd a hurt. Follow me, lady.
Turn out that eyeless villain; throw this slave
Upon the dunghill. Regan, I bleed apace:
95 Untimely comes this hurt. Give me your arm.
                    [*Exit* Cornwall, *led by* Regan
Second Servant
I'll never care what wickedness I do
If this man come to good.
Third Servant
                                    If she live long,
And in the end meet the old course of death,
Women will all turn monsters.

83 *enkindle . . . nature*: arouse all natural
passions.
84 *quit*: pay back.

86 *made the overture*: first disclosed.

88 *abus'd*: wronged.
89 *that*: i.e. his misjudgement of Edgar.

90 *out at gates*: out of the gates.

91 *How look you*: how are you feeling.

94 *apace*: very fast.
95 *Untimely . . . hurt*: this is a bad time for
me to be wounded.

94–106 These lines are present *only* in the
Quarto text of *King Lear*; see p. xli.

98 *old*: natural.
99 *all turn monsters*: i.e. because they will
never need to fear retribution.

100 *Bedlam*: Poor Tom.
101-2 *roguish . . . thing*: he is allowed to do all sorts of things because he is a vagabond and a madman.
103 *flax*: a fibrous plant, dressed to make 'bandage' material.
105s.d. *severally*: in different directions.

Second Servant

100 Let's follow the old earl, and get the Bedlam
To lead him where he would: his roguish madness
Allows itself to any thing.

Third Servant

Go thou; I'll fetch some flax and whites of eggs
To apply to his bleeding face. Now, heaven help him!

[*Exeunt severally*

Act 4

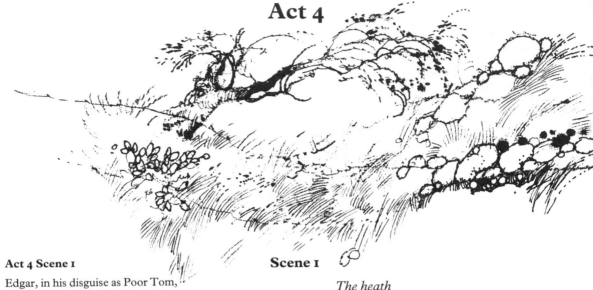

Act 4 Scene 1

Edgar, in his disguise as Poor Tom, encounters his blinded father. He undertakes to lead him to the top of Dover cliff, where Gloucester means to put an end to his misery.

1–2 'It is better to be like this (i.e. a Bedlam beggar), knowing that I am despised ('contemn'd'), than to be flatter'd and at the same time despised—which is worst of all.'

3 *most . . . Fortune*: most rejected by Fortune.

4 *Stands . . . esperance*: is always hoping for something better.

6 *returns to laughter*: i.e. the change is for the better.

6–9 *Welcome . . . blasts*: om. Q.

7 *unsubstantial*: empty.

8–9 *The wretch . . . blasts*: I do not owe anything to the winds that blew such a wretch as I was to an even worse condition.

10 *poorly led*: brought on like a beggar.

11–12 'If it were not for the fact that we come to hate the world because of all these changes in it, we would never be reconciled to the knowledge that we must grow old.'

16 *comforts*: attempts to assist me.

Scene 1

The heath
Enter Edgar

Edgar
Yet better thus, and known to be contemn'd,
Than, still contemn'd and flatter'd, to be worst.
The lowest and most dejected thing of Fortune
Stands still in esperance, lives not in fear:
5   The lamentable change is from the best;
The worst returns to laughter. Welcome, then,
Thou unsubstantial air that I embrace:
The wretch that thou hast blown unto the worst
Owes nothing to thy blasts. But who comes here?

Enter Gloucester, *led by an* Old Man

10 My father, poorly led? World, world, O world!
But that thy strange mutations make us hate thee,
Life would not yield to age.

Old Man
                                    O my good lord!
I have been your tenant, and your father's tenant,
These fourscore years.

Gloucester
15 Away, get thee away; good friend, be gone:
Thy comforts can do me no good at all;
Thee they may hurt.

Old Man

                               You cannot see your way.

Gloucester

I have no way, and therefore want no eyes;

I stumbled when I saw. Full oft 'tis seen,

20 Our means secure us, and our mere defects

Prove our commodities. Oh! dear son Edgar,

The food of thy abused father's wrath;

Might I but live to see thee in my touch,

I'd say I had eyes again.

Old Man

                           How now! Who's there?

Edgar

25 [*Aside*] O gods! Who is't can say 'I am at the worst'?

I am worse than e'er I was.

Old Man

                              'Tis poor mad Tom.

Edgar

[*Aside*] And worse I may be yet; the worst is not

So long as we can say 'This is the worst.'

Old Man

Fellow, where goest?

Gloucester

                       Is it a beggar-man?

Old Man

30 Madman and beggar too.

Gloucester

He has some reason, else he could not beg.

I'th'last night's storm I such a fellow saw,

Which made me think a man a worm. My son

Came then into my mind; and yet my mind

35 Was then scarce friends with him. I have heard more
     since:

As flies to wanton boys, are we to th'gods;

They kill us for their sport.

Edgar

[*Aside*]   How should this be?

Bad is the trade that must play fool to sorrow,

Ang'ring itself and others. [*Aloud*] Bless thee, master!

Gloucester

40 Is that the naked fellow?

Old Man

                                Ay, my lord.

---

20 *Our . . . us*: having possessions makes us over-confident.

20–21 *mere defects . . . commodities*: total disadvantages turn out to be assets.

22 'The food which fed your father's anger while he was deceived about you ('abused').'

23 *see*: recognize.

27–8 *the worst . . . the worst*: the worst has not happened as long as we can comfort ourselves by thinking that it has already happened (and that things are going to get better).

31 *has some reason*: must have some intelligence.

33 *worm*: i.e. the lowest of all creatures.

35 *scarce friends with him*: did not think well of him.

36 'The gods play with human beings just as careless [and cruel] boys play with flies.'

37 *sport*: amusement.
   How . . . be?: what has happened?

38 *Bad is the trade*: it's a bad business.
   play fool to sorrow: Edgar prepares to resume his role as 'Poor Tom'.

42 *o'ertake*: catch up with us.
   twain: two.
43 *I'th'way*: in the direction of.
   ancient love: former loyalty.

46 *times' plague*: the trouble these days.

48 *the rest*: all.

49 *'parel*: apparel, clothing.
50 *come on't what will*: no matter what
   happens.

51 *daub it further*: carry on with this pretence
   (the metaphor is from plastering walls).

53 *And . . . must*: om. F.
55 *horse-way*: bridle-path.
57–62 *Five . . . master*: om. F.
57 *Five fiends*: The fiends are named in
   Harsnett; see p. 141.
60–61 *mopping and mowing*: grimacing and
   pulling faces.
61 *possesses*: Harsnett reports the
   examination of three chambermaids
   possessed by devils.
64 *humbled to all strokes*: made you bear the
   strokes (of Fortune, or of Heaven) so
   humbly.
65 *Heavens*: may the heavens.
   still: always.
66 *the . . . man*: any man whose possessions
   are excessive and who can get
   whatsoever he desires.
67 *That . . . ordinance*: who treats what the
   heavens have given him as though it is his
   to command.
67–8 *will not . . . feel*: will not see the needs
   of others because he does not feel them
   himself.
69 'Sharing things out would stop anybody
   from having too much.'

Gloucester
Then, prithee, get thee away. If, for my sake,
Thou wilt o'ertake us, hence a mile or twain,
I'th'way toward Dover, do it for ancient love;
And bring some covering for this naked soul,
45 Which I'll entreat to lead me.
        Old Man
                              Alack, sir! he is mad.
        Gloucester
'Tis the times' plague, when madmen lead the blind.
Do as I bid thee, or rather do thy pleasure;
Above the rest, be gone.
        Old Man
I'll bring him the best 'parel that I have,
50 Come on't what will.
                                            [*Exit*
        Gloucester
                    Sirrah, naked fellow,—
        Edgar
Poor Tom's a-cold. [*Aside*] I cannot daub it further.
        Gloucester
Come hither, fellow.
        Edgar
[*Aside*] And yet I must. Bless thy sweet eyes, they bleed.
        Gloucester
Know'st thou the way to Dover?
        Edgar
55 Both stile and gate, horse-way and foot-path. Poor
Tom hath been scar'd out of his good wits: bless thee,
good man's son, from the foul fiend! Five fiends have
been in Poor Tom at once; as Obidicut, of lust;
Hoberdidance, prince of dumbness; Mahu, of stealing;
60 Modo, of murder; Flibbertigibbet, of mopping and
mowing; who since possesses chambermaids and
waiting-women. So, bless thee, master!
        Gloucester
Here, take this purse, thou whom the heav'ns' plagues
Have humbled to all strokes: that I am wretched
65 Makes thee the happier. Heavens, deal so still!
Let the superfluous and lust-dieted man,
That slaves your ordinance, that will not see
Because he does not feel, feel your power quickly;
So distribution should undo excess,
70 And each man have enough. Dost thou know Dover?

Edgar
Ay, master.
Gloucester
There is a cliff, whose high and bending head
Looks fearfully in the confined deep;
Bring me but to the very brim of it,
75 And I'll repair the misery thou dost bear
With something rich about me; from that place
I shall no leading need.
Edgar
                                        Give me thy arm:
Poor Tom shall lead thee.

                                              [*Exeunt*

72 *bending*: leaning over its base.
73 *fearfully*: The cliff is personified.
   confined deep: At Dover the sea—the
   English Channel—is held back by cliffs.
74 *but to the very brim*: right to the very edge.
76 *about me*: that I have with me.

Act 4 Scene 2

Goneril and Edmund have become very
friendly, but Oswald describes a change in the
nature of Goneril's husband, Albany. Albany
expresses his horror at the treatment Lear has
received; and there is a quarrel between
husband and wife. News is brought of
Cornwall's death, and of the blinding of
Gloucester. Goneril begins to be jealous of
her sister.

2 *on the way*: i.e. as they were returning
   from Gloucester's castle.
8 *sot*: fool.
9 *turn'd . . . out*: got things the wrong way
   round (Albany knows that Gloucester is
   not a traitor, and that Edmund was not
   acting as a loyal subject).
12 *cowish*: cowardly.
13 *undertake*: take any responsibility upon
   himself.
13–14 *he'll not . . . answer*: he will pretend to
   ignore any injuries which (if he noticed
   them) would demand his retaliation.
14 *Our wishes on the way*: what we were
   hoping for on the journey here.
15 *May prove effects*: might come true.
   my brother: i.e. brother-in-law, Cornwall.
16 *Hasten his musters*: make him call up his
   armies quickly.
   conduct his powers: lead his forces.

Scene 2

Albany's *palace*
Enter Goneril *and* Edmund

Goneril
Welcome, my lord; I marvel our mild husband
Not met us on the way.

Enter Oswald

                        Now, where's your master?
Oswald
Madam, within; but never man so chang'd.
I told him of the army that was landed;
5 He smil'd at it: I told him you were coming;
His answer was 'The worse': of Gloucester's treachery,
And of the loyal service of his son,
When I inform'd him, then he call'd me sot,
And told me I had turn'd the wrong side out:
10 What most he should dislike seems pleasant to him;
What like, offensive.
Goneril
[*To* Edmund]   Then shall you go no further.
It is the cowish terror of his spirit
That dares not undertake; he'll not feel wrongs
Which tie him to an answer. Our wishes on the way
15 May prove effects. Back, Edmund, to my brother;
Hasten his musters and conduct his powers:

17 *must change arms*: Goneril must exchange
arms with Albany: she will wield the
masculine sword herself, and hand the
feminine distaff (used in spinning) to her
husband.

19 *like*: likely.

20 *venture in your own behalf*: do something
for yourself.

21 *Wear this*: Goneril gives Edmund a token
(e.g. a scarf or chain) to wear as a sign of
her favour.
spare speech: do not say anything.

22 *Decline your head*: i.e. to receive a favour
or her kiss.

23 *stretch*: raise; Goneril's words are sexually
suggestive, and Edmund responds with a
pun.

24 *Conceive*: understand what I mean.

25 *ranks of death*: until I die, *and in the
enjoyment of sexual orgasm*.

26 *of man and man*: between one man (i.e.
Edmund) and another (i.e. Albany).

27 'You deserve all that a woman can do for
a man.'

28 *A fool*: i.e. Albany.
usurps my bed: has got possession of my
bed.

29 *worth the whistle*: Goneril refers to the
proverb, 'It is a poor dog that is not
worth whistling for'; she reproaches her
husband for not coming to meet her.

30 *rude*: rough, uncivil.

31 *fear your disposition*: am fearful about
your temperament.

32 *contemns it origin*: despises its own
beginnings.

33 'Cannot be trusted to stay within normal
bounds.'

34 *sliver and disbranch*: cut off and sever
connections; Albany compares Goneril
to the branch of a tree.

35 *material*: essential.
perforce: inevitably.

36 *deadly use*: a bad end.

37 *text*: subject on which Albany has been
preaching.

39 *Filths . . . themselves*: to the filthy, all
things seem filthy.

42 *the head-lugg'd bear*: the bear which is
dragged along by the ring through its
nose.

43 *madded*: driven mad.

45 *benefited*: given such benefits.

46 *visible spirits*: spirits in visible form.

I must change arms at home, and give the distaff
Into my husband's hands. This trusty servant
Shall pass between us; ere long you are like to hear,
20 If you dare venture in your own behalf,
A mistress's command. Wear this; spare speech;

Giving a favour

Decline your head: this kiss, if it durst speak,
Would stretch thy spirits up into the air.
Conceive, and fare thee well.

Edmund
25 Yours in the ranks of death.

Goneril
My most dear Gloucester!
[*Exit* Edmund

Oh, the difference of man and man!
To thee a woman's services are due:
A fool usurps my bed.

Oswald
Madam, here comes my lord.
[*Exit*

Enter Albany

Goneril
I have been worth the whistle.

Albany
O Goneril!
30 You are not worth the dust which the rude wind
Blows in your face. I fear your disposition:
That nature, which contemns it origin,
Cannot be border'd certain in itself;
She that herself will sliver and disbranch
35 From her material sap, perforce must wither
And come to deadly use.

47 *vilde*: vile; Shakespeare's form of the word seems also to have undertones of 'wild'.
   offences: offenders.
48 *It will come*: it must happen; the half-line allows Albany to make a dramatic pause before speaking his prophecy.
49–50 *Humanity . . . deep*: Albany warns that the violation of natural order will lead to cannibalism—just as fishes in the sea devour each other.
50 *Milk-liver'd man*: coward (with a white, bloodless liver).
51 *a cheek for blows*: i.e. only so that you can be struck on the face.
52–3 *an eye . . . suffering*: that can tell the difference between what can be honourably endured and what should be resented.
53–9 *that . . . so*: *om*. F.
54–5 *Fools . . . mischief*: only fools feel sorry for those villains who are punished *before* they have performed their villainy. (Goneril refers to Lear, implying that he is now in league with France and a threat to their kingdom.)
55 *thy drum*: i.e. to summon armies.
56 *noiseless*: undefended—because the drum is silent.
57 *plumed helm*: helmets with plumes.
   thy . . . threat: poses a threat to your kingdom.
58 *moral*: moralizing.
59 *See thyself*: take a good look at yourself.
60–61 *Proper . . . woman*: the diabolic appearance does not look so hideous in the devil to whom it belongs (is 'Proper') as it does in a woman.
62 *changed and self-cover'd thing*: Goneril's nature seems to be transformed (she no longer seems to be human), and even her outward appearance (she is perhaps scowling at her husband) makes her look like a fiend.
63 *Be-monster not thy feature*: stop looking like a monster.
   Were't my fitness: if it were appropriate for me.
64 *blood*: instinct, passion.
65 *apt*: ready.
66 *howe'er*: but although.
68 Goneril dismisses Albany's masculinity with a contemptuous oath ('Marry' = by [the Virgin] Mary) and the cry of a kitten ('mew').

Goneril
No more; the text is foolish.
Albany
Wisdom and goodness to the vile seem vile;
Filths savour but themselves. What have you done?
40 Tigers, not daughters, what have you perform'd?
A father, and a gracious aged man,
Whose reverence even the head-lugg'd bear would lick,—
Most barbarous, most degenerate!—have you madded.
Could my good brother suffer you to do it?
45 A man, a prince, by him so benefited!
If that the heavens do not their visible spirits
Send quickly down to tame these vilde offences,
It will come,
Humanity must perforce prey on itself,
50 Like monsters of the deep.
Goneril
                                   Milk-liver'd man!
That bear'st a cheek for blows, a head for wrongs;
Who hast not in thy brows an eye discerning
Thine honour from thy suffering; that not know'st
Fools do those villains pity who are punish'd
55 Ere they have done their mischief. Where's thy drum;
France spreads his banners in our noiseless land,
With plumed helm thy state begins to threat,
Whil'st thou, a moral fool, sits still, and cries
'Alack! why does he so?'
Albany
                                   See thyself, devil!
60 Proper deformity shows not in the fiend
So horrid as in woman.
Goneril
                         O vain fool!
Albany
Thou changed and self-cover'd thing, for shame,
Be-monster not thy feature. Were't my fitness
To let these hands obey my blood,
65 They are apt enough to dislocate and tear
Thy flesh and bones; howe'er thou art a fiend,
A woman's shape doth shield thee.
Goneril
Marry, your manhood—mew!

Enter a Messenger

Albany

What news?

Messenger

70 O my good lord, the Duke of Cornwall's dead—
Slain by his servant, going to put out
The other eye of Gloucester!

Albany

Gloucester's eyes!

Messenger

A servant that he bred, thrill'd with remorse,
Oppos'd against the act, bending his sword
75 To his great master; who, thereat enrag'd,
Flew on him, and amongst them fell'd him dead;
But not without that harmful stroke, which since
Hath pluck'd him after.

Albany

This shows you are above,
You justicers, that these our nether crimes
80 So speedily can venge! But, O poor Gloucester!
Lost he his other eye?

Messenger

Both, both, my lord.
This letter, madam, craves a speedy answer;
'Tis from your sister.

Presents a letter

Goneril

[*Aside*]   One way I like this well;
But being widow, and my Gloucester with her,
85 May all the building in my fancy pluck
Upon my hateful life: another way,
The news is not so tart. [*Aloud*] I'll read, and answer.

[*Exit*

Albany

Where was his son when they did take his eyes?

Messenger

Come with my lady hither.

Albany

He is not here.

Messenger

90 No, my good lord; I met him back again.

Albany

Knows he the wickedness?

---

73 *thrill'd with remorse*: stirred to action by pity.
74 *bending*: turning.
75 *To*: against.
76 *fell'd*: struck.
77 *that harmful stroke*: i.e. the wound he had received from the servant.
78 *pluck'd him after*: taken him to follow his servant (i.e. to death).

79 *justicers*: judges.
nether crimes: crimes committed on earth (under the heavens).
80 *venge*: avenge.

85 *building in my fancy*: everything I have dreamed up.
pluck: pull down.
86 *hateful*: i.e. her life will then be hateful because Regan will be able to have Edmund, while Goneril will be left with her husband.
87 *tart*: bitter.

90 *back again*: on his way back.

Messenger
Ay, my good lord; 'twas he inform'd against him,
And quit the house on purpose that their punishment
Might have the freer course.

Albany

Gloucester, I live
95 To thank thee for the love thou show'dst the king,
And to revenge thine eyes. Come hither, friend:
Tell me what more thou know'st.

[*Exeunt*

Act 4 Scene 3

The Gentleman who was sent to meet
Cordelia (in *Act 3*, Scene 1) has returned to
Kent, and describes Cordelia's reactions to
the news of her sisters' cruelty and her father's
sufferings. Kent (still in disguise) leads the
way to his master. This scene is not present in
the Folio text of the play.

3–4 *Something . . . of*: he left some state
  business unfinished and he has
  remembered this since he has been away.
4 *imports*: threatens.

7 *general*: as general, in command.

9 *your letters*: The Gentleman seems to
  have given Kent's 'just report' (see *3, 1,
  37*) in writing.
  pierce: move.

12 *trill'd*: trickled.

14 *passion*: emotion.

16 *patience*: self-control.
17 *express her goodliest*: make her seem more
  lovely; the Gentleman does not know
  whether to wonder more at Cordelia's
  emotion or at her self-control.

93 *quit*: left.

Scene 3

The French camp near Dover
Enter Kent *and a* Gentleman

Kent
Why the King of France is so suddenly gone back
know you no reason?

Gentleman
Something he left imperfect in the state, which since
his coming forth is thought of; which imports to the
5 kingdom so much fear and danger that his personal
return was most requir'd and necessary.

Kent
Who hath he left behind him general?

Gentleman
The Marshall of France, Monsieur La Far.

Kent
Did your letters pierce the queen to any demonstra-
10 tion of grief?

Gentleman
Ay, sir; she took them, read them in my presence;
And now and then an ample tear trill'd down
Her delicate cheek; it seem'd she was a queen
Over her passion; who, most rebel-like,
15 Sought to be king o'er her.

Kent

O, then it mov'd her!

Gentleman
Not to a rage; patience and sorrow strove
Who should express her goodliest. You have seen

19 *Were . . . way*: were just like this, but in a better way.
    smilets: little smiles.
21 *which*: i.e. the guests—her tears.
22 *pearls . . . dropp'd*: i.e. Cordelia's eyes were shining like diamonds and her tears, flowing from her eyes, resembled pearls.
24 *If . . . it*: if it made everyone look so lovely.
    Made . . . question?: didn't she say anything?
25 *Faith*: in faith; yes, indeed.
    heav'd: uttered with difficulty.
26 *press'd*: weighed heavily on.

30 *the holy water*: See Commentary, p. xxix.
31 *and clamour moisten'd*: The meaning seems to be that Cordelia's exclamations of pity and outrage were drowned in her tears.

33 *conditions*: characters.
34 *one self mate and make*: the very same wife and husband.
35 *issues*: children.

39 *sometime*: sometimes.
    better tune: more lucid intervals.

42 *sovereign*: overpowering.
    elbows him: holds him back.
43 *turn'd her*: turned her out.
44 *foreign casualties*: chances of life in a foreign land.
    dear rights: the precious things (not only her share of the kingdom, but also a father's love) which are hers by right.
45 *dog-hearted*: pitiless.

Sunshine and rain at once; her smiles and tears
Were like, a better way; those happy smilets
20 That play'd on her ripe lip seem'd not to know
What guests were in her eyes; which parted thence,
As pearls from diamonds dropp'd. In brief,
Sorrow would be a rarity most belov'd,
If all could so become it.

    Kent
                             Made she no verbal question?

Gentleman
25 Faith, once or twice she heav'd the name of 'father'
Pantingly forth, as if it press'd her heart;
Cried 'Sisters! sisters! Shame of ladies! sisters!
Kent! father! sisters! What? i'th'storm! i'th'night?
Let pity not believe it!' There she shook
30 The holy water from her heavenly eyes,
And clamour moisten'd, then away she started
To deal with grief alone.

    Kent
                               It is the stars,
The stars above us, govern our conditions;
Else one self mate and make could not beget
35 Such different issues. You spoke not with her since?

    Gentleman
No.

    Kent
Was this before the king return'd?

    Gentleman
                              No, since.

    Kent
Well, sir, the poor distressed Lear's i'th'town;
Who sometime, in his better tune, remembers
40 What we are come about, and by no means
Will yield to see his daughter.

    Gentleman
                            Why, good sir?

    Kent
A sovereign shame so elbows him: his own unkindness,
That stripp'd her from his benediction, turn'd her
To foreign casualties, gave her dear rights
45 To his dog-hearted daughters, these things sting
His mind so venomously that burning shame
Detains him from Cordelia.

Gentleman

Alack! poor gentleman.

Kent

Of Albany's and Cornwall's powers you heard not?

Gentleman

'Tis so, they are afoot.

Kent

50 Well, sir, I'll bring you to our master Lear,
And leave you to attend him. Some dear cause
Will in concealment wrap me up awhile;
When I am known aright, you shall not grieve
Lending me this acquaintance. I pray you,
55 Go along with me.

[*Exeunt*

---

48 *powers*: armies.

49 *afoot*: on the march.

51–2 *Some . . . awhile*: 'There is a good reason why I should stay disguised for a time'; we are never told what Kent's 'cause' could be.
53 *aright*: for who I really am.
54 *Lending . . . acquaintance*: for having befriended me.

Act 4 Scene 4

Cordelia describes her father's madness, and asks for the Doctor's help. She is told that the British armies are approaching, and she prepares to take up arms in defence of her father's rights.

os.d. *colours*: military banners.
1 *'tis he*: he (Lear) is exactly as he has been described (i.e. mad).
even now: just now.
2 *vex'd*: raging.
3–5 The weeds that make up Lear's wreath are not easily identified.
3 *rank fumiter*: fumitory (also called 'earth-smoke') which grows abundantly.
furrow-weeds: weeds that grow in the furrows of ploughed land.
4 *hardocks*: hoar dockleaves.
cuckoo-flowers: This name is given to various wild flowers in different parts of England.
5 *Darnel*: tares, weeds growing among the corn.
idle: useless.
6 *sustaining*: life supporting.
century: division of a hundred soldiers (under the command of a centurion).
7 *the high-grown field*: Cordelia's description indicates that the time is now the height of summer.

Scene 4

The camp
Enter, with drum and colours, Cordelia,
Doctor, *and* Soldiers.

Cordelia

Alack, 'tis he! why, he was met even now
As mad as the vex'd sea; singing aloud;
Crown'd with rank fumiter and furrow-weeds,
With hardocks, hemlock, nettles, cuckoo-flowers,
5 Darnel, and all the idle weeds that grow
In our sustaining corn. A century send forth;
Search every acre in the high-grown field,
And bring him to our eye.

[*Exit an* Officer

8–9 *What . . . sense?*: what does human
science know that can restore the
balance of his mind?
10 *helps*: cures.
outward worth: possessions.

12 'What cherishes and protects human
nature is rest.'
13 *provoke*: induce.
14 *simples operative*: effective medicinable
herbs.

15 *bless'd*: blessed; Cordelia invokes the
powers of natural—'white'—magic.
16 *unpublish'd virtues*: unknown powers.
17 *aidant and remediate*: helpfully remedial;
the Latinate words emphasize the
formality of Cordelia's prayer.
19 *ungovern'd rage*: uncontrolled frenzy.
dissolve: destroy.
20 *wants*: lacks.
the means: i.e. his reason.

22 *before*: already.
preparation: armed troops ready to fight.

24 'I am going in your service.' See
Commentary, p. xxx.
25 *France*: i.e. the King of France,
Cordelia's husband.
26 *importun'd*: importunate, beseeching.
27 'We are not taking up arms out of any
inflated ambition of conquest.'

                         What can man's wisdom
In the restoring his bereaved sense?
10 He that helps him take all my outward worth.
    Doctor
There is means, madam;
Our foster-nurse of nature is repose,
The which he lacks; that to provoke in him,
Are many simples operative, whose power
15 Will close the eye of anguish.
    Cordelia
                          All bless'd secrets,
All you unpublish'd virtues of the earth,
Spring with my tears! be aidant and remediate
In the good man's distress! Seek, seek for him,
Lest his ungovern'd rage dissolve the life
20 That wants the means to lead it.

        Enter a Messenger

    Messenger
                          News, madam;
The British powers are marching hitherward.
    Cordelia
'Tis known before; our preparation stands
In expectation of them. O dear father!
It is thy business that I go about;
25 Therefore great France
My mourning and importun'd tears hath pitied.
No blown ambition doth our arms incite,
But love, dear love, and our ag'd father's right.
Soon may I hear and see him!
                              [*Exeunt*

Act 4 Scene 5

Oswald has delivered to Regan the letter that Goneril promised to send (*4, 2, 87*), and he tries to deliver Goneril's letter to Edmund. Regan explains that Edmund has gone to look for his father and to kill him. Regan is now very jealous of Goneril: she wants Edmund as her own husband.

1 *set forth*: started out.
2 *with much ado*: after a lot of persuasion; Albany was evidently unsure where his loyalties should lie.
6 'Why was my sister writing to him?'

8 *posted*: ridden away in a hurry.
serious matter: important business.
9 *ignorance*: political folly.
10 *where* : wherever.

12 *in pity*: taking pity.
dispatch: put an end to.
13 *nighted*: darkened—because he is blind.
descry: ascertain.

18 *charg'd my duty*: was very insistent that I should do what she ordered.
20 *Belike*: probably.
21 *Some things*: Regan is suspicious.
I'll love thee much: I'll be very grateful to you (and show my gratitude).

Scene 5

Gloucester's castle
Enter Regan and Oswald

Regan
But are my brother's powers set forth?
 Oswald
          Ay, madam.
 Regan
Himself in person there?
 Oswald
       Madam, with much ado:
Your sister is the better soldier.
 Regan
Lord Edmund spake not with your lord at home?
 Oswald
5 No, madam.
 Regan
What might import my sister's letter to him?
 Oswald
I know not, lady.
 Regan
Faith, he is posted hence on serious matter.
It was great ignorance, Gloucester's eyes being out,
10 To let him live; where he arrives he moves
All hearts against us. Edmund, I think, is gone,
In pity of his misery, to dispatch
His nighted life; moreover, to descry
The strength o'th'enemy.
 Oswald
15 I must needs after him, madam, with my letter.
 Regan
Our troops set forth to-morrow; stay with us,
The ways are dangerous.
 Oswald
         I may not, madam;
My lady charg'd my duty in this business.
 Regan
Why should she write to Edmund? Might not you
20 Transport her purposes by word? Belike,
Some things—I know not what. I'll love thee much,
Let me unseal the letter.

Oswald

                                                  Madam, I had rather—
Regan

I know your lady does not love her husband;
I am sure of that: and at her late being here
25 She gave strange oeilliads and most speaking looks
To noble Edmund. I know you are of her bosom.
Oswald

I, madam!
Regan

I speak in understanding; y'are, I know't:
Therefore I do advise you, take this note:
30 My lord is dead; Edmund and I have talk'd
And more convenient is he for my hand
Than for your lady's. You may gather more.
If you do find him, pray you give him this,
And when your mistress hears thus much from you,
35 I pray desire her call her wisdom to her:
So, fare you well.
If you do chance to hear of that blind traitor,
Preferment falls on him that cuts him off.
Oswald

Would I could meet him, madam: I should show
40 What party I do follow.
Regan

                                                  Fare thee well.
                                                  [*Exeunt*

24 *at . . . here*: when she was here recently.
25 *oeilliads*: amorous glances; the word (pronounced 'eeliads') was used by other writers of this period.
   speaking: meaningful.
26 *of her bosom*: in her confidence.

28 *speak in understanding*: know what I am talking about.
29 *take this note*: take note of what I say.
30 *have talk'd*: have come to an understanding.
31 *convenient*: fitting.
   my hand: to marry me.
32 *You . . . more*: you can make more deductions yourself.
33 *this*: Regan gives Oswald some token— perhaps a ring— to take to Edmund.
34 *thus much*: what I have told you.
35 *desire . . . to her*: tell her to come to her senses.
38 *Preferment*: promotion, advancement.
   cuts him off: kills him.
39 *Would*: I wish.

Act 4 Scene 6

Edgar persuades his father that they are at the top of Dover cliff, and Gloucester tries to commit suicide. Edgar then pretends to find him at the foot of the cliff. The king appears, in his total madness, and talks with Gloucester. Cordelia's servants come looking for Lear, but he runs away from them. There are more rumours of war. Oswald, who is carrying Goneril's letter to Edmund, tries to kill Gloucester; but Edgar, now speaking like a peasant, defends his father. He kills Oswald, and reads the letter—and learns that Goneril wants Edmund to kill her husband so that she can become Edmund's wife. Edgar takes his father to a place of safety.

1 *that same hill*: that hill we were talking about—i.e. Dover cliff.

5–6 *your . . . anguish*: the pain of your eyes.

8 *in better phrase and matter*: with better words and more sense.

Scene 6

The countryside near Dover
Enter Gloucester *and* Edgar *dressed like a peasant*

Gloucester
When shall I come to th'top of that same hill?
    Edgar
You do climb up it now; look how we labour.
    Gloucester
Methinks the ground is even.
    Edgar
                                Horrible steep:
Hark! do you hear the sea?
    Gloucester
                       No, truly.
    Edgar
5 Why, then your other senses grow imperfect
By your eyes' anguish.
    Gloucester
                      So may it be, indeed.
Methinks thy voice is alter'd, and thou speak'st
In better phrase and matter than thou didst.
    Edgar
You're much deceiv'd; in nothing am I chang'd
10 But in my garments.
    Gloucester
                  Methinks you're better spoken.

13 *choughs*: jackdaws.
14 *gross*: big.
15 *sampire*: samphire, a herb used in pickling.

18 *tall anchoring bark*: fine ship riding at anchor.
19 'Reduced to the size of her cock-boat (= rowing-boat), and the cock-boat itself is only the size of a buoy.'
20 *surge*: tide.
21 *unnumber'd*: numberless.
   idle pebble: barren pebbles.
22 *so high*: because we are so high up.
23 *brain turn*: mind becomes giddy.
23–4 *and . . . headlong*: and my sight fails so that I overbalance and fall down headlong.

26 *extreme verge*: very edge.
27 *leap upright*: i.e. even if he jumped straight up in the air he would probably fall over the edge of the cliff.

29 *fairies*: good fairies; Gloucester, still superstitious, alludes to the belief that the fairies who guard hidden treasure would also multiply it for the finder.

33–4 *Why . . . cure it*: the reason I am taking his despair so lightly is so that I may cure it.

37–8 *fall to quarrel*: start to rebel.
38 *opposeless*: irresistible.
39–40 *My snuff . . . out*: the last remains ('snuff' = the smouldering wick of a candle) of my hateful life should wear out naturally.

Edgar
Come on, sir; here's the place: stand still. How fearful
And dizzy 'tis to cast one's eyes so low!
The crows and choughs that wing the midway air
Show scarce so gross as beetles; halfway down
15 Hangs one that gathers sampire, dreadful trade!
Methinks he seems no bigger than his head.
The fishermen that walk upon the beach
Appear like mice, and yond tall anchoring bark
Diminish'd to her cock, her cock a buoy
20 Almost too small for sight. The murmuring surge,
That on th'unnumber'd idle pebble chafes,
Cannot be heard so high. I'll look no more,
Lest my brain turns, and the deficient sight
Topple down headlong.
Gloucester
                                Set me where you stand.
Edgar
25 Give me your hand; you are now within a foot
Of th'extreme verge: for all beneath the moon
Would I not leap upright.
Gloucester
                                Let go my hand.
Here, friend, 's another purse; in it a jewel
Well worth a poor man's taking: fairies and gods
30 Prosper it with thee! Go thou further off;
Bid me farewell, and let me hear thee going.
Edgar
Now fare ye well, good sir.
Gloucester
                                With all my heart.
Edgar
[*Aside*] Why I do trifle thus with his despair
Is done to cure it.
Gloucester
[*Kneeling*]   O you mighty gods!
35 This world I do renounce, and in your sights
Shake patiently my great affliction off;
If I could bear it longer, and not fall
To quarrel with your great opposeless wills,
My snuff and loathed part of nature should
40 Burn itself out. If Edgar live, O, bless him!
Now, fellow, fare thee well.

Edgar

Gone, sir: farewell.

Gloucester throws himself forward and falls

42 *conceit*: imagination.

43 *treasury*: treasure.

44 *Yields*: consents.

45 *thought been past*: he would not be
capable of any more thought.

46 *Ho, you sir!*: Edgar adopts another
persona.

47 *pass*: die.

And yet I know not how conceit may rob
The treasury of life when life itself
Yields to the theft; had he been where he thought
45 By this had thought been past. Alive or dead?
Ho, you sir! friend! Hear you, sir! speak!
Thus might he pass indeed; yet he revives.
What are you, sir?

Gloucester

Away, and let me die.

Edgar

Hadst thou been aught but gossamer, feathers, air,

50 *precipitating*: falling headlong.

51 *shiver'd*: smashed into pieces.

52 *heavy*: solid.
sound: whole—i.e. no bones are broken.

53 *Ten . . . altitude*: the masts of ten ships,
one on top of the other, would not be as
high as that cliff.

54 *fell*: fallen.

50 So many fathom down precipitating,
Thou'dst shiver'd like an egg; but thou dost breathe,
Hast heavy substance, bleed'st not, speak'st, art sound.
Ten masts at each make not the altitude
Which thou hast perpendicularly fell:
55 Thy life's a miracle. Speak yet again.

Gloucester

But have I fall'n or no?

Edgar

57 *chalky bourn*: boundary (of the sea) made
by the chalk cliffs of Dover.

58 *a-height*: on high.
shrill-gorg'd: shrill-voiced.

From the dread summit of this chalky bourn.
Look up a-height: the shrill-gorg'd lark so far
Cannot be seen or heard: do but look up.

62 *'Twas yet*: it has always been.
63–4 *When . . . will*: i.e. by committing
     suicide.
63 *beguile*: cheat.

65 *Feel you*: have you any feeling in?

68 *parted*: departed.
71 *whelk'd*: twisted.
   enridged: furrowed.
72 *happy father*: you lucky old man. Edgar's
   use of this form of address is deliberately
   ambiguous: certainly he is not revealing
   his identity to Gloucester.
73 *clearest*: most righteous.
73–4 *make them . . . impossiblities*: get
   honour by doing things which are
   impossible to men.
76–7 *till . . . die*: till affliction recognizes
   that I have borne enough and allows me
   to die a natural death.

80 *free*: free from guilt or self-reproach.

81–2 *The safer . . . thus*: a man in his right
   senses would never appear like this.

83 *touch*: arrest.
   coining: coining money (one of the rights
   of the monarch).

85 *side-piercing*: heart-rending.

Gloucester

60   Alack! I have no eyes.
      Is wretchedness depriv'd that benefit
      To end itself by death? 'Twas yet some comfort,
      When misery could beguile the tyrant's rage,
      And frustrate his proud will.
      Edgar
                                          Give me your arm:
65   Up: so; how is't? Feel you your legs? You stand.
      Gloucester
      Too well, too well.
      Edgar
                              This is above all strangeness.
      Upon the crown o'th'cliff what thing was that
      Which parted from you?
      Gloucester
                              A poor unfortunate beggar.
      Edgar
      As I stood here below methought his eyes
70   Were two full moons; he had a thousand noses,
      Horns whelk'd and wav'd like the enridged sea:
      It was some fiend; therefore, thou happy father,
      Think that the clearest gods, who make them honours
      Of men's impossibilities, have preserved thee.
      Gloucester
75   I do remember now; henceforth I'll bear
      Affliction till it do cry out itself
      'Enough, enough,' and die. That thing you speak of
      I took it for a man; often 'twould say
      'The fiend, the fiend': he led me to that place.
      Edgar
80   Bear free and patient thoughts. But who comes here?

      Enter Lear, *fantastically dressed with wild
      flowers*

      The safer sense will ne'er accommodate
      His master thus.
      Lear
      No, they cannot touch me for coining; I am the king
      himself.
      Edgar
85   O thou side-piercing sight!

86 *Nature's . . . respect*: a born king can never lose his natural rights.

87 *press-money*: money paid to recruits when they were impressed (= forcibly enrolled) into the army.

88 *crow-keeper*: scarecrow.
me: for me.
clothier's yard: an arrow the length of a yard (i.e. 36 inches, 90 centimetres) of cloth.

89 *mouse*: probably imaginary, (like the dogs in *3, 6, 62*).

90 *gauntlet*: glove thrown down as a challenge.
prove it on: defend my case against.

91 *Bring . . . bills*: call up the foot-soldiers armed with pikes (which were painted brown to prevent rusting).
well flown bird: Lear praises the shooting of the arrow with the falconer's call of approval to his hawk.

92 *i'th'clout*: right in the centre of the arrow's target.
hewgh: Lear imitates the sound of an arrow.
word: password.

93 *Sweet marjoram*: The herb was said to be remedial for diseases of the brain.

96 *Goneril . . . beard*: Lear (obsessed with his daughters' cruelty) mistakes Gloucester for Goneril.

96–7 *flattered me like a dog*: as a dog fawns on his master.

97–8 *told me . . . there*: said that I had the wisdom of old age before I was even old enough to have grown a beard.

98–9 *To say . . . said*: to agree with everything I said.

99 *no good divinity*: not good theology.

100 *once*: on one occasion.

101 *peace*: hold its peace, be silent.

102 *found 'em*: learned what they (the flatterers) were really like.

104 *ague-proof*: immune to feverish colds.

105 *trick*: inflection.

108 *cause*: offence.

111 *goes to't*: enjoys it (i.e. copulation).

112 *lecher*: fornicate.

Lear
Nature's above art in that respect. There's your press-money. That fellow handles his bow like a crow-keeper: draw me a clothier's yard. Look, look! a mouse. Peace, peace! this piece of toasted cheese will do't. There's my gauntlet; I'll prove it on a giant. Bring up the brown bills. O! well flown bird; i'th'clout, i'th'clout: hewgh! Give the word.

Edgar
Sweet marjoram.

Lear
Pass.

Gloucester
I know that voice.

Lear
Ha! Goneril, with a white beard! They flattered me like a dog, and told me I had the white hairs in my beard ere the black ones were there. To say 'ay' and 'no' to every thing that I said 'ay' and 'no' to was no good divinity. When the rain came to wet me once and the wind to make me chatter, when the thunder would not peace at my bidding, there I found 'em, there I smelt 'em out. Go to, they are not men o'their words: they told me I was every thing; 'tis a lie, I am not ague-proof.

Gloucester
The trick of that voice I do well remember:
Is't not the king?

Lear
                        Ay, every inch a king:
When I do stare, see how the subject quakes.
I pardon that man's life. What was thy cause?
Adultery?
Thou shalt not die: die for adultery! No:
The wren goes to't, and the small gilded fly
Does lecher in my sight.

114 *kinder*: more natural *and* more loving.
115 *Luxury*: lustfulness.
    pell-mell: as hard as you can, promiscuously; the word is also used to describe soldiers rushing into battle, and so leads to Lear's next notion.
116 *lack soldiers*: Lear seems to be suggesting that promiscuity will somehow provide men for his army.
117 'Who looks as though she is quite chaste.'
    forks: legs.
    pressages snow: is a warning of coldness— i.e. chastity.
118 *minces virtue*: pretends to be fastidiously virtuous.
    shake the head: give signs of disapproval or embarrassment.
119 *pleasure's name*: the name of (sexual) pleasure.
120 *fitchew*: pole-cat (a name often applied to prostitutes).
    soiled horse: horse over-fed with spring grass, frisky.
122 *Centaurs*: Mythical creatures that were half-human (as far as the waist), and half-horse; they were notoriously lecherous.
124 *But . . . inherit*: only the top half of the human body belongs to the gods.
    girdle: waist.
125 *Beneath is all the fiend's*: The priests exposed by Harsnett claimed to exorcize devils from the lower parts of the body; see p. 141.
127 *consumption*: destruction.
128 *civet*: perfume.
    apothecary: Lear addresses Gloucester.
132 *This great world*: the whole universe.
133 *so wear out to naught*: collapse into ruin, like Lear.
134 *squiny*: squint.
135 *blind Cupid*: Lear takes Gloucester for the classical god of love who was traditionally depicted as being blind.
136 *challenge*: Lear's mind reverts to the 'challenge' of line 90.
    the penning of it: the way it is written.
138 'I would not believe anyone who told me about the scene I am now witnessing.'
    it is: it is really happening.
141 *case*: sockets (which had once held his eyes).
142 *are . . . me?*: is that what you mean?

Let copulation thrive; for Gloucester's bastard son
Was kinder to his father than my daughters
115 Got 'tween the lawful sheets. To't, Luxury, pell-mell!
For I lack soldiers. Behold yond simp'ring dame,
Whose face between her forks presages snow;
That minces virtue, and does shake the head
To hear of pleasure's name;
120 The fitchew nor the soiled horse goes to't
With a more riotous appetite.
Down from the waist they are Centaurs
Though women all above:
But to the girdle do the gods inherit,
125 Beneath is all the fiend's: there's hell, there's darkness,
There is the sulphurous pit—burning, scalding,
Stench, consumption; fie, fie, fie! pah, pah!
Give me an ounce of civet, good apothecary,
To sweeten my imagination.
130 There's money for thee.

Gloucester
               O, let me kiss that hand!

Lear
Let me wipe it first; it smells of mortality.

Gloucester
O ruin'd piece of Nature! This great world
Shall so wear out to naught. Dost thou know me?

Lear
I remember thine eyes well enough. Dost thou squiny
    at me?
135 No, do thy worst, blind Cupid; I'll not love.
Read thou this challenge; mark but the penning of it.

Gloucester
Were all thy letters suns, I could not see.

Edgar
[*Aside*] I would not take this from report; it is,
And my heart breaks at it.

Lear
140 Read.

Gloucester
What, with the case of eyes?

Lear
O, ho! are you there with me? No eyes in your head, nor
no money in your purse? Your eyes are in a heavy case,
your purse in a light: yet you see how this world goes.

143-4 *Your eyes . . . light*: your eyes are in a serious condition, your purse in a happy one.

144 *how this world goes*: what is happening in this world.

145 *feelingly*: Gloucester means both 'by my sense of touch' *and* 'keenly'.

148 *justice*: magistrate.
rails upon: scolds.
simple: poor, common.

149 *handy-dandy*: i.e. take your choice—as in a guessing game where an object is concealed in one hand.

153 *creature*: human being.

155 *A dog's obey'd in office*: even the most servile creature must be obeyed when it is given authority.

156 *beadle*: parish constable.
hold: stop; see the New Testament story of the woman taken in adultery, John 8:7.

158 *kind*: manner.

159 *The usurer . . . cozener*: the magistrate who is himself guilty of large-scale usury condemns the petty cheat.

160 *Thorough*: through.

161-6 *Plate . . . lips*: *om.* Q.

161 *Plate*: clothe in plate armour.

162 *hurtless*: without harming.

163 *it*: i.e. sin.

164 *able*: vouch for—and so exempt from punishment.

165 *that*: that piece of information.

166 *glass eyes*: spectacles.

167 *scurvy politician*: vile deceiver.

170 *matter and impertinency*: sense and nonsense.

175 *smell*: breathe.

176 *wawl*: wail.

Gloucester
145 I see it feelingly.

Lear
What, art mad? A man may see how this world goes with no eyes. Look with thine ears: see how yond justice rails upon yond simple thief. Hark, in thine ear: change places, and, handy-dandy, which is the
150 justice, which is the thief? Thou hast seen a farmer's dog bark at a beggar?

Gloucester
Ay, sir.

Lear
And the creature run from the cur? There thou might'st behold
The great image of Authority:
155 A dog's obey'd in office.
Thou rascal beadle, hold thy bloody hand!
Why dost thou lash that whore? Strip thine own back;
Thou hotly lusts to use her in that kind
For which thou whipp'st her. The usurer hangs the cozener.
160 Thorough tatter'd clothes small vices do appear;
Robes and furr'd gowns hide all. Plate sin with gold,
And the strong lance of justice hurtless breaks;
Arm it in rags, a pigmy's straw does pierce it.
None does offend, none, I say, none; I'll able 'em:
165 Take that of me, my friend, who have the power
To seal th'accuser's lips. Get thee glass eyes;
And, like a scurvy politician, seem
To see the things thou dost not. Now, now, now, now;
Pull off my boots; harder, harder; so.

Edgar
170 [*Aside*] O, matter and impertinency mix'd!
Reason in madness.

Lear
If thou wilt weep my fortunes, take my eyes;
I know thee well enough; thy name is Gloucester;
Thou must be patient; we came crying hither:
175 Thou know'st the first time that we smell the air
We wawl and cry. I will preach to thee: mark.

Gloucester
Alack, alack the day!

Lear
When we are born, we cry that we are come
To this great stage of fools. This' a good block!
180   It were a delicate stratagem to shoe
A troop of horse with felt; I'll put't in proof,
And when I have stol'n upon these son-in-laws,
Then, kill, kill, kill, kill, kill, kill!

Enter a Gentleman, *with* Attendants

Gentleman
O, here he is! lay hand upon him. Sir,
185   Your most dear daughter—
Lear
No rescue? What, a prisoner? I am even
The natural fool of Fortune. Use me well;
You shall have ransom. Let me have surgeons;
I am cut to th'brains.
Gentleman
You shall have any thing.
Lear
190   No seconds? all myself?
Why this would make a man a man of salt,
To use his eyes for garden water-pots,
Ay, and laying autumn's dust. I will die bravely,
Like a smug bridegroom. What, I will be jovial!
195   Come, come; I am a king, masters, know you that?
Gentleman
You are a royal one, and we obey you.
Lear
Then there's life in't. Come and you get it, you shall
get it by running. Sa, sa, sa, sa.
                                   [*Exit running.* Attendants *follow*
Gentleman
A sight most pitiful in the meanest wretch,
200   Past speaking of in a king! Thou hast one daughter,
Who redeems nature from the general curse
Which twain have brought her to.
Edgar
Hail, gentle sir!
Gentleman
Sir, speed you: what's your will?
Edgar
Do you hear aught, sir, of a battle toward?

179   *stage of fools*: Shakespeare, like many other Elizabethan writers, was fond of the metaphor equating the world and the stage (see *As You Like It*, 2, 7, 139–166). *This' a good block*: it's a well-made hat.
180   *delicate stratagem*: neat scheme.
181   *in proof*: make a trial of it.

187   *The natural fool of Fortune*: born for Fortune to make a fool of me.

189   *cut to th'brains*: vexed to madness; Lear calls for a surgeon to heal an imaginary wound in his head.

190   *seconds*: supporters.
191   *a man of salt*: i.e. of salt tears.

193   *die*: end my life (with a pun on *die* = achieve sexual climax).
       bravely: courageously; *and* handsomely, in fine clothes.
194   *smug*: neatly dressed.
       jovial: majestic (like Jove); *and* merry, convivial.

197   *there's life in't*: things are not desperate yet.
       and: if.
       it: i.e. the ransom.
198   *Sa, sa, sa, sa*: the hunting cry used to encourage the hounds.

201   *general*: universal.
202   *twain*: two others.
       her: i.e. (human) nature.

203   *speed you*: may God prosper you.

204   *toward*: that is going to happen.

205 *sure and vulgar*: certain and commonly known.
206 *distinguish sound*: understand what is being said.

207 *the other army*: i.e. that of Goneril and Regan.

208 *speedy foot*: advancing rapidly.
208–9 *the main . . . hourly thought*: we expect to catch sight of the main body of the army at any hour.

210 *on special cause*: for a particular reason.

213 *my worser spirit*: i.e. my bad angel.
214 *to die before you please*: to commit suicide.

216 *tame*: submissive.
217 *by . . . sorrows*: because I have had the teaching which comes from knowing and experiencing grief.
218 *pregnant*: capable of feeling.
219 *biding*: resting place.

220 *benison*: blessing.
221 *To boot, and boot*: to reward you, in addition to my thanks.
proclaim'd: The accent is on the first syllable.
happy: fortunate; there is also something of a pun with 'hap' = chance.

222 *fram'd*: made into.

224 *thyself remember*: think of your sins (to make your peace with heaven).
out: out of its scabbard.

Gentleman
205 Most sure and vulgar; every one hears that,
Which can distinguish sound.
Edgar
But, by your favour,
How near's the other army?
Gentleman
Near, and on speedy foot; the main descry
Stands on the hourly thought.
Edgar
I thank you, sir: that's all.
Gentleman
210 Though that the queen on special cause is here,
Her army is mov'd on.
Edgar
I thank you sir.
[*Exit* Gentleman
Gloucester
You ever-gentle gods, take my breath from me:
Let not my worser spirit tempt me again
To die before you please!
Edgar
Well pray you, father.
Gloucester
215 Now, good sir, what are you?
Edgar
A most poor man, made tame to Fortune's blows;
Who, by the art of known and feeling sorrows,
Am pregnant to good pity. Give me your hand,
I'll lead you to some biding.
Gloucester
Hearty thanks:
220 The bounty and the benison of heaven
To boot, and boot!

Enter Oswald

Oswald
A proclaim'd prize! Most happy!
That eyeless head of thine was first fram'd flesh
To raise my fortunes. Thou old unhappy traitor,
Briefly thyself remember: the sword is out
225 That must destroy thee.

225 *friendly*: welcome (because it gives him the death he desires).

227 *support*: protect.
publish'd: proclaimed.

230–40 *Chill . . . foins*: Edgar assumes a 'rustic' dialect to disguise himself from Oswald.
230 *Chill*: I will.
'casion: occasion, cause.
232–7 *Good gentleman . . . with you*: 'Good sir, you get on your own way ('gait') and let ordinary people go past. If I could have been scared out of my life by swaggering like yours, I would never have lived so long—not by a whole fortnight. Now, don't you come any closer to the old man; keep away or—I promise you ('che vor ye') I'll test which is the harder, your head ('costard' = a kind of apple) or my cudgel ('ballow'). I'm telling you straight.'
238 *dunghill*: born on a dunghill.
239–40 *no matter . . . foins*: I don't care about your sword thrusts (perhaps Oswald is threatening with a dagger, and Edgar scorns the weapon as no more than a toothpick).
241 *Villain*: serf.

245 *Upon*: among.

247 *serviceable villain*: rogue who will do any (dishonest) job.

Gloucester

 Now let thy friendly hand
Put strength enough to't.

Edgar interposes

Oswald

 Wherefore, bold peasant
Dar'st thou support a publish'd traitor? Hence;
Lest that th'infection of his fortune take
Like hold on thee. Let go his arm.

Edgar

230 Chill not let go, zir, without vurther 'casion.

Oswald

Let go, slave, or thou die'st.

Edgar

Good gentleman, go your gait, and let poor volk pass.
And 'chud ha' bin zwagger'd out of my life, 'twould not ha' bin zo long as 'tis by the vortnight. Nay, come
235 not near th'old man; keep out, che vor' ye, or ise try whither your costard or my ballow be the harder.
Chill be plain with you.

Oswald

Out, dunghill!

Edgar

Chill pick your teeth, zir. Come; no matter vor your
240 foins.

They fight, and Edgar knocks him down

Oswald

Slave, thou hast slain me. Villain, take my purse.
If ever thou wilt thrive, bury my body;
And give the letters which thou find'st about me
To Edmund Earl of Gloucester; seek him out
245 Upon the British party: O! untimely death.
Death!

 [*Dies*

Edgar

I know thee well: a serviceable villain;
As duteous to the vices of thy mistress
As badness would desire.

Gloucester

 What! is he dead?

Edgar

250 Sit you down, father; rest you.
     Let's see these pockets: the letters that he speaks of
     May be my friends. He's dead; I am only sorry
     He had no other deathsman. Let us see:
     Leave, gentle wax; and, manners, blame us not:
255 To know our enemies' minds, we rip their hearts;
     Their papers is more lawful.

                                                  [*Reads*
        Let our reciprocal vows be remembered. You have many
        opportunities to cut him off; if your will want not, time
        and place will be fruitfully offer'd. There is nothing done if
260 *he return the conqueror; then am I the prisoner, and his*
        bed my gaol; from the loathed warmth whereof deliver me,
        and supply the place for your labour.
              Your wife, so I would say—
                    Affectionate servant,
265   *Goneril*

     O indistinguish'd space of woman's will!
     A plot upon her virtuous husband's life,
     And the exchange my brother! Here, in the sands,
     Thee I'll rake up, the post unsanctified
270 Of murtherous lechers; and in the mature time
     With this ungracious paper strike the sight
     Of the death-practis'd duke. For him 'tis well
     That of thy death and business I can tell.

Gloucester

     The king is mad: how stiff is my vile sense
275 That I stand up, and have ingenious feeling
     Of my huge sorrows! Better I were distract:
     So should my thoughts be sever'd from my griefs,
     And woes by wrong imaginations lose
     The knowledge of themselves.

                    Drum afar off

Edgar

                                        Give me your hand:
280 Far off, methinks, I hear the beaten drum.
     Come, father, I'll bestow you with a friend.
                                                  [*Exeunt*

---

253 *deathsman*: executioner.
254 *Leave*: by your leave; Edgar breaks open the waxen seal on the letter.
256 *Their papers*: i.e. to rip open their letters.
257 *reciprocal vows*: the pact we have made with each other.
258 *cut him off*: kill him—i.e. Albany.
     want: lack.
259 *fruitfully*: plentifully.
259–60 *There . . . conqueror*: We shall have achieved nothing if he (Albany) returns victorious.
262 *for*: as a reward for.
264 *servant*: lover.

266 Edgar exclaims against Goneril's lust ('will') which seems to know no limits.

268 *the exchange*: i.e. Goneril will exchange the virtuous Albany's life so that she can have Edmund's love.
269 *rake up*: cover up with sand (see Commentary, p. xxxiii), as embers of the domestic fire are covered in ashes at night.
     the post: the messenger.
270 *in the mature time*: when the time is ripe.
271 *ungracious*: wicked.
272 *death-practis'd*: whose death is plotted.
274 *stiff*: obstinate.
     vile sense: Gloucester calls his sense 'vile' because it will not allow him to escape from his sorrows by relaxing into madness.
275 *ingenious*: conscious.
276–79 *Better . . . themselves*: Gloucester wishes that he were mad ('distract') like Lear, so that he would lose consciousness of his sufferings in a world of mistaken illusions ('wrong imaginations').
276 *distract*: mad.
278 *wrong imaginations*: illusions.
280 *the beaten drum*: i.e. the battle is approaching.
281 *bestow*: accommodate.

Act 4 Scene 7

Kent has revealed himself to Cordelia, and they wait for Lear to wake up. At first he is confused, but at last he recognizes Cordelia as his daughter. The war is coming closer.

3 'Everything I can do will be too small.'
4 'It is more than enough reward just to be recognized by you for what I have done.'

5–6 *All . . . so*: everything I have told you is the simple truth, with nothing added and nothing taken away ('clipp'd')—just as it was.
6 *better suited*: better dressed; Kent still wears the servant's livery with which he disguised himself as 'Caius'.
7 *weeds*: clothes.
   memories: reminders.
9 *shortens . . . intent*: interferes with the plan I have made.
10 *boon*: request.
11 *meet*: appropriate.
15 *great . . . nature*: breakdown of his whole personality caused by such cruel treatment.
16 *untuned*: out of harmony.
   wind up: put in tune (by tightening the strings of, for example, a lute).

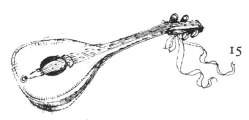

17 *child-changed*: changed back to a child, *or* changed by his children.
   So . . . majesty: if your majesty (Cordelia is Queen of France) will permit.
20 *I'th'sway*: according to.
21 *in the . . . sleep*: whilst he was fast asleep.

Scene 7

The French camp
Enter Cordelia, Kent, Doctor, *and* Gentleman

Cordelia
O thou good Kent! how shall I live and work
To match thy goodness? My life will be too short,
And every measure fail me.
　　Kent
To be acknowledg'd, madam, is o'er-paid.
5 All my reports go with the modest truth,
No more nor clipp'd, but so.
　　Cordelia
　　　　　　　Be better suited:
These weeds are memories of those worser hours:
I prithee, put them off.
　　Kent
　　　　　　Pardon, dear madam;
Yet to be known shortens my made intent:
10 My boon I make it that you know me not
Till time and I think meet.
　　Cordelia
Then be't so, my good lord. [*To the* Doctor] How
   does the king?
　　Doctor
Madam, sleeps still.
　　Cordelia
O you kind gods,
15 Cure this great breach in his abused nature!
Th'untuned and jarring sense, O, wind up
Of this child-changed father!
　　Doctor
　　　　　　So please your majesty
That we may wake the king? he hath slept long.
　　Cordelia
Be govern'd by your knowledge, and proceed
20 I'th'sway of your own will. Is he array'd?

Enter Lear *in a chair carried by* Servants

　　Gentleman
Ay, madam, in the heaviness of sleep
We put fresh garments on him.

23 *by*: close by.
24 *temperance*: sanity.

Doctor
Be by, good madam, when we do awake him;
I doubt not of his temperance.
   Cordelia
                Very well.

Music

26–7 *Restoration . . . lips*: may my lips carry the medicine that will restore you.

29 *reverence*: reverend person.

Doctor
25 Please you, draw near. Louder the music there!
   Cordelia
O my dear father! Restoration hang
Thy medicine on my lips, and let this kiss
Repair those violent harms that my two sisters
Have in thy reverence made!
   Kent
               Kind and dear princess!
   Cordelia

30 *white flakes*: thin white hair.
31 *challenge*: claim.

30 Had you not been their father, these white flakes
Did challenge pity of them. Was this a face
To be oppos'd against the warring winds?
To stand against the deep dread-bolted thunder?
In the most terrible and nimble stroke

33 *deep dread-bolted thunder*: loud noise of dreaded thunderbolts.
33-6 *To stand . . . helm*: om. F.
35 *cross*: forked.
   watch: stay out on guard.
   perdu: lonely sentry; *and perhaps also* lost soul.
36 *helm*: helmet—i.e. his head.
38 *Against*: in front of.
   wast thou fain: were you compelled to.
39 *rogues*: outcast vagabonds.
40 *short and musty straw*: stale straw spread thin for animal litter.
42 *concluded all*: given up altogether.
43 *do you*: you speak to him.

35 Of quick, cross lightning? to watch—poor *perdu!*—
With this thin helm? Mine enemy's dog,
Though he had bit me, should have stood that night
Against my fire. And wast thou fain, poor father,
To hovel thee with swine and rogues forlorn,
40 In short and musty straw? Alack, alack!
'Tis wonder that thy life and wits at once
Had not concluded all. He wakes; speak to him.
   Doctor
Madam, do you; 'tis fittest.
   Cordelia
How does my royal lord? How fares your majesty?
   Lear

45 *do . . . grave*: hurt me by restoring me to life.
46 *bliss*: heavenly blessedness.
47 *wheel of fire*: One of the torments of the damned in medieval representations of hell.
   that: so that.

45 You do me wrong to take me out o'th'grave;
Thou art a soul in bliss; but I am bound
Upon a wheel of fire, that mine own tears
Do scald like molten lead.
   Cordelia
             Sir, do you know me?
   Lear
You are a spirit, I know; where did you die?

50 *wide*: wandering in his mind.

53 *abus'd*: deluded.
   e'en: just about.

56 *Would*: I wish.

60 *fond*: in my dotage.

65 *mainly*: entirely.

Cordelia
50 Still, still, far wide.
   Doctor
   He's scarce awake; let him alone awhile.
   Lear
   Where have I been? Where am I? Fair daylight?
   I am mightily abus'd. I should e'en die with pity
   To see another thus. I know not what to say.
55 I will not swear these are my hands: let's see;
   I feel this pin prick. Would I were assur'd
   Of my condition!
   Cordelia
                              O, look upon me, sir,
   And hold your hand in benediction o'er me.
   No, sir, you must not kneel.
   Lear
                              Pray, do not mock me:
60 I am a very foolish fond old man,
   Fourscore and upward, not an hour more or less;
   And, to deal plainly,
   I fear I am not in my perfect mind.
   Methinks I should know you and know this man;
65 Yet I am doubtful: for I am mainly ignorant
   What place this is, and all the skill I have
   Remembers not these garments; nor I know not
   Where I did lodge last night. Do not laugh at me;
   For, as I am a man, I think this lady
70 To be my child Cordelia.
   Cordelia
                              And so I am, I am.
   Lear
   Be your tears wet? Yes, faith! I pray, weep not:
   If you have poison for me, I will drink it.
   I know you do not love me; for your sisters
   Have, as I do remember, done me wrong:
75 You have some cause, they have not.
   Cordelia
                              No cause, no cause.
   Lear
   Am I in France?
   Kent
                              In your own kingdom, sir.

77 *abuse*: deceive.

78 *rage*: madness, delirium.

80 *even o'er*: try to remember, piece together.

82 *Till further settling*: until he is calmer.

83 *walk*: i.e. withdraw.

85–97   These lines appear only in the Quarto text.
85 *Holds it true*: is it still believed.

88 *conductor*: leader.

92 *Report is changeable*: there are varying reports.
93 *apace*: very quickly.
94 *arbitrement*: final settlement.

95 *my point and period*: my last full stop—i.e. the completion of his life's work.
throughly wrought: thoroughly finished.
96 *Or . . . ill*: either for good or for ill.

Lear
Do not abuse me.
    Doctor
Be comforted, good madam; the great rage,
You see, is kill'd in him: and yet it is danger
80 To make him even o'er the time he has lost.
Desire him to go in; trouble him no more
Till further settling.
    Cordelia
Will't please your highness walk?
    Lear
                     You must bear with me.
Pray you now, forget and forgive: I am old and foolish.
       [*Exeunt* Lear, Cordelia, Doctor, *and* Servants
    Gentleman
85 Holds it true, sir, that the Duke of Cornwall was so
slain?
    Kent
Most certain, sir.
    Gentleman
Who is conductor of his people?
    Kent
As 'tis said, the bastard son of Gloucester.
    Gentleman
90 They say Edgar, his banish'd son, is with the Earl of
Kent in Germany.
    Kent
Report is changeable. 'Tis time to look about; the
powers of the kingdom approach apace.
    Gentleman
The arbitrement is like to be bloody. Fare you well, sir.
                                      [*Exit*
    Kent
95 My point and period will be throughly wrought,
Or well or ill, as this day's battle's fought.
                                      [*Exit*

Act 5

Act 5 Scene 1

War is imminent. Regan speaks plainly to Edmund and declares her intentions. There is a coldness between the two sisters, as both Goneril and Regan are jealous for Edmund's love. Edgar gives Albany a letter to be opened after the battle. Edmund reveals his latest schemes.

os.d. *drum and colours*: a drum beating and banners unfurled: this is the usual stage direction to indicate an army prepared for war.

1 *last purpose*: most recent intention i.e. to fight with Regan and Edmund against Cordelia.

2 *advis'd by aught*: warned by anything.

3 *course*: plan of action.
full of alteration: always changing his mind.

4 *self-reproving*: self-reproach.
constant pleasure: firm decision.

5 *sister's man*: i.e. Oswald; when Regan last saw Oswald (in *Act 4*, Scene 5), he was going to find Edmund.
miscarried: met with some accident.

6 *doubted*: feared.

Scene 1

The British camp near Dover
Enter, with drum and colours, Edmund,
Regan, Officers, Soldiers, *and Others*

Edmund
Know of the duke if his last purpose hold,
Or whether since he is advis'd by aught
To change the course; he's full of alteration
And self-reproving; bring his constant pleasure.
[*To an* Officer, *who goes out*

Regan
5 Our sister's man is certainly miscarried.

Edmund
'Tis to be doubted, madam.

Regan
                  Now, sweet lord,
You know the goodness I intend upon you:
Tell me, but truly, but then speak the truth,
Do you not love my sister?

Edmund
                      In honour'd love.

7 'You know what good things I have in
  store for you.'
9 *honour'd*: honourable.
10–11 *have you . . . place*: have you never
  taken my brother's place (i.e. in
  Goneril's bed), which is forbidden
  ('forfended') by the commandment
  against adultery.
11 *abuses*: is unworthy of.
12 *doubtful*: afraid.
  conjunct: joined together with.
13 'Taken into her fullest confidence';
  Regan implies that there has also been
  some physical intimacy.
15 *endure her*: i.e. as a rival.

16 *Fear me not*: trust me.

19 *loosen*: come between.

20 *be-met*: encountered.

22 *rigour of our state*: harshness of our
  government.
23–8 *Where . . . nobly*: om. F.
23 *Where*: in a situation where.
24 *for*: as for.
25 *touches*: concerns.
25–6 *as France . . . king*: Albany is prepared
  to fight the French army because it
  constitutes an invasion of his territory,
  not because it gives encouragement
  ('bolds') to King Lear.
28 *Why is this reason'd?*: why are you giving
  all these reasons?
29 *Combine together*: let us join forces to
  fight.
30 *domestic and particular broils*: private
  family squabbles.

32 *th'ancient of war*: the most experienced
  soldiers.

Regan
10 But have you never found my brother's way
To the forfended place?
    Edmund
                              That thought abuses you.
    Regan
I am doubtful that you have been conjunct
And bosom'd with her, as far as we call hers.
    Edmund
No, by mine honour, madam.
    Regan
15 I never shall endure her: dear my lord,
Be not familiar with her.
    Edmund
                         Fear me not.
She and the duke her husband!

Enter, with drum and colours, Albany,
Goneril, *and* Soldiers

    Goneril
[*Aside*] I had rather lose the battle than that sister
Should loosen him and me.
    Albany
20 Our very loving sister, well be-met.
Sir, this I hear; the king is come to his daughter,
With others whom the rigour of our state
Forc'd to cry out. Where I could not be honest,
I never yet was valiant: for this business,
25 It touches us, as France invades our land,
Not bolds the king, with others, whom, I fear,
Most just and heavy causes make oppose.
    Edmund
Sir, you speak nobly.
    Regan
                      Why is this reason'd?
    Goneril
Combine together 'gainst the enemy;
30 For these domestic and particular broils
Are not the question here.
    Albany
                      Let's then determine
With th'ancient of war on our proceeding.

33 *presently*: immediately.

Edmund
I shall attend you presently at your tent.
Regan
Sister, you'll go with us?
Goneril
35 No.
Regan
'Tis most convenient; pray go with us.
Goneril
[*Aside*] O, ho! I know the riddle. I will go.

37 *I know the riddle*: I can see what you are thinking: Goneril thinks that Regan does not want to lose sight of her.

As they are going out enter Edgar, *disguised.*

Edgar
If e'er your grace had speech with man so poor,
Hear me one word.
Albany
                              I'll overtake you.
[*Exeunt* Edmund, Regan, Goneril, Officers,
                              Soldiers, *and* Attendants
                                                    Speak
Edgar
40 Before you fight the battle, ope this letter.
If you have victory, let the trumpet sound
For him that brought it: wretched though I seem,
I can produce a champion that will prove
What is avouched there. If you miscarry,
45 Your business of the world hath so an end,
And machination ceases. Fortune love you!
Albany
Stay till I have read the letter.
Edgar
                              I was forbid it.
When time shall serve, let but the herald cry,
And I'll appear again.
Albany
                              Why, fare thee well:
50 I will o'erlook thy paper.
[*Exit* Edgar

40 *ope*: open.
   this letter: i.e. the letter from Goneril to Edmund that Edgar took from Oswald's pocket in *4, 6, 251*.

43 *champion*: defender; Edgar seems to be setting up a medieval tournament.
44 *avouched*: maintained.
   miscarry: lose the battle.
45 *so*: in that way.
46 *machination*: plots and counter-plots.
50 *o'erlook*: have a look at.

Enter Edmund

Edmund
The enemy's in view; draw up your powers.
Here is the guess of their true strength and forces

51 *powers*: troops.
52 *guess*: estimate.

53 *By diligent discovery*: obtained by careful reconnaissance.

54 *greet the time*: be ready to cope when the time is ripe; unlike Edmund, Albany is not over-eager to join battle.

56 *jealous*: suspicious.
the stung: those who have been stung.

61 *carry out my side*: succeed in my ambitions.
62 *Now then*: let me see; Edmund has to think fast.
63 *countenance*: authority.
65 *His speedy taking off*: how to get rid of him quickly.
66 *to*: to show to.
68 *Shall*: they shall.
68–9 *for . . . debate*: it is very important for me now to fight for my position, not talk about it.

By diligent discovery; but your haste
Is now urged on you.
> **Albany**
>   We will greet the time. [*Exit* Albany
> **Edmund**
55 To both these sisters have I sworn my love;
Each jealous of the other, as the stung
Are of the adder. Which of them shall I take?
Both? one? or neither? Neither can be enjoy'd
If both remain alive: to take the widow
60 Exasperates, makes mad her sister Goneril;
And hardly shall I carry out my side,
Her husband being alive. Now then, we'll use
His countenance for the battle; which being done,
Let her who would be rid of him devise
65 His speedy taking off. As for the mercy
Which he intends to Lear and to Cordelia,
The battle done, and they within our power,
Shall never see his pardon; for my state
Stands on me to defend, not to debate.

>   [*Exit*

Act 5 Scene 2

Gloucester shelters under a tree whilst the battle is fought. Cordelia's army is defeated.

os.d. *drum and colours*: Shakespeare now shows the army of Cordelia and Lear prepared for battle.

1 *father*: old man; Edgar has still not revealed himself to Gloucester.
2 *good host*: entertainer.
4 *comfort*: good news.
4s.d. *Alarum*: the trumpet-call to start a battle.
4s.d. *retreat*: the trumpet-call indicating that the battle is over.

Scene 2

> *Between the two camps*
> *Alarum within*
>
> *Enter, with drum and colours,* Lear, Cordelia, *and their Forces; and Exeunt*
>
> *Enter* Edgar *and* Gloucester

> **Edgar**
Here, father, take the shadow of this tree
For your good host; pray that the right may thrive.
If ever I return to you again,
I'll bring you comfort.
> **Gloucester**
>   Grace go with you, sir!
>   [*Exit* Edgar
>
> *Alarum; afterwards a retreat. Enter* Edgar

Edgar

5 Away, old man! give me thy hand: away!
King Lear hath lost, he and his daughter ta'en.
Give me thy hand; come on.

Gloucester

No further, sir; a man may rot even here.

Edgar

What! in ill thoughts again? Men must endure
10 Their going hence, even as their coming hither:
Ripeness is all. Come on.

Gloucester

And that's true too.
[*Exeunt*

6 *ta'en*: captured.

10 'Dying, just like being born.'
11 *Ripeness is all*: all that matters is to be
ready for it.

Scene 3

The British camp
Enter, in conquest, with drum and colours,
Edmund, *with* Lear *and* Cordelia *prisoners;*
Officers, Soldiers, *etc.*

Edmund

Some officers take them away: good guard,
Until their greater pleasures first be known
That are to censure them.

Cordelia

We are not the first
Who, with best meaning, have incurr'd the worst.
5 For thee, oppressed king, I am cast down;
Myself could else out-frown false Fortune's frown.
Shall we not see these daughters and these sisters?

Lear

No, no, no, no! Come, let's away to prison;
We two alone will sing like birds i'th'cage:
10 When thou dost ask me blessing, I'll kneel down,
And ask of thee forgiveness: so we'll live,
And pray, and sing, and tell old tales, and laugh
At gilded butterflies, and hear poor rogues
Talk of court news; and we'll talk with them too,
15 Who loses and who wins; who's in, who's out;
And take upon's the mystery of things,
As if we were gods' spies: and we'll wear out,

Act 5 Scene 3

Lear and Cordelia are taken to prison.
Edmund gives instructions to an Officer.
Albany denounces Edmund and issues a
challenge. Regan is taken ill. Edgar comes to
confront his brother; they fight, and Edmund
is wounded. Goneril is mad with grief, and
rushes out to kill herself. Edgar tells of
Gloucester's death. When Edmund sees the
bodies of the two sisters, he tries to rescue
Cordelia. Lear carries in her body. He grieves,
then dies himself. Edgar speaks the play's last
words.

1 *good guard*: keep them well guarded.
2 *their greater pleasures*: the wishes of those
in command.
3 *censure*: judge.
4 *with . . . worst*: with the best intentions,
have received the worst punishment.
5 *cast down*: i.e. by Fortune.
6 *Myself*: for my own part—i.e. if she alone
were affected.
else: otherwise.
out-frown: frown back at.
false: Fortune is always untrustworthy.
8 *let's away*: let us go away.
9 *i'th'cage*: in the cage—i.e. in their prison
cell.
12 *old tales*: stories of the olden days.
13 *gilded butterflies*: gaily dressed courtiers.
poor rogues: other wretched creatures—
probably Lear refers to fellow prisoners.

14 *court news*: news at court.

15 *who's in, who's out*: who is in, or out of, the king's favour.

16 *take upon's*: act as though we could understand.
the mystery of things: the mysterious course of events.

17 *gods' spies*: There is no apostrophe in either Q or F, and both use a capital G, but Lear refers to plural 'gods' in line 21; the 'spies' may be agents (like guardian angels) who survey and report to the deities on the lives of human beings.
wear out: outlast.

18 *packs and sects*: political cliques and parties.

19 *ebb . . . moon*: i.e. suffer shifts in political power just as the tides are affected by the moon.

20 *such sacrifices*: i.e. their renunciation of the world.

21 *The . . . incense*: i.e. the gods themselves perform the priestly functions.
caught thee: made you weep.

22 *He . . . heaven*: anyone who separates us will have to bring fire from heaven—i.e. no earthly power will ever part us.

23 *fire . . . foxes*: drive us out (with fire and smoke) as foxes are driven from their lairs.

24 *good years*: bogeymen, evil spirits (the derivation of the phrase is uncertain—it comes possibly from the Dutch *goet iaer*).
flesh and fell: altogether (both flesh and skin).

28 *this note*: i.e. the death warrant of Lear and Cordelia.

29 *advance'd*: promoted.

32 *Are as the time is*: have to behave in whatever way suits the time.

33 *Does . . . sword*: is not appropriate for a man who wields a sword.

34 *Will not bear question*: is not to be questioned.

36 *About it*: get on with the job.
write happy: call yourself a happy man (because you can expect great reward).

37 *carry it so*: do it exactly.

In a wall'd prison, packs and sects of great ones
That ebb and flow by th'moon.

Edmund
                                        Take them away.

    Lear
20 Upon such sacrifices, my Cordelia,
The gods themselves throw incense. Have I caught
   thee?
He that parts us shall bring a brand from heaven,
And fire us hence like foxes. Wipe thine eyes;
The good years shall devour them, flesh and fell,
25 Ere they shall make us weep; we'll see 'em starv'd first.
Come.

    [*Exeunt* Lear *and* Cordelia, *guarded*

     Edmund
Come hither, captain; hark.
Take thou this note;

    Giving a paper

        Go follow them to prison.
One step I have advanc'd thee; if thou dost
30 As this instructs thee, thou dost make thy way
To noble fortunes; know thou this, that men
Are as the time is; to be tender-minded
Does not become a sword; thy great employment
Will not bear question; either say thou'lt do't,
35 Or thrive by other means.

    Officer
            I'll do't, my lord.

    Edmund
About it; and write happy when th'hast done.
Mark,—I say, instantly, and carry it so
As I have set it down.

39 *I . . . oats*: I am not a horse.

40s.d. *Flourish*: A triumphant call on the trumpets.

41 *strain*: lineage, *and* disposition.
42 *Fortune led you well*: you have been lucky.
43 *opposites*: opponents.
44–6 *I . . . determine*: I want you to treat them as they deserve but with consideration for our safety.

48 *retention*: confinement.
49 *Whose*: i.e. the king's.
   title: entitlement, legal right.
50 'To win the hearts of the common people over to his side.'
51 *impress'd lances*: conscripted soldiers (fighting with lances).
53 *My . . . same*: for just the same reason.
54 *further space*: some later time.
55 *session*: trial.

57 *quarrels*: causes.
   in the heat: i.e. of passion (Edmund implies that Lear and Cordelia might not get fair trial in the present circumstances).

60 *by your patience*: if you don't mind.
61–2 Now that the fighting is over, Edmund must not presume to think that he is Albany's social equal.

62 *list*: please.
63 'You might have asked what I wanted'; Regan uses the royal plural.
64 *spoke so far*: said so much.
65 'Carried the authority of my position and represented me personally.'
66 *immediacy*: direct connection.

67 *Not so hot*: go easily—don't get so excited.

Officer
I cannot draw a cart nor eat dried oats;
40 If it be man's work I'll do't.
                                    [*Exit*

Flourish. Enter Albany, Goneril, Regan,
Officers, *and* Soldiers

Albany
Sir, you have show'd to-day your valiant strain,
And Fortune led you well; you have the captives
Who were the opposites of this day's strife;
I do require them of you, so to use them
45 As we shall find their merits and our safety
May equally determine.
Edmund
                          Sir, I thought it fit
To send the old and miserable king
To some retention and appointed guard;
Whose age had charms in it, whose title more,
50 To pluck the common bosom on his side,
And turn our impress'd lances in our eyes
Which do command them. With him I sent the queen;
My reason all the same; and they are ready
To-morrow, or at further space, t'appear
55 Where you shall hold your session. At this time
We sweat and bleed; the friend hath lost his friend,
And the best quarrels, in the heat, are curs'd
By those that feel their sharpness;
The question of Cordelia and her father
60 Requires a fitter place.
Albany
                          Sir, by your patience,
I hold you but a subject of this war,
Not as a brother.
Regan
                    That's as we list to grace him;
Methinks our pleasure might have been demanded,
Ere you had spoke so far. He led our powers,
65 Bore the commission of my place and person;
The which immediacy may well stand up,
And call itself your brother.
Goneril
                          Not so hot;

68 *grace*: abilities.
69 *your addition*: any title you give him.

In his own grace he doth exalt himself
More than in your addition.

       Regan

                     In my rights,

70 *compeers*: equals.

70 By me invested, he compeers the best.

       Albany

71 *husband*: be your husband.

That were the most, if he should husband you.

       Regan

72 *Jesters . . . prophets*: 'There's many a true
    word spoken in jest.'

Jesters do oft prove prophets.

       Goneril

                Holla, holla!

73 *That . . . a-squint*: you can't see straight.

That eye that told you so look'd but a-squint.

       Regan

Lady, I am not well, else I should answer

75 *From a full-flowing stomach*: with a great
    many angry words.
77 *the walls are thine*: everything is yours.

75 From a full-flowing stomach. General,
Take thou my soldiers, prisoners, patrimony;
Dispose of them, of me; the walls are thine;
Witness the world, that I create thee here
My lord and master.

       Goneril

79 *enjoy him*: take him for your lover.

                Mean you to enjoy him?

       Albany

80 *The let-alone . . . will*: it is not in your
    power to forbid it.

80 The let-alone lies not in your good will.

       Edmund

Nor in thine, lord.

       Albany

81 *half-blooded fellow*: bastard.

                Half-blooded fellow, yes.

       Regan

82 *strike*: strike up.

[*To* Edmund] Let the drum strike, and prove my title
    thine.

       Albany

83 *thee*: Albany now uses the degrading
    second-person singular pronoun to
    express his contempt for Edmund.
84 *attaint*: impeachment, arrest.
85 *gilded*: beautified.

Stay yet; hear reason. Edmund, I arrest thee
On capital treason; and, in thy attaint,
85 This gilded serpent.

       Pointing to Goneril

                For your claim, fair sister,
I bar it in the interest of my wife;

87 *sub-contracted*: only 'sub-contracted'
    because she is already contracted (in
    marriage) to Albany.
88 *banes*: banns (of marriage).
89 *make your loves*: make your courtship.
90 *bespoke*: spoken for (by Edmund).

'Tis she is sub-contracted to this lord,
And I, her husband, contradict your banes.
If you will marry, make your loves to me,
90 My lady is bespoke.

90 *An interlude*: What a performance!

92 *prove upon thy person*: i.e. by fighting you.
94 *pledge*: gage (Albany throws down his gauntlet).
   make: prove.
97 *medicine*: i.e. poison.
98 *exchange*: i.e. the glove thrown down in exchange for Albany's 'pledge'.
   What: whoever and of whatsoever rank.

101 *maintain*: justify.
103 *single virtue*: complete integrity.

Goneril
                                    An interlude!
   Albany
Thou art arm'd, Gloucester; let the trumpet sound:
If none appear to prove upon thy person
Thy heinous, manifest, and many treasons,
There is my pledge;

                        Throws down a glove

                                    I'll make it on thy heart,
95 Ere I taste bread, thou art in nothing less
Than I have here proclaim'd thee.
   Regan
                                    Sick! O, sick!
   Goneril
[*Aside*] If not, I'll ne'er trust medicine.
   Edmund
There's my exchange:

                        Throws down a glove

                        What in the world he is
That names me traitor, villain-like he lies.
100 Call by the trumpet: he that dares approach,
On him, on you, who not? I will maintain
My truth and honour firmly.
   Albany
                        A herald, ho!
Trust to thy single virtue; for thy soldiers,
All levied in my name, have in my name
105 Took their discharge.
   Regan
                        My sickness grows upon me.
   Albany
She is not well; convey her to my tent.

                                    [*Exit* Regan, *led*

                Enter a Herald

Come hither, herald,—Let the trumpet sound,—
And read out this.
   Officer
Sound, trumpet!

                        A trumpet sounds

110 *quality or degree*: i.e. a knight with the
proper status.
lists: limits.
111 *maintain upon*: accuse.
112 *manifold*: manifest.
116s.d. *trumpet before him*: preceded by a
trumpeter.

119 *quality*: rank.
121 *bare-gnawn and canker-bit*: eaten bare, as
though by caterpillars.

123 *cope*: encounter.

127 *mine*: i.e. his sword.
128–9 *it is . . . profession*: Edgar claims the
right to draw his sword by his
knighthood ('honours'), loyalty ('oath'),
and religion ('profession').

Herald

110 [*Reads*] *If any man of quality or degree within the lists of
the army will maintain upon Edmund, supposed Earl of
Gloucester, that he is a manifold traitor, let him appear by
the third sound of the trumpet. He is bold in his defence.*
Sound!

First trumpet

115 Again!

Second trumpet

Again!

Third trumpet

[*Trumpet answers within*

Enter Edgar, *armed, with a trumpet before
him*

Albany
Ask him his purposes, why he appears
Upon this call o'th'trumpet.

Herald
                                                    What are you?
Your name? your quality? and why you answer
120 This present summons?

Edgar
                                        Know, my name is lost;
By treason's tooth bare-gnawn, and canker-bit:
Yet am I noble as the adversary
I come to cope.

Albany
                        Which is that adversary?

Edgar
What's he that speaks for Edmund Earl of
Gloucester?

Edmund
125 Himself: what say'st thou to him?

Edgar
                                                    Draw thy sword,
That, if my speech offend a noble heart,
Thy arm may do thee justice; here is mine:
Behold, it is the privilege of mine honours,
My oath, and my profession: I protest,

130 *Maugre*: in spite of.
eminence: high position.
131 *victor*: victorious.
fire-new: brand new.
132 *heart*: courage.
134 *Conspirant*: one who conspires.

135 *extremest upward*: very top.

136 *descent*: lowest part.

137 *toad-spotted*: stained with infamy (as the toad is spotted and venomous).

138 *bent*: determined.
140 *In wisdom*: i.e. because he was not in honour bound to fight with a man of lower rank.
141 *outside*: appearance.
142 'Your speech shows some sign ('say') of education.'
143 *safe and nicely*: quite properly.
144 *rule of knighthood*: code of knightly conduct.
146 *hell-hated*: hated like hell.
147 *Which*: i.e. the terrible charges.
for: since.
glance: glide.
148 *instant way*: an immediate outlet (i.e. back into the accuser's heart).
149 *rest*: be silent; Edmund's success in the fight will prove that his accuser is the traitor, and so the charges of treason will be silenced with the death of the adversary.
150 *Save him*: Albany wants to save Edmund's life so that a full confession can be obtained.
practice: treachery.
152 *opposite*: opponent.
153 *cozen'd and beguil'd*: cheated and deceived.
154 *this paper*: i.e. the letter of 5, 1, 40.
stople: put a stopper in.
Hold, sir: just a moment.

130 Maugre thy strength, place, youth, and eminence,
Despite thy victor sword and fire-new fortune,
Thy valour and thy heart, thou art a traitor,
False to thy gods, thy brother, and thy father,
Conspirant 'gainst this high illustrious prince,
135 And, from th'extremest upward of thy head
To the descent and dust below thy foot,
A most toad-spotted traitor. Say thou 'No,'
This sword, this arm, and my best spirits are bent
To prove upon thy heart, whereto I speak,
140 Thou liest.

Edmund
                    In wisdom I should ask thy name;
But since thy outside looks so fair and war-like,
And that thy tongue some say of breeding breathes,
What safe and nicely I might well delay
145 By rule of knighthood, I disdain and spurn;
Back do I toss these treasons to thy head,
With the hell-hated lie o'erwhelm thy heart,
Which, for they yet glance by and scarcely bruise,
This sword of mine shall give them instant way,
Where they shall rest for ever. Trumpets, speak.

Alarums. They fight. Edmund *falls*

Albany
150 Save him! save him!
Goneril
                    This is practice, Gloucester:
By th'law of war thou wast not bound to answer
An unknown opposite; thou art not vanquish'd,
But cozen'd and beguil'd.
Albany
                    Shut your mouth, dame,
Or with this paper shall I stople it. Hold, sir;
155 Thou worse than any name, read thine own evil:
No tearing, lady; I perceive you know it.
Goneril
Say, if I do, the laws are mine, not thine:
Who can arraign me for't?
Albany
                    Most monstrous! O!
Know'st thou this paper?

157 *mine, not thine*: Goneril asserts her
    position as queen; Albany is merely her
    consort.

Goneril

                    Ask me not what I know.
                                    [*Exit*

Albany

160 Go after her: she's desperate; govern her.
                            [*Exit an* Officer

Edmund

161 *charg'd me with*: accused me of.

What you have charg'd me with, that have I done,
And more, much more; the time will bring it out:
'Tis past, and so am I. But what art thou

164 *hast this fortune on me*: have had the good
    luck to conquer me.

That hast this fortune on me? If thou'rt noble,

165 *Let's exchange charity*: i.e. Edgar is now
    prepared to forgive Edmund.

165 I do forgive thee.

Edgar

                    Let's exchange charity.

169 *our pleasant vices*: the sins we take
    pleasure in.

I am no less in blood than thou art, Edmund;
If more, the more th'hast wrong'd me.
My name is Edgar, and thy father's son.

171 *The dark and vicious place*: i.e. the bed
    where he committed adultery.
    got: begot.

The gods are just, and of our pleasant vices

173 *The wheel is come full circle*: Edmund
    refers to the wheel of Fortune, which
    raised him from the lowly point at which
    he started (in *Act 1*, Scene 1) to his
    successful position as commander and
    lover; he is now brought low again.

170 Make instruments to plague us;
The dark and vicious place where thee he got
Cost him his eyes.

Edmund

                    Th'hast spoken right, 'tis true.
The wheel is come full circle; I am here.

Albany

Methought thy very gait did prophesy

175 A royal nobleness: I must embrace thee:
Let sorrow split my heart, if ever I
Did hate thee or thy father.

Edgar

                    Worthy prince, I know't.

Albany

Where have you hid yourself?
How have you known the miseries of your father?

Edgar

174 *gait*: manner of walking.
177 *Worthy*: noble.
180 *List*: listen to.
182 'In order to escape the proclamation of
    death.'

180 By nursing them, my lord. List a brief tale;
And when 'tis told, O, that my heart would burst!
The bloody proclamation to escape
That follow'd me so near,—O, our lives' sweetness,
That we the pain of death would hourly die

183 *near*: closely.
184–5 *we . . . once*: we would rather suffer the
    pain of death every hour of our lives than
    actually die once (and get it over).

185 Rather than die at once!—taught me to shift
Into a madman's rags, t'assume a semblance

185 *shift*: change.
186 *semblance*: appearance.
187 *The very dogs*: even the dogs.

That very dogs disdain'd: and in this habit

188 *rings*: eye-sockets (without the jewels that were his eyes).

191 *O fault*: that was a terrible mistake.

192 *some half-hour past*: about half an hour ago.
was arm'd: had put on my armour.

193 *success*: result.

195 *flaw'd*: already overstrained.

196 *conflict*: i.e. between joy at finding Edgar and grief for Edgar's suffering.

198 *Burst smilingly*: i.e. he died of joy.

202 *dissolve*: melt into tears.

203–20 *This would . . . slave*: om. F.

203 *period*: highest point.

204 *but*: only.
another: i.e. sorrow.

205 *To amplify too much*: would go beyond all bounds.

206 *top extremity*: exceed the limit.

207 *big*: ready to burst out.

208 *my worst estate*: poorest condition (i.e. as 'Poor Tom').

212 *As*: as if.
threw him: threw himself.

215 *puissant*: powerful.
the strings of life: heart strings; the man's heart was beginning to fail.

217 *tranc'd*: senseless.

219 *enemy*: hostile.

Met I my father with his bleeding rings,
Their precious stones new lost; became his guide,
190 Led him, begg'd for him, sav'd him from despair;
Never—O fault!—reveal'd myself unto him,
Until some half-hour past, when I was arm'd;
Not sure, though hoping, of this good success,
I ask'd his blessing, and from first to last
195 Told him my pilgrimage: but his flaw'd heart,
Alack, too weak the conflict to support!
'Twixt two extremes of passion, joy and grief,
Burst smilingly.

Edmund
        This speech of yours hath mov'd me,
And shall perchance do good; but speak you on;
200 You look as you had something more to say.

Albany
If there be more, more woeful, hold it in;
For I am almost ready to dissolve,
Hearing of this.

Edgar
        This would have seem'd a period
To such as love not sorrow; but another,
205 To amplify too much, would make much more,
And top extremity.
Whilst I was big in clamour came there in a man,
Who, having seen me in my worst estate,
Shunn'd my abhorr'd society; but then, finding
210 Who 'twas that so endur'd, with his strong arms
He fasten'd on my neck, and bellow'd out
As he'd burst heaven; threw him on my father;
Told the most piteous tale of Lear and him
That ever ear receiv'd; which in recounting
215 His grief grew puissant, and the strings of life
Began to crack: twice then the trumpets sounded,
And there I left him tranc'd.

Albany
        But who was this?

Edgar
Kent, sir, the banish'd Kent; who in disguise
Follow'd his enemy king, and did him service
220 Improper for a slave.

Enter a Gentleman, *with a bloody knife*

Gentleman
Help, help! O, help!

Edgar
                              What kind of help?

Albany
                                        Speak, man.

Edgar
What means this bloody knife?

Gentleman
                              'Tis hot, it smokes;
It came even from the heart of—O, she's dead!

Albany
Who dead? speak, man.

Gentleman
225   Your lady, sir, your lady: and her sister
By her is poison'd; she confesses it.

Edmund
I was contracted to them both: all three
Now marry in an instant.

Edgar
                              Here comes Kent.

Enter Kent

Albany
Produce the bodies, be they alive or dead;
                              [*Exit* Gentleman
230   This judgment of the heavens, that makes us tremble,
Touches us not with pity.
                              [*To* Kent] O, is this he?
The time will not allow the compliment
Which very manners urges.

Kent
                              I am come
To bid my king and master aye good night;
235   Is he not here?

Albany
                              Great thing of us forgot!
Speak, Edmund, where's the king? and where's
    Cordelia?
Seest thou this object, Kent?

The bodies of Goneril *and* Regan *are brought
in*

222 *smokes*: steams.

228 *marry*: are united.

232 *compliment*: ceremony.
233 *very manners urges*: it is merely good
manners.

234 *aye*: for ever.

237 *object*: spectacle.

Kent
Alack! why thus?

Edmund
                    Yet Edmund was belov'd:
The one the other poison'd for my sake,
240 And after slew herself.

Albany
Even so. Cover their faces.

Edmund
I pant for life; some good I mean to do
Despite of mine own nature. Quickly send,
Be brief in it, to th'castle; for my writ
245 Is on the life of Lear and on Cordelia.
Nay, send in time.

Albany
                            Run, run! O, run!

Edgar
To who, my lord? Who has the office? send
Thy token of reprieve.

Edmund
Well thought on: take my sword,
250 Give it the captain.

Edgar
                            Haste thee, for thy life.
                                    [*Exit* Officer

Edmund
He hath commission from thy wife and me
To hang Cordelia in the prison, and
To lay the blame upon her own despair,
That she fordid herself.

Albany
                            The gods defend her!
255 Bear him hence awhile.
                            [Edmund *is borne off*

Enter Lear, *with* Cordelia *dead in his arms;*
Officer

Lear
Howl, howl, howl! O, you are men of stones!
Had I your tongues and eyes, I'd use them so
That heaven's vault should crack. She's gone for ever.
I know when one is dead, and when one lives;
260 She's dead as earth. Lend me a looking-glass;

238 *Yet Edmund was belov'd*: after all, someone did love me.

240 *after*: afterwards.

244 *Be brief in it*: don't waste time about it.
    writ: order of execution.
245 *on*: against.

248 *token of reprieve*: some authority for a reprieve.

254 *fordid*: destroyed; see p. 140.

261 *stone*: crystal, *or* a polished stone used as a mirror.
262 *the promis'd end*: i.e. the end of the world.
263 *image*: representation.
Fall and cease: let the heavens fall and all things come to an end.
264 *This feather*: Lear holds a feather to Cordelia's lips.

265–6 *It is . . . felt*: This piece of good luck will make up for everything I have ever suffered.
271 *ever*: always.
275 *biting falchion*: light sword with its point bending inwards.

277 *these . . . me*: all these troubles ruin me as a swordsman.
278 *straight*: honestly.

279–80 *If . . . behold*: If Fortune should boast of the way she has treated two people, giving one great success and the other greatest misery, we are now looking at one of these.
281 *dull sight*: miserable spectacle.

If that her breath will mist or stain the stone,
Why, then she lives.

Kent   Is this the promis'd end?

Edgar
Or image of that horror?

Albany   Fall and cease.

Lear
This feather stirs; she lives! if it be so,
265 It is a chance which does redeem all sorrows
That ever I have felt.

Kent
[*Kneeling*]   O my good master!

Lear
Prithee, away.

Edgar   'Tis noble Kent, your friend.

Lear
A plague upon you, murderers, traitors all!
I might have sav'd her; now she's gone for ever!
270 Cordelia, Cordelia! stay a little. Ha!
What is't thou say'st? Her voice was ever soft,
Gentle and low, an excellent thing in woman.
I kill'd the slave that was a-hanging thee.

Officer
'Tis true, my lords, he did.

Lear   Did I not, fellow?
275 I have seen the day, with my good biting falchion
I would have made them skip: I am old now,
And these same crosses spoil me. Who are you?
Mine eyes are not o'th'best: I'll tell you straight.

Kent
If Fortune brag of two she lov'd and hated,
280 One of them we behold.

Lear
This is a dull sight. Are you not Kent?

Kent   The same;
Your servant Kent. Where is your servant Caius?

286 *I'll . . . straight*: I'll attend to that in a
moment.

287 *first . . . decay*: the very beginning of the
change and decline in your fortunes.

289 *Nor no man else*: that's really who I am
(i.e. Caius—Kent is anxious that Lear
should make the connection).
290 *fordone*: destroyed.
291 *desperately*: in despair.

292–3 *vain . . . him*: it's useless to try to
explain things to him.

293 *Very bootless*: no good at all.

294 *here*: in this situation.

296 *this great decay*: this ruin of a great piece
of humanity—i.e. Lear.
come: be given.
297 *resign*: Albany gives back his kingdom,
and Lear is once more the king.
299–301 *You . . . merited*: Edgar and Kent,
once banished, are restored to their
former positions with such extra rewards
('boot') and titles as their noble deeds
('honours') have deserved.

304 *poor fool*: a term of endearment for
Cordelia.

Lear
He's a good fellow, I can tell you that;
He'll strike, and quickly too. He's dead and rotten.
Kent
285 No, my good lord; I am the very man,—
Lear
I'll see that straight.
Kent
That from your first of difference and decay,
Have follow'd your sad steps,—
Lear
You are welcome hither.
Kent
Nor no man else. All's cheerless, dark, and deadly:
290 Your eldest daughters have foredone themselves,
And desperately are dead.
Lear
Ay, so I think.
Albany
He knows not what he says, and vain is it
That we present us to him.
Edgar
Very bootless.

Enter an Officer

Officer
Edmund is dead, my lord.
Albany
That's but a trifle here.
295 You lords and noble friends, know our intent;
What comfort to this great decay may come
Shall be appli'd: for us, we will resign,
During the life of this old majesty,
To him our absolute power: [*To* Edgar *and* Kent
You, to your rights,
300 With boot and such addition as your honours
Have more than merited. All friends shall taste
The wages of their virtue, and all foes
The cup of their deservings. O see, see!
Lear
And my poor fool is hang'd! No, no, no life!
305 Why should a dog, a horse, a rat, have life,
And thou no breath at all? Thou'lt come no more,

308 *this button*: Lear feels again the sense of suffocation which he described as 'Hysterica passio' in 2, 4, 55.

309 *Look*: Lear thinks that Cordelia is breathing.

Never, never, never, never, never!
Pray you, undo this button: thank you, sir.
Do you see this? Look on her, look, her lips,
310 Look there, look there!

[*Dies*

Edgar
He faints! My lord, my lord!

Kent
Break, heart; I prithee, break!

Edgar
Look up, my lord.

312 *ghost*: departing spirit.
pass: i.e. die.

313 *rack*: instrument of torture which stretched the body until everything broke.
tough: rigid, cruel.

314 *longer*: for any longer time.

Kent
Vex not his ghost: O, let him pass! he hates him
That would upon the rack of this tough world
Stretch him out longer.

Edgar
He is gone, indeed.

316 *usurp'd his life*: lived longer than he ought to have done.

Kent
315 The wonder is he hath endur'd so long:
He but usurp'd his life.

Albany
Bear them from hence. Our present business

318 *general woe*: public mourning for all.

Is general woe. [*To Kent and Edgar*] Friends of my
soul, you twain

319 *gor'd state*: wounded kingdom.

Rule in this realm, and the gor'd state sustain.

Kent

320 *journey*: i.e. to another world.

320 I have a journey, sir, shortly to go;
My master calls me, I must not say no.

Edgar

322 *weight*: grief.

The weight of this sad time we must obey;
Speak what we feel, not what we ought to say.
The oldest hath borne most: we that are young
325 Shall never see so much, nor live so long.

[*Exeunt, with a dead march*

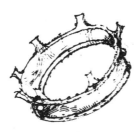

Appendix A

Quarto and Folio

The differences between the Quarto and Folio texts of *King Lear* can best be studied when the two plays are printed side by side, as they are in *'King Lear': A Parallel Text Edition*, edited by Rene Weis (1993). For the present school edition, four separate passages are presented as parallel texts. Those words which are uniquc to either text are printed in bold type, and spaces show where something has been omitted from one text or else added in the other. The modernized texts are taken from *William Shakespeare: The Complete Works*, edited by Gary Taylor and Stanley Wells (Oxford, 1986).

Quarto: Act 1, Scene 1	Folio: Act 1, Scene 1
Sound a sennet	*Sennet*
The King is coming.	The King is coming.
*Enter **one bearing a coronet, then** King Lear, **then the Dukes of** Albany **and** Cornwall; **next** Gonoril, Regan, Cordelia, **with followers***	*Enter King Lear, the Dukes of Cornwall and Albany, Goneril, Regan, Cordelia, **and attendants***
Lear	**Lear**
Attend **my** lords of France and Burgundy, Gloucester.	Attend **the** lords of France and Burgundy, Gloucester.
Gloucester	**Gloucester**
I shall, my **liege**. [*Exit*	I shall, my **lord**. [*Exit*
Lear	**Lear**
Meantime we **will** express our darker **purposes**.	Meantime we **shall** express our darker **purpose**.
The map there. Know we have divided	**Give me** the map there. Know **that** we have divided
In three our kingdom, and 'tis our **first** intent	In three our kingdom, and 'tis our **fast** intent
To shake all cares and business **off** our **state**,	To shake all cares and business **from** our **age**,
Confirming them on younger **years**.	**Conferring** them on younger **strengths while we Unburdened crawl toward death. Our son of Cornwall,**
	And you, our no less loving son of Albany,
	We have this hour a constant will to publish
	Our daughters' several dowers, that future strife
The **two great** princes, France and Burgundy—	**May be prevented now**. The princes France and Burgundy—
Great rivals in our youngest daughter's love—	Great rivals in our youngest daughter's love—
Long in our court have made their amorous sojourn,	Long in our court have made their amorous sojourn,
And here are to be answered. Tell me, my daughters,	And here are to be answered. Tell me, my daughters—
	Since now we will divest us both of rule,
	Interest of territory, cares of state—
Which of you shall we say doth love us most,	Which of you shall we say doth love us most,
That we our largest bounty may extend	That we our largest bounty may extend
Where **merit doth most** challenge **it**?	Where **nature doth with merit** challenge? Goneril,
Gonoril, our eldest born, speak first.	Our eldest born, speak first.

Quarto: Act 1, Scene 2

Gloucester
He cannot be such a monster.
Edmund
Nor is not, sure.
Gloucester
**To his father, that so tenderly and entirely loves him—
heaven and earth!** Edmund seek him out, wind me into
him. I pray you, frame **your** business after your own
wisdom. I would unstate myself to be in a due resolution.
Edmund
I **shall** seek him, sir, presently, convey the business as I shall
see means, and acquaint you withal.
Gloucester
These late eclipses in the sun and moon portend no good to
us. Though the wisdom of nature can reason   thus and
thus, yet nature finds itself scourged by the sequent effects.
Love cools, friendship falls off, brothers divide; in cities
mutinies, in countries **discords**   palaces treason,   the
bond cracked **between** son and father.

Find out this villain, Edmund; it shall lose thee nothing. Do
it carefully. And the noble and true-hearted Kent banished,
his offence honesty! **Strange**, strange!

                        [*Exit*

Folio: Act 1, Scene 2

Gloucester
He cannot be such a monster.

Edmond, seek him out, wind me into him, I pray you.
Frame **the** business after your own wisdom. I would unstate
myself to be in a due resolution.
Edmond
I **will** seek him, sir, presently, convey the business as I shall
find means, and acquaint you withal.
Gloucester
These late eclipses in the sun and moon portend no good to
us. Though the wisdom of nature can reason **it** thus and
thus, yet nature finds itself scourged by the sequent effects.
Love cools, friendship falls off, brothers divide; in cities,
mutinies; in countries, **discord; in** palaces, treason; **and**
the bond cracked **'twixt** son and father. **This villain of
mine comes under the prediction: there's son against
father. The King falls from bias of nature: there's
father against child. We have seen the best of our
time. Machinations, hollowness, treachery, and all
ruinous disorders follow us disquietly to our graves.**
Find out this villain, Edmond; it shall lose thee nothing. Do
it carefully. And the noble and true-hearted Kent banished,
his offence honesty! **'Tis** strange.

                        [*Exit*

Quarto: Act 2, Scene 2

Cornwall
[*calling*]   Fetch forth the stocks!—
As I have life and honour, there shall he sit till noon.
    Regan
Till noon?—till night, my lord, and all night too.
    Kent
Why, madam, if I were your father's dog
You **could** not use me so.
    Regan
                Sir, being his knave, I will.
        [*Stocks brought out*]
    Cornwall
This is a fellow of the selfsame **nature**
Our sister speaks of.—Come, bring away the stocks.
    Gloucester
Let me beseech your grace not to do so.
His fault is much, and the good King his master
Will check him for't. Your purposed low correction
Is such as basest and contemnèd wretches
For pilf'rings and most common trespasses
Are punished with. The King   must take it ill
That **he's** so slightly valued in his messenger,
Should have him thus restrained.
    Cornwall
             I'll answer that.
    Regan
My sister may receive it much more worse
To have her gentlemen abused, assaulted,
For following her affairs. Put in his legs.
    They put Kent in the stocks
Come, my good lord, away!
      Exeunt all but Gloucester and Kent

Folio: Act 2, Scene 2

Cornwall
[*calling*]   Fetch forth the stocks!—
As I have life and honour, there shall he sit till noon.
    Regan
Till noon?—till night, my lord, and all night too.
    Kent
Why, madam, if I were your father's dog
You **should** not use me so.
    Regan
                Sir, being his knave, I will.
    Stocks brought out
    Cornwall
This is a fellow of the selfsame **colour**
Our sister speaks of.—Come, bring away the stocks.
    Gloucester
Let me beseech your grace not to do so.

The King **his master needs** must take it ill
That **he**, so slightly valued in his messenger,
Should have him thus restrained.
    Cornwall
             I'll answer that.
    [*They put Kent in the stocks*]
    Regan
My sister may receive it much more worse
To have her gentlemen abused, assaulted.

    Cornwall
Come, my good lord, away!
      Exeunt all but Gloucester and Kent

Quarto: Act 5, Scene 3

Lear
And my poor fool is hanged. No, no life.
Why should a dog, a horse, a rat have life,
And thou no breath at all? **O, thou wilt** come no more.
Never, never, never   —Pray you, undo
This button. Thank you, sir, **O, O, O, O**!

Edgar
He faints. [*To Lear*] My lord, my lord!
Lear
Break, heart, I prithee break.
Edgar
Look up, my lord.
Kent
Vex not his ghost. O, let him pass. He hates him
That would upon the rack of this tough world
Stretch him out longer.
                    [*Lear dies*]
Edgar
                              O, he is gone indeed.
Kent
The wonder is he hath endured so long.
He but usurped his life.
Albany
[*to attendants*] Bear them from hence. Our present business
Is **to** general woe. [*To Kent and Edgar*] Friends of my soul
    you twain
Rule in this **kingdom**, and the gored state sustain.
Kent
I have a journey, sir, shortly to go:
My master calls, **and** I must not say no.
Albany
The weight of this sad time we must obey,
Speak what we feel, not what we ought to say.
The oldest **have** borne most. We that are young
Shall never see so much, nor live so long.
                                    Exeunt carrying the bodies

Folio: Act 5, Scene 3

Lear
And my poor fool is hanged. No, no, **no** life.
Why should a dog, a horse, a rat have life,
And thou no breath at all? **Thou'lt** come no more.
Never, never, never, **never, never.**
[*To Kent*] Pray you, undo this button. Thank you, sir.
Do you see this? Look on her. Look, her lips.
Look there, look there.   *He dies*
Edgar
He faints. [*To Lear*] My lord, my lord!
Kent
[*to Lear*] Break, heart, I prithee break.
Edgar
[*to Lear*]   Look up, my lord.
Kent
Vex not his ghost. O, let him pass. He hates him
That would upon the rack of this tough world
Stretch him out longer.
Edgar
                              He is gone indeed.
Kent
The wonder is he hath endured so long.
He but usurped his life.
Albany
Bear them from hence. Our present business
Is   general woe. [*To Edgar and Kent*] Friends of my soul,
    you twain
Rule in this **realm**, and the gored state sustain.
Kent
I have a journey, sir, shortly to go:
My master calls **me**; I must not say no.
Edgar
The weight of this sad time we must obey,
Speak what we feel, not what we ought to say.
The oldest **hath** borne most. We that are young
Shall never see so much, nor live so long.
            *Exeunt **with a dead march**, carrying the bodies*

Appendix B

Shakespeare's Sources

The passages printed here are intended to afford some slight indication of the nature and variety of the literary works which gave inspiration to Shakespeare in the making of his *King Lear*.

A comprehensive collection of Shakespeare's sources is to be found in *Narrative and Dramatic Sources of Shakespeare*, Vol. VII, ed. Geoffrey Bullough (London, 1973). The Arden edition of the play (ed. Kenneth Muir, 1952, revised 1972) prints substantial extracts, and there is a good account of the way Shakespeare worked with his raw material in *Shakespeare's Sources*, by Kenneth Muir (Methuen, 1977).

1. Extracts from the anonymous play of *King Leir*.
2. Passage from Holinshed's *Chronicles of England*.
3. Stanzas from Spenser's *Faerie Queene*.
4. Extract from Sir Philip Sidney's *Arcadia*.
5. Samuel Harsnett and *King Lear*.

1. *The Chronicle History of King Leir.*

> **Leir**
> Resolve a doubt which much molests my mind:
> Which of you three to me would prove most kind,
> Which loves me most, and which at my request,
> Would soonest yield unto their father's hest?
> **Gonerill**
> I hope my gracious father makes no doubt
> Of any of his daughters' love to him:
> Yet for my part, to show my zeal to you,
> Which cannot be in windy words rehearsed:
> I prize my love to you at such a rate,
> I think my life inferior to my love . . .
> **Leir**
> How thy words revive my dying soul!
> **Cordella**
> Oh, how I do abhor this flattery!

Leir

But what says Ragan to her father's will?

Ragan

Oh, that my simple utterance could suffice
To tell the true intention of my heart,
Which burns in zeal of duty to your grace,
And never can be quenched, but by desire
To show the same in outward forwardness.
Oh, that there were some other maid that dars't
But make a challenge of her love with me,
I'd make her soon confess she never loved
Her father half so well as I do you . . .

Leir

Did never Philomel sing so sweet a note.

Cordella

Did never flatterer tell so false a note.

Leir

Speak now, Cordella, make my joys at full,
And drop down nectar from thy honey lips.

Cordella

I cannot paint my duty forth in words,
I hope my deed shall make report for me.
But look what love the child doth owe the father,
The same to you I bear, my gracious Lord.

Gonerill

Here is an answer answerless indeed:
Were you my daughter, I should scarcely brook it.

Ragan

Does thou not blush, proud peacock as thou art,
To make our father such a slight reply?

Leir

Why how now, Minion, are you grown so proud?
Does our dear love make you thus peremptory?
What, is your love become so small to us,
As that you scorn to tell us what it is?
Do you love us, as every child doth love
    their father? . . .

Cordella

Dear father, do not so mistake my words,
Nor my plain meaning be misconstrued;
My tongue was never used to flattery.

Gonerill

You were not best say I flatter: if you do,

My deeds shall show, I flatter not with you.
I love my father better than thou canst.

Cordella

The praise were great, spoke from another mouth;
But it should seem your neighbours dwell far off.

Ragan

Nay, here is one, that will confirm as much
As she has said, both for myself and her.
I say, thou does not wish my father's good.

Cordella

Dear father—

Leir

Peace, bastard imp, no issue of King Leir,
I will not hear thee speak one tittle more.
Call me not father, if thou love thy life,
Nor these thy sisters once presume to name:
Look for no help henceforth from me nor mine;
Shift as thou wilt, and trust unto thyself:
My kingdom will I equally divide
'Twixt thy two sisters to their royal dowcr,
And will bestow them worthy their deserts:
This done, because thou shall not have a hope,
To have a child's part in the time to come,
I presently will dispossess myself,
And set up these upon my princely throne.

Gonerill

I ever thought that pride would have a fall.

Ragan

Plain dealing, sister, your beauty is so sheen,
You need no dowry to make you be a queen.

*   *   *   *   *

Leir

Now I am constrained to seek relief
Of her, to whom I have been so unkind;
Whose censure, if it do award me death,
I must confess she pays me but my due:
But if she shows a loving daughter's part,
It comes of God and her, not my desert.

Cordella

No doubt she will, I dare be sworn she will.

Leir

How know you that, not knowing what she is?

Cordella
My self a father have a great way hence,
Used me as ill as ever you did her;
Yet, that his reverend age I once might see,
I'd creep along, to meet him on my knee.
   Leir
O, no men's children are unkind but mine.
   Cordella
Condemn not all, because of others' crimes:
But look, dear father, look, behold and see
Thy loving daughter speaketh unto thee.

                                        (She kneels)

   Leir
O, stand thou up, it is my part to kneel,
And ask forgiveness for my former faults.

                                        (He kneels)

   Cordella
O, if you wish I should enjoy my breath,
Dear father rise, or I receive my death.
   Leir
Then I will rise, to satisfy your mind,

                                    (He rises)

But kneel again, till pardon be resigned.

                                      (He kneels)

   Cordella
I pardon you: the word beseems not me.
But I do say so, for to ease your knee.
You gave me life, you were the cause that I
Am what I am, who else had never been.

2.   Holinshed's *Chronicles of England*.

Holinshed tells how King Leir 'had by his wife three daughters, without other issue, whose names were Gonorilla, Ragan and Cordeilla; which daughters he greatly loved—but specially Cordeilla the youngest far above the two elder. When this Leir therefore was come to great years and began to wax unweildy through age, he thought to understand the affections of his daughters towards him, and prefer her whom he best loved to the succession of the kingdom. Whereupon he first asked Gonorilla how well she loved him: who, calling the gods to report, professed that she loved him more than her own life . . . With which answer the father being well pleased, turned to the second and demanded of her how well she loved him: who answered, confirming her sayings with great oaths, that she loved him more than tongue could express and far above any other creatures of the world. Then called he his youngest daughter Cordeilla before him and asked her what account she made of him, to which she made this answer as follows: "Knowing the great love and fatherly zeal you have always borne towards me . . . I protest unto you that I have loved you ever and will continually (while I live) love you as my natural father . . .". The father, being nothing content with this answer, married his two eldest daughters, the one unto the Duke of Cornwall and the other unto the Duke of Albania; betwixt whom he willed and ordained that his land should be divided after his death, and the one half thereof immediately should be assigned to them in hand. But to the third daughter Cordeilla he reserved nothing. Nevertheless it fortuned that one of the princes of Gallia, which now is called France, whose name was Aganippus, hearing of the beauty, womanhood, and good condition of the said Cordeilla desired to have her in marriage and sent over to her father requiring that he might have her to wife.

To whom answer was made, that he might have her in marriage but as for any dower, he could have none for all was promised and assured to her other sisters already. Aganippus, not withstanding this answer of denial to receive anything by way of dower with Cordeilla, took her to wife, only moved thereto for respect to her person and amiable virtues . . .

After that Leir was fallen into age, the two Dukes that had married his two eldest daughters, thinking it long ere the government of the land did come into their hands, arose against him in armour and reft from him the governance of the land, upon conditions to be continued for term of life: by the which he was put to his portion—that is, to live after a rate assigned to him for the maintenance of his estate, which in the process of time was diminished as well by [the Duke of Cornwall] as by [the Duke of Albania]. But the greatest grief that Leir took was to see the unkindness of his daughters, which seemed to think that all was too much that their father had, the same being never so little; in so much that going from one to the other he was brought to that misery, that scarcely they would allow him one servant to wait upon him.'

3.   Stanzas 31 and 32 from *The Faerie Queene* by Edmund Spenser, Book Two, Canto X.

> The wretched man gan then advise too late,
>   That love is not where most it is profess'd,
>   Too truly tried in his extremest state;
>   At last resolv'd likewise to prove the rest,
>   He to Cordelia himself addressed,
>   Who with entire affection him received,
>   As for her Sire and King she seemed best;
>   And after all an army strong she leav'd,
> To war on those which him had of his realm bereav'd
>
> So to his crown she him restored again,
>   In which he died, made ripe for death by eld,
>   And after will'd it should to her remain:
>   Who peacably the same long time did weld,
>   And all mens' hearts in due obedience held.
>   Till that her sisters' children, waxen strong
>   Through proud ambition, against her rebelled
>   And overcomen, kept in prison long,
> Till weary of that vretched life, herself she hung.

4.   Extract from Sir Philip Sidney's *Arcadia*, 11.10. *The pitiful state, and story of the* Paphlagonian *unkind King and his kind son.*

'Having had in lawful marriage, and by a mother fit to bear royal children, this son . . . I was carried by a bastard son of mine . . . first to dislike, then to hate, lastly to destroy, to do my best to destroy, this son . . . undeserving destruction. What ways he used to bring me to it, if I should tell you, I should tediously trouble you with as much poisonous hypocrisy, desperate fraud, smooth malice, hidden ambition, and smiling envy, as in any living person could be harboured. . . . The conclusion is, that I gave order to some servants of mine, whom I thought as apt for such charities as myself, to lead him out into a forest and there to kill him.

But those thieves (better natured to my son than myself) spared his life, letting him go to learn to live poorly. Which he did, giving himself to be a private soldier in a country hereby . . . But . . . he heard news of me, who (drunk in my affection to that unnatural and unlawful son of mine) suffered myself to be so governed by him, that all favours and punishments passed by him, all offices and places of importance distributed to his favourites, so that ere I was aware, I had left myself nothing but the name of King. Which

he shortly weary of too, with many indignities . . . threw me out of
my seat, put out my eyes, and then (proud in his tyranny) let me
go. Neither imprisoning nor killing me, but rather delighting to
make me feel my misery . . .'

[The good son came to his father's aid, and the King tells how]

'I craved of him to lead me to the top of this rock, indeed I must
confess with meaning to free him from so serpentine a companion
as I am. But he finding what I purposed . . . showed himself
disobedient unto me. And now Gentlemen . . . if it may be, let me
obtain that of you, which my son denies me: for never was there
more pity in saving any than in ending me . . . because therein my
agonies shall end.'

5.   Samuel Harsnett and *King Lear.*

*A Declaration of Egregious Popishe Impostures . . . Practised
by Edmunds . . . a Jesuit.*

Harsnett was Chaplain to the Bishop of London, and his
publication was intended to attack the belief in witches and
diabolic 'possession'. He reported his investigations into a certain
Jesuit priest who was claiming to exorcise the devils who had taken
over control of certain feeble-minded or hysterical servants in the
household of Edward Peckham. The influence of his book is
diffused throughout Shakespeare's play.

The Jesuit Edmunds probably gave his name to Gloucester's
younger son, and the servant 'Mainy' shared his complaint with
King Lear: 'Maynie had a spice of the *Hysterica passio,* as seems,
from his youth, hee himselfe termes it the Moother' (see 2, 4,
54–6). Even the name of the servant may be reflected in
Shakespeare's use (line 34 of the same scene) of the unusual word
'meiny' for Gloucester's household. Two allusions to Harsnett are
combined in Lear's abuse of the entire female sex, 'But to the
girdle do the gods inherit, Beneath is all the fiend's' (4, 6, 124–7).
Harsnett recounts how the *girdle* of Edmund Campion was used
by the exorcist as he pretended to drive out the devils which, he
said, 'did rest in the most secret part' of one maidservant's body.

The idea of bringing all the madmen together on the desolate
heath in the thunderstorm might have been suggested by
Harsnett's account of another servant, Marwood—'a pittiful
creature' who 'being pinched with penurie and hunger, did lie but
a night, or two, abroad in the fieldes, and beeing a melancholicke
person, was scared with lightning, and thunder, that happened in
the night'.

   The madness assumed by Edgar in his disguise as Poor Tom
owes much to Harsnett's descriptions: the devils he names, for
example, are the same familiar spirits that possessed the servants
interviewed by Harsnett—Frateretto, Flibberdigibbet, Hoberdidance, Moho, Mahu, Smulkin, and Purr—and they are similarly
associated with animals. Edgar's description of the fiend who
tempted his father to suicide (4, 6, 69–72) owes something to
Harsnett's description of a popular folk-devil who had 'ougly
hornes on his head, fire in his mouth . . . eyes like a bason, fangs
like a dogge, clawes like a Beare, skinne like a Neger, and a voyce
roaring like a Lyon'.

What the Critics have said

Some of the greatest of all English men of letters have written about *King Lear*, and their thoughts—although coming from the past—are still deserving of our consideration today. These are a very few of the most famous ones.

Samuel Johnson

'The tragedy of Lear is deservedly celebrated among the dramas of Shakespeare. There is perhaps no play which keeps the attention so strongly fixed; which so much agitates our passions and interests our curiosity. The artful involutions of distinct interests, the striking opposition of contrary characters, the sudden changes of fortune, and the quick succession of events, fill the mind with a perpetual tumult of indignation, pity, and hope.

There is no scene which does not contribute to the aggravation of the distress or conduct of action, and scarce a line which does not conduce to the progress of the scene. So powerful is the current of the poet's imagination that the mind which once ventures within it is hurried irresistibly along.

But . . . Shakespeare has suffered the virtue of Cordelia to perish in a just cause, contrary to the natural ideas of justice, to the hope of the reader, and, what is yet more strange, to the faith of chronicles . . . A play in which the wicked prosper and the virtuous miscarry may doubtless be good, because it is a just representation of the common events of human life; but since all reasonable beings naturally love justice, I cannot easily be persuaded that the observation of justice makes a play worse; or that, if other excellencies are equal, the audience will not always rise better pleased from the final triumph of persecuted virtue.

In the present case the public has decided. Cordelia, from the time of Tate[1], has always retired with victory and felicity. And, if my sensations could add anything to the general suffrage, I might relate that I was many years ago so shocked by Cordelia's death that I know not whether I ever endured to read again the last

[1]   See p. vii

scenes of the play till I undertook to revise them as an editor.'
Notes from The Plays of William Shakespeare (1765)

Charles Lamb

'So to see Lear acted, —to see an old man tottering about the stage with a walking-stick, turned out of doors by his daughters in a rainy night, has nothing in it but what is painful and disgusting. We want to take him into shelter and relieve him. That is all the feeling which the acting of Lear ever produced in me. But the Lear of Shakespeare cannot be acted. The contemptible machinery by which they mimic the storm which he goes out in, is not more adequate to represent the horrors of the real elements, than any actor can be to represent Lear . . . The greatness of Lear is not in corporal dimension, but in intellectual: the explosions of his passion are terrible as a volcano; they are storms turning up and disclosing to the bottom that sea, his mind, with all its vast riches. It is his mind which is laid bare. This case of flesh and blood seems too insignificant to be thought on; even as he himself neglects it. On the stage we see nothing but corporal infirmities and weakness, the impotence of rage: while we read it, we see not Lear, but we are Lear,—we are in his mind, we are sustained by a grandeur which baffles the malice of daughters and storms; in the aberrations of his reason, we discover a mightily irregular power of reasoning, immethodized from the ordinary purposes of life, but exerting its powers, as the wind bloweth where it listeth, at will upon the corruptions and abuses of mankind.'
On the Tragedies of Shakespeare, Considered with Reference
to Their Fitness for Stage Representation (1812)

William Hazlitt

'We wish that we could pass this play over, and say nothing about it. All that we can say must fall far short of the subject; or even of what we ourselves conceive of it. To attempt to give a description of the play itself or of its effect upon the mind is mere impertinence . . .

The mind of Lear, staggering between the weight of attachment and the hurried movements of passion, is like a tall ship driven about by the winds, buffeted by the furious waves, but that still rides above the storm, having its anchor fixed in the bottom of the sea; or it is like the sharp rock circled by the eddying whirlpool that foams and beats against it, or like the solid promontory pushed from its basis by the force of an earthquake.'
Characters of Shakespeare's Plays (1817)

John Keats

'The excellence of every Art is its intensity, capable of making all disagreeables evaporate, from their being in close relationship with Beauty & Truth—Examine *King Lear*—you will find this exemplified throughout.'

Letter to George and Tom Keats, 1 December 1817

Richard G. Moulton

'It appears, then, that the Centrepiece of the play is occupied with the contact of two madnesses, the madness of Lear and the madness of Edgar; that of Lear gathering up into a climax trains of passion from all three tragedies of the main plot, and that of Edgar holding a similar position to the three tragedies of the underplot. Further, these madnesses do not merely go on side by side by side; as they meet they mutually affect one another, and throw up each other's intensity. By the mere sight of the Bedlamite, Lear, already tottering upon the verge of insanity, is driven really and incurably mad; while in the case of Edgar, the meeting with Lear, and through Lear with Gloucester, converts the burden of feigning idiocy from a cruel stroke of unjust fate into a hardship voluntarily undergone for the sake of ministering to a father now forgiven and pitied. And so far as the general effect of the play is concerned this central Climax presents a terrible *duet of madness*, the wild ravings and mutual interworkings of two distinct strains of insanity, each answering and outbidding the other. The distinctness is greater as the two are different in kind. In Lear we have the madness of passion, exaggeration of ordinary emotions; Edgar's is the madness of idiocy, as idiocy was in early ages when the cruel neglect of society added physical hardship to mental affliction. In Edgar's frenzy we trace rapid irrelevance with gleams of unexpected relevance, just sufficient to partly answer a question and go off again into wandering; a sense of ill-treatment and of being an outcast; remorse and thoughts as to close connection of sin and retribution; visions of fiends as in bodily presence; cold, hunger: these alternating with mere gibberish, and all perhaps within the compass of a few lines.

But this is not all. When examined more closely this Centrepiece exhibits not a duet but a *trio of madness*; with the other two there mingles a third form of what may be called madness, the professional madness of the court fool.'

How Climax Meets Climax in the Centre Of 'Lear', (1885)

A. C. Bradley

'How is it now, that this defective drama so overpowers us that we are either unconscious of its blemishes or regard them as almost irrelevant? As soon as we turn to this question we recognize, not merely that *King Lear* possesses purely dramatic qualities which far outweigh its defects, but that its greatness consists partly in imaginative effects of a wider kind. And, looking for the sources of these effects, we find among them some of those very things which appeared to us dramatically faulty or injurious. Thus, to take at once two of the simplest examples of this, that very vagueness of locality which we have just considered, and again that excess in the bulk of the material and the number of figures, events and movements, while they interfere with the clearness of vision, have at the same time a positive value for imagination. They give the feeling of vastness, the feeling not of a scene or particular place, but of a world; or, to speak more accurately, of a particular place which is also a world. This world is dim to us, partly from its immensity, and partly because it is filled with gloom; and in the gloom shapes approach and recede, whose half-seen faces and motions touch us with dread, horror or the most painful pity,— sympathies and antipathies which we seem to be feeling not only for them but for the whole race.'

Shakespearean Tragedy, (1904)

Classwork and Examinations

The works of Shakespeare are studied all over the world, and this classroom edition is being used in many different countries. Teaching methods vary from school to school and there are many different ways of examining a student's work. Some teachers and examiners expect detailed knowledge of Shakespeare's text; others ask for imaginative involvement with his characters and their situations; and there are some teachers who want their students to share in the theatrical experience of directing and performing a play. Most people use a variety of methods. This section of the book offers a few suggestions for approaches to *King Lear* which could be used in schools and colleges to help with students' understanding and *enjoyment* of the play.

    A Discussion
    B Character Study
    C Activities
    D Context Questions
    E Comprehension Questions
    F Essays
    G Projects

A Discussion

Talking about the play—about the issues it raises and the characters who are involved—is one of the most rewarding and pleasurable aspects of the study of Shakespeare. It makes sense to discuss each scene as it is read, sharing impressions—and perhaps correcting misapprehensions. It can be useful to compare aspects of this play with other fictions—plays, novels, films—or with modern life.

Suggestions

A1   Abdication—does the king (or any other appointed ruler) have the right to 'shake all cares and business from [his/her] age' (*1*, 1, 38)?

A2 'According to my bond'; in this way Cordelia describes her love for her father (*1*, 1, 92). How would you define the extents and limitations of filial duty?

A3 Edmund rebels against 'the plague of custom' and 'The curiosity of nations' (*1*, 2, 3–4). What is the value of customs, conventions, and traditions in any society?

A4 Edmund scoffs at astrology: 'we make guilty of our disasters the sun, the moon, and stars; as if we were villains on necessity, fools by heavenly compulsion . . . and all that we are evil in, by a divine thrusting on' (*1*, 2, 114–120). But Kent seems to disagree: 'It is the stars, The stars above us, govern our conditions' (*4*, 3, 32–3) Do you share either of these opinions? What is your 'birth sign'? Do you read your horoscope?

A5 'Monster Ingratitude!' (*1*, 5, 35). Is ingratitude always as detestable as Lear believes?

A6 O! reason not the need; our basest beggars
Are in the poorest thing superfluous:
Allow not nature more than nature needs,
Man's life is cheap as beast's. (*2*, 4, 261–4)
What determines 'need' in different societies?

A7 Do you agree with the Fool (*3*, 2, 10–11) that 'court holy-water in a dry house is better than this rain-water out o'door'?

A8   Take physic, Pomp;
Expose thyself to feel what wretches feel,
That thou mayst shake the superflux to them,
And show the heavens more just. (*3*, 4, 33–6)
Discuss Lear's scheme for the redistribution of wealth.

A9 Who alone suffers, suffers most i' th' mind,
Leaving free things and happy shows behind;
But then the mind much sufferance doth o'erskip,
When grief hath mates, and bearing fellowship.
                    (*3*, 6, 102–5)
Do you share Edgar's philosophy of suffering?

A10 The Folio edition of *King Lear* does not print the comments of the servants after Gloucester's eyes have been put out (*3*, 7, 96–104). Does this omission do any serious damage to the scene, or to the play as a whole? Discuss the possible reasons for the omissions and additions of other passages (indicated in the

Notes), and the likely effects that these may have on the different scenes and characters.

B Character Study

Shakespeare is famous for his creation of characters who seem like real people. We can judge their actions and we can try to understand their thoughts and feelings—just as we criticize and try to understand the people we know. As the play progresses, we learn to like or dislike, love or hate, them—just as though they lived in *our* world. Characters can be studied *from the outside*, by observing what they do, and listening sensitively to what they say. This is the scholar's method; the scholar—or any reader—has access to the whole play, and can see the function of every character within the whole scheme of that play. Another approach works *from the inside*, taking a single character and looking at the action and the other characters from his/her point of view. This is an actor's technique when creating a character—who can have only a partial view of what is going on—for performance; and it asks for a student's inventive imagination. The two methods—both useful in different ways—are really complementary to each other.

Suggestions

a) from 'outside' the character

B1 Two members of the *dramatis personae* are especially valuable as instruments of the dramatist; describe the characters and functions of

a) Kent
b) Oswald

B2 Is the Fool a comedian or a half-wit? Describe his function in the play.

B3 Show how Lear learns to have compassion on others.

B4 Contrast the characters of Albany and Cornwall.

B5 Differentiate between Goneril and Regan.

B6 Write obituaries for

a) Lear
b) Cordelia
c) Edmund

B7 Trace the development of the characters of
a) Gloucester
b) Albany
c) Edgar

b) from 'inside' the character

B8 In the character of Kent, give your opinion of Gloucester and his bastard son after your first meeting with Edmund.

B9 At the end of *Act 1*, write Edmund's account (in his personal diary) of his father and his brother, and of the deceptions he has practised on them.

B10 How would Cordelia describe (perhaps in a confidential diary before leaving for France) her father's behaviour in dividing his kingdom and making the 'test' of his daughters' love?

B11 Oswald always keeps his own counsel and never expresses an opinion of the work he is asked to do. But (confiding his thoughts to a letter, diary, or close friend) what does he really think of each of the different episodes in which he is involved?

B12 Imagine you are Lear's Fool. Describe your thoughts and feelings about your master, his daughters, and all that has happened to you since the division of the kingdom.

B13 Devise new jests for the Fool, and re-write his prophecy (*Act 3*, Scene 2) using modern instances.

B14 Write the letters for
a) Goneril to Regan (*Act 1*, Scene 4)
b) Kent to Cordelia, and her reply to him (*Act 2*, Scene 1)
c) Goneril to Regan and Edmund (*Act 4*, Scene 2).

B15 In *Act 3*, Scene 5 Edmund, the loyal subject, betrays his father to Cornwall; give an account of this scene *a*) as Edmund might have recorded it in his diary; and *b*) as Cornwall would have noted it.

B16 In the character of one of the Servants present at the scene (*Act 3*, Scene 7), describe what happened when Gloucester was arrested and brought before Cornwall.

B17 Write the diary of Albany recording the changes he has seen in Goneril and describing the way his attitude to his wife is also changing.

B18 In the character of Cordelia, express (in a diary, letter, or perhaps a poem) your feelings on the discovery of your father and your reunion with him.

B19 As the Doctor, record your professional encounter with King Lear—your diagnosis of the patient's condition and the therapy prescribed (also the result of the treatment).

B20 In the character of Gloucester, speak your thoughts aloud as you shelter under the tree in *Act 5*, Scene 2.

C Activities

These can involve two or more students, preferably working *away from* the desk or study-table and using gesture and position ('body-language') as well as speech. They can help students to develop a sense of drama and the dramatic aspects of Shakespeare's play—which was written to be *performed*, not studied in a classroom. Students who have the necessary equipment can record the Activities and invite the criticism of colleagues in their own, or neighbouring, schools.

C1   Act the play—at least one or two scenes.

C2   Transpose the first scene into the twentieth century and the language of our own time. Prepare to give full media coverage—newspaper, radio, television—to Lear's division of the kingdom. Arrange for political commentators to give their views—and don't forget about the man/woman in the street! If possible, organize signing for the deaf, and translations for foreign readers/viewers.

C3   Using your own words, enact the conversation between Goneril and Regan at the end of *Act 1*, Scene 1, and between Albany and Goneril in *Act 4*, Scene 2. Speak—aloud—any of Edmund's soliloquies using your own words.

C4   Devise a scene in which Albany and Cornwall discuss the division of the kingdom and the portions they have each received.

C5   Enact the scene between Edgar and his father at Dover cliff (*Act 4*, Scene 6), transposing it to a different setting—e.g. try to persuade someone who cannot see that he/she is at the top, and then at the bottom, of a very high building.

D Context Questions

In written examinations, these questions present you with short passages from the play, and ask you to explain them. They are intended to test your knowledge of the play and your understanding of its words. Usually you have to make a choice of passages: there may be five on the paper, and you are asked to choose three. Be very sure that you know exactly how many passages you must choose. Study the ones offered to you, and select those you feel most certain of. Make your answers accurate and concise—don't waste time writing more than the examiner is asking for.

D1   Milk-liver'd man!
That bear'st a cheek for blows, a head for wrongs;
Who hast not in thy brows an eye discerning
Thine honour from thy suffering.

   (i)   Who is the speaker, and what has caused the speaker's anger?
   (ii) Who is being spoken to, and what is his relationship to the speaker?
   (iii) With whom is the speaker in love?

D2   Nature in you stands on the very verge
Of her confine: you should be rul'd and led
By some discretion that discerns your state
Better than you yourself.

   (i)   Who is the speaker, and what has occasioned the speaker's displeasure?
   (ii) Who is addressed as 'you', and what is his relationship to the speaker?
   (iii) Who supports the speaker in making this criticism?

D3   I have o'erheard a plot of death upon him.
There is a litter ready; lay him in't
And drive toward Dover, friend, where thou shalt meet
Both welcome and protection.

   (i)   Who is the speaker and who is the person addressed as 'friend'?
   (ii) Who is the person referred to as 'him', and who is plotting against his life?
   (iii) Whom will they meet at Dover?

E Comprehension Questions

These also present passages from the play and ask questions about them; and again you often have a choice of passages. But the extracts are much longer than those presented as context questions. A detailed knowledge of the language of the play is asked for here, and you must be able to express unusual or archaic phrases in your own words; you may also be asked to comment critically on the effectiveness of Shakespeare's language.

E1 *Edgar*
　　Yet better thus, and known to be contemn'd,
　　Than, still contemn'd and flatter'd, to be worst.
　　The lowest and most dejected thing of Fortune
　　Stands still in esperance, lives not in fear:
　　The lamentable change is from the best;　　　　　　5
　　The worst returns to laughter. Welcome, then,
　　Thou unsubstantial air that I embrace:
　　The wretch that thou hast blown unto the worst
　　Owes nothing to thy blasts. But who comes here?
　　　　　Enter Gloucester, *led by an Old Man.*
　　My father, poorly led? World, world, O world!　　10
　　But that thy strange mutations make us hate thee,
　　Life would not yield to age.

　　　(i)　Give the meaning of 'contemn'd' (line 1); 'esperance' (line 4); 'mutations' (line 11).
　　(ii)　Express in your own words the sense of lines 1–2, 'Yet . . . worst'; lines 5–6, 'The lamentable . . . laughter'; and lines 11–12, 'But that . . . age'.
　(iii)　What does this passage show us of Edgar's character?
　(iv)　Comment on the stagecraft revealed in these lines.

E2 *Lear*
　　I'll pray, and then I'll sleep.
　　Poor naked wretches, whereso'er you are,
　　That bide pelting of this pitiless storm,
　　How shall your houseless heads and unfed sides,
　　Your loop'd and window'd raggedness, defend you　　5
　　From seasons such as these? O, I have ta'en
　　Too little care of this! Take physic, Pomp;
　　Expose thyself to feel what wretches feel,
　　That thou mayst shake the superflux to them,
　　And show the heavens more just.　　　　　　　　　10

     (i) Explain the meanings in this context of 'bide' (line 3), 'loop'd and window'd' (line 5), 'just' (line 10).

    (ii) In your own words, express the sense of lines 4–6, 'How. . . these'; line 7, 'Take physic, Pomp'; line 9, 'shake . . . to them'.

   (iii) Why is this speech important for our understanding of the character of King Lear?

F Essays

These will usually give you a specific topic to discuss, or perhaps a question that must be answered, in writing, *with a reasoned argument*. They *never* want you to tell the story of the play—s don't! Your examiner—or teacher—has read the play, and doe not need to be reminded of it. Relevant quotations will always hel you to make your points more strongly.

F1 'King Lear is "a very foolish, fond old man" who deserv everything he gets.' Do you agree?

F2 To what extent are the two plots of *King Lear* really parallel?

F3 How important is laughter in *King Lear*?

F4 Do you agree that '*King Lear* is a play which has a great d to say to our own time'?

F5 'The Fool is an unnecessary distraction.' Is this your opinion?

F6 'In *King Lear* good does not vanquish evil: it is evil that destroys itself.' Is this true?

F7 Animal imagery in *King Lear*.

G Projects

In some schools, students are asked to do more 'free-ranging' work, which takes them outside the text—but which should always be relevant to the play. Such Projects may demand skills other than reading and writing: design and artwork, for instance, may be involved. Sometimes a 'portfolio' of work is assembled over a considerable period of time; and this can be presented to the examiner as part of the student's work for assessment.

    The availability of resources will, obviously, do much to determine the nature of the Projects; but this is something that only the local teachers will understand. However, there is always help to be found in libraries, museums, and art galleries.

Suggested Topics

G1 Court fools and jesters.
G2 Famous performers in *King Lear*.
G3 Adaptations of *King Lear*.
G4 Beggars and vagabonds in Shakespeare's England.

Background

England c. 1604

When Shakespeare was writing *King Lear,* many people still believed that the sun went round the earth. They were taught that this was a divinely ordered scheme of things, and that—in England—God had instituted a Church and ordained a Monarchy for the right government of the land and the people.

'The past is a foreign country; they do things differently there.'

L. P. Hartley

Government

For most of Shakespeare's life, the reigning monarch of England was Queen Elizabeth I; when she died, she was succeeded by King James I. He was also king of Scotland (James VI), and the two kingdoms were united in 1603 by his accession to the English throne. With his counsellors and ministers, James governed the nation (population less than six million) from London, although not more than half a million people inhabited the capital city. In the rest of the country, law and order were maintained by the land-owners and enforced by their deputies. The average man had no vote—and his wife had no rights at all.

Religion

At this time, England was a Christian country. All children were baptized, soon after they were born, into the Church of England; they were taught the essentials of the Christian faith, and instructed in their duty to God and to humankind. Marriages were performed, and funerals conducted, only by the licensed clergy and in accordance with the Church's rites and ceremonies. Attendance at divine service was compulsory; absences (without good—medical—reason) could be punished by fines. By such means, the authorities were able to keep some check on the populace—recording births, marriages, and deaths; being alert to any religious nonconformity, which could be politically dangerous; and ensuring a minimum of orthodox instruction through the official 'Homilies' which were regularly preached from the pulpits of all parish churches throughout the realm. Following Henry VIII's break away from the Church of Rome, all people in England were able to hear the church services *in their own language*. The Book of Common Prayer was used in every church, and an English translation of the Bible was read aloud in public. The Christian religion had never been so well taught before!

Education

School education reinforced the Church's teaching. From the age of four, boys might attend the 'petty school' (French '*petite école*') to learn the rudiments of reading and writing along with a few prayers; some schools also included work with numbers. At the age of seven, the boy was ready for the grammar school (if his father was willing and able to pay the fees).

A thorough grounding in Latin grammar was followed by translation work and the study of Roman authors, paying attention as much to style as to matter. The arts of fine writing were thus inculcated from early youth. A very few students proceeded to university; these were either clever scholarship boys, or else the sons of noblemen. Girls stayed at home, and acquired domestic and social skills—cooking, sewing, perhaps even music. The lucky ones might learn to read and write.

Language

At the start of the sixteenth century the English had a very poor opinion of their own language: there was little serious writing in English, and hardly any literature. Latin was the language of international scholarship, and Englishmen admired the eloquence of the Romans. They made many translations, and in this way they extended the resources of their own language, increasing its vocabulary and stretching its grammatical structures. French, Italian, and Spanish works were also translated, and—for the first time—there were English versions of the Bible. By the end of the century, English was a language to be proud of: it was rich in synonyms, capable of infinite variety and subtlety, and ready for all kinds of word-play—especially the *puns*, for which Shakespeare's English is renowned.

Drama

The great art-form of the Elizabethan and Jacobean age was its drama. The Elizabethans inherited a tradition of play-acting from the Middle Ages, and they reinforced this by reading and translating the Roman playwrights. At the beginning of the sixteenth century, plays were performed by groups of actors, all-male companies (boys acted the female roles) who travelled from town to town, setting up their stages in open places (such as inn-yards) or, with the permission of the owner, in the hall of some noble house. The touring companies continued, in the provinces, into the seventeenth century; but in London, in 1576, a new building was erected for the performance of plays. This was the Theatre, the first purpose-built playhouse in England. Other playhouses followed (including Shakespeare's own theatre, the Globe); and the English drama reached new heights of eloquence.

There were those who disapproved, of course. The theatres, which brought large crowds together, could encourage the spread of disease—and dangerous ideas. During the summer, when the plague was at its worst, the playhouses were closed. A constant censorship was imposed, more or less severe at different times. The Puritan faction tried to close down the theatres, but—partly because there was royal favour for the drama, and partly because the buildings were outside the city limits—they did not succeed until 1642.

Theatre

From contemporary comments and sketches—most particularly a drawing by a Dutch visitor, Johannes de Witt—it is possible to form some idea of the typical Elizabethan playhouse for which most of Shakespeare's plays were written. Hexagonal in shape, it had three roofed galleries encircling an open courtyard. The plain, high stage projected into the yard, where it was surrounded by the audience of standing 'groundlings'. At the back were two doors for the actors' entrances and exits; and above these doors was a balcony—useful for a musicians' gallery or for the acting of scenes 'above'. Over the stage was a thatched roof, supported on two pillars, forming a canopy—which seems to have been painted with the sun, moon, and stars for the 'heavens'.

Underneath was space (concealed by curtaining), which could be used by characters ascending and descending through a trap-door in the stage. Costumes and properties were kept backstage, in the 'tiring house'. The actors dressed lavishly, often wearing the secondhand clothes bestowed by rich patrons. Stage properties were important for defining a location, but the dramatist's own words were needed to explain the time of day, since all performances took place in the early afternoon.

Suggested Further Reading

Bayley, John, *Shakespeare and Tragedy*, (London, 1981).

Bethell, S. L., *Shakespeare and the Popular Dramatic Tradition*, (London, 1944).

Bradley, A. C., *Shakespearean Tragedy*, (London, 1904; reprinted 1978).

Danby, John F., *Elizabethan and Jacobean Poets*, (London, 1964).

——*Shakespeare's Doctrine of Nature*, (London, 1949).

Gardner, Helen, *King Lear*, (London, 1967).

Gielgud, John, *Stage Directions*, (London, 1963).

Granville-Barker, Harley, *Prefaces to Shakespeare*, First Series, (London, 1927).

Knight, G. Wilson, *The Wheel of Fire: Interpretations of Shakespearean Tragedy*, (London, 1930; rev. edn., 1949).

Knights, L. C., *Some Shakespearean Themes*, (London, 1959).

Leech, Clifford, *Shakespeare's Tragedies*, (London, 1950).

Muir, Kenneth, *'King Lear': A Critical Study*, (Harmondsworth, 1986).

——'Madness in *King Lear*', *Shakespeare Survey 13*, (1960), 30–40.

——'Samuel Harsnett and *King Lear*', *Review of English Studies* NS 2 (1951), 11–21.

——*The Sources of Shakespeare's Plays*, (Methuen, 1977).

Taylor, Gary, and Warren, Michael (eds.), *The Division of the Kingdoms*, (Oxford, 1986).

Welsford, Enid, *The Fool: His Social and Literary History*, (1935).

Weiss, Rene (ed.), *'King Lear': A Parallel Text Edition*, (Longman, 1993).

Background Reading

Blake, N. F., *Shakespeare's Language: an Introduction*, (Methuen, 1983).

Muir, K., and Schoenbaum, S., *A New Companion to Shakespeare Studies*, (Cambridge, 1971).

Schoenbaum, S., *William Shakespeare: A Documentary Life*, (Oxford, 1975).

Thomson, Peter, *Shakespeare's Theatre*, (Routledge and Kegan Paul, 1983).

William Shakespeare, 1564–1616

Elizabeth I was Queen of England when Shakespeare was born in 1564. He was the son of a tradesman who made and sold gloves in the small town of Stratford-upon-Avon, and he was educated at the grammar school in that town. Shakespeare did not go to university when he left school, but worked, perhaps, in his father's business. When he was eighteen he married Anne Hathaway, who became the mother of his daughter, Susanna, in 1583, and of twins in 1585.

There is nothing exciting, or even unusual, in this story; and from 1585 until 1592 there are no documents that can tell us anything at all about Shakespeare. But we have learned that in 1592 he was known in London, and that he had become both an actor and a playwright.

We do not know when Shakespeare wrote his first play, and indeed we are not sure of the order in which he wrote his works. If you look on page 163 at the list of his writings and their approximate dates, you will see how he started by writing plays on subjects taken from the history of England. No doubt this was partly because he was always an intensely patriotic man—but he was also a very shrewd business-man. He could see that the theatre audiences enjoyed being shown their own history, and it was certain that he would make a profit from this kind of drama.

The plays in the next group are mainly comedies, with romantic love-stories of young people who fall in love with one another, and at the end of the play marry and live happily ever after.

At the end of the sixteenth century the happiness disappears, and Shakespeare's plays become melancholy, bitter, and tragic. This change may have been caused by some sadness in the writer's life (one of his twins died in 1596). Shakespeare, however, was not the only writer whose works at this time were very serious. The whole of England was facing a crisis. Queen Elizabeth I was growing old. She was greatly loved, and the people were sad to think she must soon die; they were also afraid, for the Queen had never married, and so there was no child to succeed her.

When James I came to the throne in 1603, Shakespeare continued to write serious drama—the great tragedies and the plays based on Roman history (such as *Julius Caesar*) for which he is most famous. Finally, before he retired from the theatre, he wrote another set of comedies. These all have the same theme: they tell of happiness which is lost, and then found again.

Shakespeare returned from London to Stratford, his home town. He was rich and successful, and he owned one of the biggest houses in the town. He died in 1616.

Shakespeare also wrote two long poems, and a collection of sonnets. The sonnets describe two love-affairs, but we do not know who the lovers were. Although there are many public documents concerned with his career as a writer and a business-man, Shakespeare has hidden his personal life from us. A nineteenth-century poet, Matthew Arnold, addressed Shakespeare in a poem, and wrote 'We ask and ask—Thou smilest, and art still'.

There is not even a trustworthy portrait of the world's greatest dramatist.

Approximate order of composition of Shakespeare's works

Period	Comedies	History plays	Tragedies	Poems
I	Comedy of Errors Taming of the Shrew Two Gentlemen of Verona	Henry VI, part 1 Henry VI, part 2 Henry VI, part 3 Richard III King John	Titus Andronicus	
1594	Love's Labour's Lost			Venus and Adonis Rape of Lucrece
II	Midsummer Night's Dream Merchant of Venice	Richard II Henry IV, part 1	Romeo and Juliet	Sonnets
1599	Merry Wives of Windsor Much Ado About Nothing As You Like It	Henry IV, part 2 Henry V		
III	Twelfth Night Troilus and Cressida		Julius Caesar Hamlet Othello Timon of Athens	
1608	Measure for Measure All's Well That Ends Well		King Lear Macbeth Antony and Cleopatra Coriolanus	
IV	Pericles Cymbeline			
1613	The Winter's Tale The Tempest	Henry VIII